The Problem of Personhood

The Problem of Personhood

Giving Rights to Trees,
Corporations, and Robots

Lisa Siraganian

V
VERSO
London • New York

To my parents,
Patricia and Reuben Siraganian,
with love and gratitude

First published by Verso 2026
© Lisa Siraganian 2026
An earlier version of chapter 1 appeared in *Representations* 172 (2025), and
chapter 2 in *Public Culture* 37: 3 (2025)

The manufacturer's authorized representative in the EU for product safety
(GPSR) is LOGOS EUROPE, 9 rue Nicolas Poussin, 17000, La Rochelle, France
Contact@logoseurope.eu

The moral rights of the author have been asserted

1 3 5 7 9 10 8 6 4 2

Verso
UK: 6 Meard Street, London W1F 0EG
US: 207 East 32nd Street, New York, NY 10016
versobooks.com

Verso is the imprint of New Left Books

ISBN-13: 978-1-80429-344-7
ISBN-13: 978-1-80429-345-4 (US EBK)
ISBN-13: 978-1-80429-346-1 (UK EBK)

British Library Cataloguing in Publication Data
A catalogue record for this book is available from the British Library

Library of Congress Cataloging-in-Publication Data

Names: Siraganian, Lisa author
Title: The problem of personhood : giving rights to trees, corporations,
    and robots / Lisa Siraganian.
Description: New York : Verso, 2026. | Includes bibliographical references
    and index.
Identifiers: LCCN 2025042391 (print) | LCCN 2025042392 (ebook) | ISBN
    9781804293447 hardback | ISBN 9781804293454 ebook
Subjects: LCSH: Persons (Law) | Juristic persons
Classification: LCC K625 .S57 2026 (print) | LCC K625 (ebook) | DDC
    346.01/2--dc23/eng/20250912
LC record available at https://lccn.loc.gov/2025042391
LC ebook record available at https://lccn.loc.gov/2025042392

Typeset in Minion Pro by MJ & N Gavan, Truro, Cornwall
Printed in the UK by CPI Group (UK) Ltd, Croydon, CR0 4YY

Contents

List of Illustrations

Preface

In the process of writing this book, in the context not only of current events but their longer history, facing the problem of unrecognized personhood became unavoidable to me. A common, understandable reaction might be to recognize and count persons, everywhere. As a way to counteract the dehumanization, dispossession, and victimization that so many people have suffered, ensuring equality between different groups of people has been the go-to, default solution. We know how this story has gone, and how it should go: more recognition for the oppressed. Persons are legion, and surely more and different kinds can be identified every day. So recognize every human being—of course.

Yet here is the problem: A critical transformation is needed to extend rights to *nonhumans*. It looks, at first, merely like an extension of what came before; actually, it is a huge shift. As will become clear in the chapters to follow, this book is deeply skeptical that expanding personhood, as a legal or moral concept, will help us resolve this or other pressing issues of our time—including that of failing to redress suffering, harm, and inequality. Instead, I want to urge us, counterintuitively, to abandon the practice of extending personhood beyond human beings when we feel that temptation. Expansive personhood has become the problem, not the solution. And we should aim for something else in its place.

This book seeks to understand why legal personhood, as a concept detached, hovering on its own, has been so tempting and yet unable to solve the kinds of legal, moral, and political problems we want it to. My hunch is that we have been looking at that legal concept, personhood, on its own, when it makes no sense without a community of people—neighbors with a sense of their obligations to others. But even that is not enough. All the right moral choices, at critical moments, will not remedy a world filled with individual losses and unluckiness. Only an entire social and political world of neighbors could start to do that. Only a group of people can make persons meaningful.

More than an abstract sense of collective personhood, we need a concept of shared interests and actions on behalf of a collectivity. This book attempts to clear some ground for that solidarity. It hopes for, and begins to imagine, a world full of persons but *without* personhood at the forefront of our most fascinating stories.

Introduction: Unbecoming Us

Collectively Passing into Things

Until the 1990s, the term "personhood"—the quality or condition of being an individual person—appeared rarely, sometimes in bioethics or moral and religious philosophy, occasionally in legal scholarship. But, over the last twenty-five years, the concept has seeped into the political, legal, and cultural realms, generating confusion, fascination, and unease. Personhood has become essential to debates about providing corporations human privileges, releasing animals from zoos, limiting access to abortion, permitting trees the standing to sue, and giving algorithms free speech protections. For many, these movements are variously disturbing or hopeful. Controversies about each of them have been examined with journalistic vigor and scholarly care. But why exactly has *personhood* become the critical term for all these cultural, legal, and political debates? And what are the consequences of that trend? What happens when we turn more things, ideas, and entities into persons?

This book seeks to answer these questions, revealing the unsettling connections between the many different imagined persons, and their sought-after rights, that proliferate today. Synthesizing the political, legal, and philosophical debates on personhood, *The Problem of Personhood: Giving Rights to Trees, Corporations, and Robots* uncovers the unexpected, disturbing, and sometimes dangerous alignments among them. I show how our new forms of personhood emerged out of, and are variations on, an old version of legal "fictional" personhood: the corporate one. Starting in the nineteenth century, law sought to tackle the representation and apportionment of collective thoughts and actions at scale, in societies and commercial firms that were becoming unwieldy. Anglo-American legal systems developed corporate personhood to project large business entities on the model of rationally contracting individuals, and perversely did so, in the United States, with constitutional amendments intended to protect formerly enslaved people. For better and sometimes worse, today's multifaceted personhood movement is a complex culmination of those legal and business aims that foregrounded rights over responsibilities, individual freedoms over collective obligations. To put it a little differently, other, nonhuman entities are permitted, in law, to amass and exercise rights without having anything much in the way of duties, because (like corporate persons) they do not have the capacity to *ought* to do something. This lack of duties will emerge as a central theme in the chapters to follow, as we begin to grasp the extent to which our personhood is constituted by our obligations. And, as distinctive and as politically divergent as contemporary personhood movements might seem, they all began with a type of person that developed into its modern form not in the past few decades, but in the nineteenth century.

Both a history of, and an intervention into, these ongoing personhood debates, *The Problem of Personhood* perches at the intersection of intellectual and legal history, political theory, and art. To animate this story, each of its five central chapters homes in on a single aspect of this group biography to profile a different "person": corporate, fetal, animal, environmental, and AI. By integrating a variety of different source material, ranging from court cases, legal theory, and philosophy to performance art, children's books, and prestige television, my aim is to introduce the fascinating and contentious topic of contemporary legal personhood to everyone. Those who have been baffled or outraged by the US Supreme Court's *Citizens United v. FEC* (2010) decision, holding that corporations may exercise their free speech rights as persons by "speaking" with campaign donations, will grasp its long backstory in the legal and philosophical disputes about collective personality.[1] Others, curious to know why, in 2019, the citizens of Toledo, Ohio, voted to grant Lake Erie the rights of a legal person in order to combat a toxic algae bloom, will understand the arguments leading to the charter's initial success, and—for now—its overturning.[2] And readers who may question the alignment between corporations and lakes, or who want to know

---

1   *Citizens United v. Federal Election Commission*, 558 US 310 (2010).
2   Devon Alexandra Berman, "Lake Erie Bill of Rights Gets the Ax: Is Legal Personhood for Nature Dead in the Water?," *Sustainable Development Law and Policy* 20 (2019): 15.

this history to rethink our current ecosystem of persons, will begin to visualize alternatives.

For the philosopher and political activist Simone Weil in the 1940s, collective thought was a dangerous conundrum wherever we might find it. Because, she wrote, "collective thought cannot exist as thought, it passes into things (signs, machines . . .). Hence the paradox: it is the thing which thinks, and the man who is reduced to the state of a thing."[3] Weil's revelation guides my book. Collective thought's tantalizing hope, and its actual impossibility, generates a paradox of people reduced to and equated *with* things. Legal personhood is another symptom of this paradox, a way to make palpable the collective thought of corporations, and the intentions and judgments of beings that either cannot express their intentions in language (nonhuman animals, fetuses), or lack them to begin with (the environment, robots, and AI). Law makes meaning by reformulating "people" into "legal persons," and into another, thing-like form. This chapter begins to tell that story with a brief intellectual history of the recent personhood discourse and debates. With the example of one of the oldest liberty rights—habeas corpus—we will see epitomized what is unique and overlooked about these personhood debates. And we will also see how discussions about personhood both intersect with and diverge from discussions of human rights, object-oriented ontology, and other recent theories. In the process, this chapter takes a few exemplary instances to swiftly introduce the broader philosophical, legal, and cultural contexts for the book, setting up the stakes of the chapters to follow.

That You Have the "Person"

"To be visible in law," Margaret Davies and Ngaire Naffine observe, "one must be a legal person."[4] Lawyers often use the term "person" in this technical way. But not always. There are also ordinary ways we talk about a person—say, as a human being with moral standing in our community—and that common usage frequently slips into lawyers' and judges' arguments too. When an appeals court judge opines that "there is little mystery that a 'person' is 'an individual human being,'" she is invoking

---

3 Simone Weil, *Gravity and Grace*, trans. Arthur Wills (University of Nebraska Press, 1997), 210.

4 Margaret Davies and Ngaire Naffine, *Are Persons Property?: Legal Debates About Property and Personality* (Burlington, VT: Ashgate, 2001), 51.

not a legal but a more ordinary definition of "person."[5] Lawmakers, also, have been far from unanimous about the meaning of "person," sometimes insisting on strict terminology and other times encouraging common usage. As one scholar observes, statutes tend to use different definitions of the word "depending on the individual purpose of the statute," which "creates more ambiguity as to the common definition of the term." In the United States, neither the Constitution nor the highest courts have "provided a concrete definition for who qualifies as a 'person.'"[6] Under these circumstances, it is tricky to aim for a consistent meaning that develops from law, as contemporary expansive personhood has. When I mean "legal person" or "legal personhood" narrowly or technically, I try to call it that. But because discussions of expansive personhood have taken on philosophical, cultural, and political roles beyond the courtroom, seeping into our non-technical conversations, we will need to include all the various ways in which we use the word "person." Typically, I intend "expansive personhood" to embrace both its philosophical and legal sources as well as its extralegal adaptations, and lean on context to clarify which usages are in play.

All this reminds us that being a person (legal or otherwise) has meant different things in different traditions, disciplines, and contexts. As Jens David Ohlin notes, "The meaning of the term ['person'] is so difficult to nail down because it straddles not only metaphysics, biology, and religion, but also value theory, such as moral philosophy and the law."[7] Moreover, everyone's definition of personhood, whether legal, moral, philosophical, or ordinary, requires some, often divergent, set of assumptions about what persons are. To start, consider a few touchstones of "person," from contemporary law's sources in ancient Roman law, which classified all law as of three kinds: of persons, things, or actions (with a further division of persons into "free or slaves").[8] As the philosopher Antonia LoLordo observes, "The Romans distinguished the concept of a person from the concept of the individual human being," allowing one human being to "play many *personae*," in the sense of roles or characters.[9] Already it was assumed that the category of "person" and the sense

---

5   *Rasul v. Myers*, 563 F.3d 527 (DC Cir. 2009), J. Brown concurrence, 533.

6   Emily A. Fitzgerald, "(Ape)rsonhood," *Review of Litigation* 34 (Spring 2015): 341.

7   Jens David Ohlin, "Is the Concept of the Person Necessary for Human Rights?," *Columbia Law Review* 105 (2005): 214.

8   Gaius, William M. Gordon, and O. F. Robinson, *The Institutes of Gaius* (Ithaca, NY: Cornell University Press, 1988), 23.

9   Antonia LoLordo, "Introduction: The Concept of a Person from Antiquity to the

of "human being" overlapped yet were not exactly identical. Roles and characters are not the same as human beings. It is from this small but significant divergence that expansive personhood, eventually, will bloom.

Certainty, there are reductive formal accounts of legal personhood (as merely the subject of rights and duties) that we might entertain.[10] However, generally, expansive legal personhood has both a historical-legal *and* a philosophically robust support, and it is that combinatory genealogy that we will follow. Offering a synthetic mapping, LoLordo articulates the five possible characteristics that philosophers have selected, historically, to braid together the personhood concept. Persons are, or can be (1) particulars (which is to say, unique individuals); (2) roles; (3) entities with moral significance; (4) rational beings; and/ or (5) reflective, self-constituting selves.[11] Throughout this book, we will see how accounts of contemporary expansive legal personhood choose *selectively* from this list, and why that causes problems. Some of these essential attributes will be plucked from the main chord, and others will be abandoned—typically forsaken are the characteristics of (2) roles, (4) rational beings, and (5) reflective, self-constituting selves. Quite often, we find ourselves left with a concept of persons reduced to only two critical qualities: particular entities with moral significance.

To start to see the powerful ramifications of this development of expansive legal personhood, consider two recent, very different, and widely recounted cases of one of the oldest liberty rights. These are petitions for the writ of habeas corpus, literally translated as "that you have the body." The petitioners employed the same legal instrument but were very different: on the one hand, a teenage prisoner named Mohammed el Gharani at Guantánamo and, on the other, an old elephant named Happy, living in the Bronx Zoo.

The term "habeas corpus" is ancient, dating from before the Magna Carta (1215). And the right, or something comparable to it, is enshrined as foundational, whether in the UK Parliament's Habeas Corpus Act (1679), the "suspension clause" of the US Constitution (1789), the French Declaration of the Rights of Man and of the Citizen (1789), or the UN Declaration of Human Rights (1948). In most liberal democracies this so-called "Great Writ" is still employed, albeit inconsistently, as a way

---

Twenty-First Century," in *Persons: A History*, ed. Antonia LoLordo (Oxford University Press, 2019), 5.

10   See Visa A. J. Kurki, *A Theory of Legal Personhood* (Oxford University Press, 2019), 31–90.

11   LoLordo, "Introduction: The Concept of a Person," 2–3.

to bring a person physically (their body or "corpus") before a court, allowing them (through their lawyers) to scrutinize the legality of their detention. The ultimate aim is to be released from custody. In the United States, state and federal prisoners file tens of thousands of habeas petitions every year. As a civil liberty check on arbitrary police or sovereign power, the order effectively compels a government institution that is locking someone up to tell the prisoner the reasons that they have been imprisoned.[12]

However, as ordered after 9/11, this protection may be suspended for "enemy combatants" during public safety emergencies.[13] And US courts have sharply limited habeas corpus relief for prisoners of all types over the last half century, a trend accelerating recently.[14] This is the context for the first habeas case we will consider. In 2009, Mohammed el Gharani, the youngest prisoner at the US Naval Base in Guantánamo Bay, Cuba, was finally granted his petition for habeas corpus release. After 9/11, fourteen-year-old El Gharani was swept up by Pakistani authorities and then imprisoned and tortured in Guantánamo for over seven years. The US government claimed that he had been in Afghanistan, worked as a courier for senior al-Qaeda operatives, received terrorist military training, participated in a London-based al-Qaeda cell, and fought in the battle of Tora Bora.[15] The evidence established none of that. In fact, El Gharani had left his Saudi Arabian birthplace as a teenager because he was discriminated against as a native Black African and was trying to pick up some computer and English skills in Pakistan. He had never set foot in Afghanistan or London, and he had no connection to al-Qaeda.

Granting El Gharani's petition, US Federal District Judge Richard Leon made these points in his court order, rejecting the government's argument that El Gharani had supported the Taliban. The government's evidence, the judge criticized, was a "mosaic of allegations" based on the dubious and inconsistent testimony of several other Guantánamo detainees, whom government employees knew to be unreliable.

---

12   Judith Farbey, Robert J. Sharpe, and Simon Atrill, "Historical Aspects of Habeas Corpus," in *The Law of Habeas Corpus*, 3rd ed. Judith Farbey, R. J. Sharpe, and Simon Atrill (Oxford University Press, 2011), 1–17.

13   See US Constitution, Art. 1, sect. 9, cl. 2: "The privilege of the Writ of Habeas Corpus shall not be suspended, unless when in cases of Rebellion or Invasion the Public Safety may require it."

14   *Brown v. Davenport*, 212 L. Ed. 2d 463, 142 S. Ct. 1510 (2022); *Shinn v. Ramirez*, 212 L. Ed. 2d 713, 142 S. Ct. 1718 (2022).

15   *El Gharani v. Bush*, 593 F. Supp. 2d 144 (D.D.C. 2009), 144, 147.

"Accordingly, the Court must, and will, GRANT the detainee's petition for a writ of habeas corpus" and the government was "ORDERED . . . to take all necessary appropriate diplomatic steps to facilitate his release forthwith."[16] Although such habeas corpus petitions rarely succeed, El Gharani's did.

Around the time El Gharani was released, after President Barack Obama was first elected and tried to make good on his campaign promise to close the Guantánamo Bay prison, Obama's administration proposed transferring its prisoners to the Thomson Correctional Center in Illinois. This planned move never happened; Congress blocked the transfer of Guantánamo prisoners to the United States and Obama failed to close Guantánamo. As of this writing, Guantánamo remains open indefinitely and is holding prisoners. As the Thomson proposal was developing, the People for the Ethical Treatment of Animals (PETA) irreverently proposed that the Illinois prison would be better suited to permanently house their exhibit, one they called "the Thomson All Living Beings Empathy Center":

> We can't think of a more appropriate site for our Animal Liberation Project (ALP) than a prison. The ALP is a display that takes viewers through a history of the discrimination and suffering of humans and other beings—from the Crusades to human slavery and from animal circuses to factory farms—reminding people that suffering is suffering, no matter who the victim is.[17]

The Animal Liberation Project (ALP) displays, which toured various cities in the United Kingdom and the United States, made that history of suffering explicit through formally similar imagery of humans and animals. Photographs of imprisoned chimps gripping cages were juxtaposed with human beings doing the same. The texts explained the similar images: "This primate was held in confinement at a roadside zoo for people's entertainment . . . This Iranian was held in confinement in an Iraqi prison during the Iran-Iraq conflict."[18]

Working with PETA, the late Jamaican English poet, playwright, and social justice activist Benjamin Zephaniah launched ALP in 2007 by creating a series of controversial panels explicitly comparing animals held in zoos to political prisoners and enslaved people. His arguments followed

---

16   *El Gharani*, 148, 149.
17   PETA.org.
18   grist.org.

the philosopher Peter Singer's manifestoes defining "'speciesism,' by analogy with racism" (a claim discussed at more length in chapter 3). Writing in *The Guardian*, Zephaniah acknowledged ways in which the comparison might disturb and outrage viewers but maintained the claim's necessity and veracity. "It is always hard to look at today's abuses and imagine them through the critical eyes of future generations," he observed, "just as those who sold hundreds of thousands of human slaves along the Thames 200 years ago probably could not imagine how that industry would be viewed today."[19]

Zephaniah and ALP's point was that wrongful imprisonment of a living being is wrong in whatever form we find it, and graphic images enable us to see new forms for what they really are. Over the next decade, animal rights legal activists advanced versions of Zephaniah and ALP's arguments in US courts using habeas corpus petitions, the ancient "writ of liberty," as Blackstone called it—the same legal instrument that El Gharani successfully employed to petition for his release from Guantánamo.

With that context in view, now consider a second and very different case, one that deployed that legal procedure on behalf of a different individual animal: an elephant in the Bronx Zoo named Happy. In 2018, the nonprofit Nonhuman Rights Project, Inc. (NhRP) filed a writ of habeas corpus in New York state, alleging that Happy was "unlawfully imprisoned solely because she is an elephant."[20] Born in the wild in Thailand, in 1971, Happy was captured at a young age and eventually sold to the Bronx Zoo, where she was taught and forced to perform tricks.[21] Her companion of many years died in 2006 and from that time she lived alone as the only elephant in a single-acre enclosure. The NhRP argued that because Happy possessed the basic common law right to bodily liberty, she should be released immediately to a wildlife sanctuary "so as to prevent future unlawful deprivation of her liberty" and autonomy. Furthermore, they argued that "person" and "human being" are not synonyms in law, and so courts could properly adjudicate the personhood of Happy for habeas relief. In this case, the court had a duty "to recognize that modern scientific evidence and justice require that Happy be recognized as a 'person'" with liberty rights.[22]

---

19   Benjamin Zephaniah, "The Lives of Others," *The Guardian* (August 1, 2007).

20   Brief for Petitioner-Appellant, *In the Matter of . . . The Nonhuman Rights Project, Inc, on behalf of Happy v. James J. Breheny, et al.,* Appellate Case No.: 2020-02581, New York Supreme Court, Appellate Division-First Department (July 10, 2018), 2.

21   Macarena Montes Franceschini, "Animal Personhood: The Quest for Recognition," *Animal and Natural Resource Law Review* 17 (2021): 129.

22   *In the matter of . . . Happy,* 5.

NhRP's choice of Happy as a plaintiff was inspired. In 2006, she had made national news as the first elephant to be scientifically recorded spontaneously recognizing herself in a mirror, a capacity that up to that time was thought to be limited to humans (beginning around toddler-hood), chimpanzees, and sometimes dolphins.[23] Unlike most nonhuman mammals, her selfhood seemed proven by science. But, more gener-ally, elephants' complex cognitive functions were being progressively established by increasing numbers of studies. They had been shown to share human traits including "empathy, intentional communication, long-term memory allowing for the accumulation of social knowledge, goal-directness, and even mourning and awareness of death."[24]

Bucking convention, the district court judge agreed that there was merit to these arguments and set a hearing to determine whether Happy should be released. In December 2018, for the first time in the United States, a court heard arguments on both sides regarding an elephant's habeas corpus petition. That success was short-lived. Ultimately, the court rejected Happy's petition, and the appeals court upheld the lower court's ruling, arguing that "the writ of habeas corpus is limited to human beings."[25] The appeals court judges seemed especially concerned about displacing long-standing precedents without legislative guidance. Decid-ing otherwise "would lead to a labyrinth of questions that common-law processes are ill-equipped to answer," and tackling such questions was not a job for judges but for the legislature. Quite simply, "because the writ of habeas corpus is intended to protect the liberty right of *human beings* to be free of unlawful confinement, it has no applicability to Happy, a nonhuman animal who is not a 'person' subjected to illegal detention."[26]

Such a view—that a nonhuman animal cannot be a person—stretches back to the early modern period if not before. For the fifth-century phi-losopher Boethius, a person is "an individual substance of a rational nature," and it went without saying, to him, that nonhuman animals did not possess rationality.[27] Although philosophers tinkered with the

---

23   Joshua M. Plotnik, Frans B. M de Waal, and Diana Reiss, "Self-Recognition in an Asian Elephant," *Proceedings of the National Academy of Sciences - PNAS* 103, no. 45 (2006): 17053–7.

24   Gianfranco Cesareo, "The Elephant in the Room: New York's Highest Court Takes Up Animal Rights," *Georgetown Environmental Law Review Online* (February 23, 2022).

25   *Nonhuman Rights Project, Inc. v. Breheny*, 189 A.D.3d 583, 134 N.Y.S.3d 188, 189 (2020), *aff'd*, 38 N.Y.3d 555, 197 N.E.3d 921 (2022).

26   *Nonhuman Rights*, 566–9, 923–6.

27   Scott M. Williams, "Persons in Patristic and Medieval Christian Theology," in *Persons: A History*, ed. Antonia LoLordo (Oxford University Press, 2019), 52.

personhood definition for the next millennium, the view that had been consolidating for centuries was not wildly different from Boethius's. By the eighteenth century, a person was "a rational being, a self, and a locus of moral significance."[28] In rejecting Happy's petition, the New York courts leaned on this ancient history of withholding personhood from nonhuman animals, whose rationality could not be proven.

But, reflecting the broader interest in expansive personhood, two of the seven appeals court judges disagreed with this reasoning. Judge Rowan D. Wilson argued in his dissent that Happy *did* sufficiently state a case "entitling her to a hearing . . . to weigh the evidence, resolve conflicting issues and render" a decision on the merits. He quoted Jeremy Bentham's legendary warning that "the day *may* come when the rest of the animal creation may acquire those rights" that have been only tyrannically withheld from them, and the judge answered Bentham's famous rhetorical questions—"the question is not, Can they reason? nor, Can they talk? but Can they suffer?"—with a resounding: "They can and do, and that day is upon us." Incorporating discussions of Aristotle, Descartes, Malebranche, Montaigne, Darwin, and Nussbaum, among others, Wilson's dissent offers a robust historical and legal framework for the philosophical debates that we will examine later in this book. He acknowledges that, while an elephant in the eighteenth century might not have been able to petition for habeas corpus, that is "a different question from whether an elephant can do so today, because we know much more about elephant cognition, social organization, behaviors, and needs" than in the past, and our laws and norms should reflect our new understanding.[29]

While supporting Happy's petition, Wilson also stresses something else, a very different kind of point, that will be a key to this book. The entire issue of animal *personhood*, he says, perhaps surprisingly, should be abandoned: It is a distraction and irrelevant to the legal issues in play. The correct question is not whether or not Happy is a person but, quite simply, considering all that we now know about elephants, "should the law afford her certain rights through habeas corpus?" Acknowledging his background as an African American, Wilson observes something troubling about the comparison of animal to human personhood. He traces this back to PETA's advocacy campaign (created by Zephaniah, although Wilson does not mention this) comparing enslaved Black people to the

---

28   LoLordo, "Introduction: The Concept of a Person," in *Persons*, 11.
29   *Nonhuman Rights*, dissent; 578, 603.

contemporary treatment of animals. Wilson proposes abandoning the personhood arguments for animals to avoid "comparisons that have harmful racial-coding and dehumanizing effects." We should recognize Happy's right to petition for her liberty, he says, not because she is a person (or a wild animal), but because the rights we choose to confer on her, or not, reflect back on us as a society.[30]

We will have an opportunity to revisit these arguments in chapter 3, on nonhuman animal personhood. But we can already start to see an impasse forming in the expanding personhood model, one that Wilson is attempting to break through or maybe evade. Some jurists (like the majority denying Happy's petition) and legal philosophers (Yan Thomas, Anna Grear) reject expansive personhood for a range of reasons. Other legal theorists, philosophers, and animal rights activists, such as the late Robbyne Kaamil, embrace expansive personhood fully. Like Zephaniah, Kaamil makes the race-speciesism connection explicitly and without Wilson's qualms: "My great-great-grandmother was a slave," she announces in a PETA video set to Mississippi Delta guitar music and illustrated with her own Kara Walker–like silhouettes, as the image of an enslaved human being in shackles is replaced by one of an elephant shackled and behind bars. Kaamil deploys her personal genealogy to authorize her call to moral action: "Let's end slavery everywhere, anywhere, in all its forms for all living beings."[31]

But besides these two poles, there are also other intriguing positions—true third options, as with Judge Wilson's learned dissent, that attempt contradictory moves. Wilson is, on the one hand, seeking to give Happy access to habeas corpus, that venerable, fundamental right of persons. It seems to Wilson that she deserves it. And, on the other hand, Wilson is rejecting the language and concept of personhood to do so. Personhood, he feels, gets in the way and hurts Black people. How do we understand this paradoxical view? Rather than dismiss it as a logical contradiction, we can make sense of Wilson's desire because it intuits that something is going awry in these discussions of personhood, even though the conventions and protections that have developed under its purview remain vital. His careful dissent warns us to be on our guard about personhood arguments. In the next sections of this introduction, we will start to see how this notion of the expansive legal person developed. It is an individual strangely flattened yet emotionally various;

---

30   Ibid., 580–1, 612, 626.
31   Robbyne Kaamil, "Animal Captivity Is Slavery," PETA.org (2015).

gouged out, yet colossal; alienated, yet ever-present. The longer biography of this inherited, expanded form of the legal person—and how and why this reductive version came to dominate our understanding—still needs to be told.

Expanding the Circle and Impoverishing the Person

On the most basic level, arguments like NhRP's for Happy the elephant function by expanding the circle of personhood beyond the criteria of conventional rationality and language use. Think of Kaamil's call to arms to "end slavery everywhere, anywhere, in all its forms for all living beings." Her gesture is one of munificent inclusion and expansiveness. Animal intelligence will be broadly conceived, emotional depth and suffering will be newly respected, and self-awareness and sociability will be recognized and valued where we did not locate them before. All these qualities become characteristics that, if exhibited, land an individual in the plush personhood circle. And, once there, protections are newly open and potentially available to that individual: certain rights, most importantly. But, as the appeals court judges worried, other privileges could follow, including jurisdictional standing, a voice that must be listened to, maybe even features of citizenship. The nonhuman individual, like Happy the elephant, takes on significance in the world that she did not have before, the consequences of which will have to be measured and weighed against that of human beings. As the philosopher Mary Midgley observes, engaging in this process means that it will become "much harder to exclude [animals] from moral consideration."[32]

We have already seen a few ways in which personhood expanded beyond human beings could be helpful for animal rights advocates; this will be the larger subject of chapter 3. In recent decades, expansive personhood has also been used by environmental activists who are seeking to combat climate degradation by protecting the environment as a moral and legal person, providing natural entities a status that would be comprehensible and litigable in law; this is the topic of chapter 4. As hopeful as such moves might be, expansive personhood for other entities has also been disturbing to many people, in these and different realms. Corporate personhood remains one of the most disconcerting versions, particularly

---

32   Mary Midgley, *Utopias, Dolphins, and Computers: Some Problems In Philosophical Plumbing* (New York: Routledge, 1996), 115.

since, for nonlawyers at least, it appeared to arise out of the ether with the *Citizens United* decision. In fact, corporate personhood has a long history and has set the stage for subsequent conversations about personhood, as discussed next in chapter 1.

Other versions of expansive personhood are movements for "fetal personhood," often known in the United States as "Human Life Amendments," which aim to overthrow remaining state-level abortion rights protections in favor of the "unborn." This is the subject of chapter 2. And then there are those legal scholars who argue that no legitimate reason can be made to withhold legal electronic personhood, so-called "ePersonhood," from social robots or algorithms like ChatGPT, produced and owned by companies such as OpenAI, Google, and X (formerly Twitter). These arguments are challenged in chapter 5. In these varied cases (corporate, fetal, animal, environmental, AI), each the subject of a chapter to follow, the logic of expansive personhood supports the claims being made.

What sorts of premises does expanding personhood need? There are several key components. We can synthesize arguments made by various philosophers and political theorists, placing them in an earlier historical context. The most basic thesis is as follows:

Thesis 1: The expanding personhood model requires the eighteenth-century notion of perfect equality, in contrast to the status-based model of older regimes founded in Roman law.

To see the force of the equality idea we must remember what it replaced. A central function of the Roman law treatise *Gaius's Institutes* (c. 170 CE), later incorporated as a major part of the influential legal handbook known as *Justinian's Institutes* (533 CE), is to guarantee that everyone and everything have a designated and *ranked* place in the law: a proper status. This secures all the jurisdictions for adjudicating laws, whether private or public, divine or human. In Roman law, in other words, all must be accounted for and classified somewhere in its hierarchical system. No human being or object could be imagined to either drift outside law's reach or be permitted to make a reasoned claim to be judged under a different law or standard. And notwithstanding many modifications, Roman law, as legal historians have long noted, serves as the backbone for the common law still in effect in many parts of the world.

In sharp contrast to that tradition, the US Declaration of Independence (1776), the French Declaration of the Rights of Man (1789), and the countless constitutions roughly contemporaneous with them claim a very different premise and purpose: "that all men are created equal" (as the US version proclaims). The French variant expands on the theme: Article 1 of the Rights of Man states from the outset that "men are born and remain free and equal in rights. Social distinctions may be founded only upon the general good." The former hierarchical classifications, either through birth or experience, are declared void, and any further distinctions must have a general social purpose. Article 6 of the Rights of Man expands on this position, describing how it can be realized through egalitarian policies: The law "must be the same for all, whether it protects or punishes. All citizens, being equal in the eyes of the law, are equally eligible to all dignities and to all public positions and occupations, according to their abilities, and without distinction except that of their virtues and talents." Although the addition of the term "citizens" (rather than the more general "man" or "men") will complicate matters significantly, the premise of equality is the necessary first step in all such declarations.

It is an obvious point but still needs to be stated: The notion of expansive personhood we have started exploring cannot begin without this initial equalizing move. And it should also go without saying that racial and gender differences (understood as a kind of moral or legal disability) were promptly deployed to circumvent claims of equality for all human beings. But without the notion of equality, there is no consistent way to challenge *any* allegation of legal inferiority or disability. Likewise, expansive personhood needs the concept of equality because without it there will be no secure way to bring in all individuals under its protections. Otherwise, it always will be possible to make, invent, or legitimate what the Rights of Man calls "social distinctions" between individuals of different backgrounds or social classes—or between species or kinds.

Almost immediately, the force of this point was deployed on both sides of the expansiveness debate. Think of Mary Wollstonecraft's point in *A Vindication of the Rights of Woman* (1792): "Let women share the rights, and she will emulate the virtues of man." It is not woman's innately different being that holds her back but her lower social status and lack of rights, argues Wollstonecraft, and so she will "grow more perfect when emancipated."[33] As Peter Singer notes, that basic logic was

---

33   Mary Wollstonecraft, *Wollstonecraft: A Vindication of the Rights of Men and a Vindication of the Rights of Woman and Hints*, ed. Sylvana Tomaselli (Cambridge University Press, 1995), 294.

used the same year to produce a parody of not just women's asserted rights, but of the assertion of rights belonging to animals more generally.[34] Thomas Taylor's anonymously published *A Vindication of the Rights of Brutes* (1792) mocks "the equality of all things." Anything, Taylor notes, is "of inestimable value, and intrinsically equal to a thing of the least magnitude and worth."[35] Wollstonecraft sees women's rights and full flourishing as the only way for society to realize its potential, to continue "the progress of knowledge, because truth must be common to all."[36] Taylor, in contrast, predicts the dangers both to his patriarchal, elevated position and to society more generally, destroying the necessary differences that sustain the status quo. "Treatises on the rights of vegetables and minerals" are sure to follow so that "the doctrine of perfect equality will become universal" and "dominion of every kind [will] be exiled from the face of the earth."[37] All distinctions between humans and nonhumans will be erased, and vegetables will rule, somehow, as ferociously as men.

Taylor's mockery of utopian "perfect equality" gestures at an aspect of rights discourse that ripens into a real concern by the mid-twentieth century.

Thesis 2: Expansive personhood, paradoxically, requires an impoverished notion of personhood.

That is, the expanding circle of personhood logically entails a radically reductive, almost empty account of the person (without the Christian soul, at the very least), one who is *also* missing the ascriptions of conventions and status that might stitch different individuals into a coherent social fabric. Typically, this depleted version of personhood equates with rudimentary human rights.

Versions of this claim have been recognized by a range of more recent philosophers and critical theorists. Anna Grear, for example, helpfully discusses the "the decontextualisation of law's person," which surreptitiously serves "to privilege the interests of identifiable propertied capitalistic elites and their interests."[38] But personhood is not typically

---

34   Peter Singer, *Animal Liberation: A New Ethics for Our Treatment of Animals* (Random House, 1975), 1.

35   Thomas Taylor, *A Vindication of the Rights of Brutes* (London: Edward Jeffery, 1792), 11–12.

36   Wollstonecraft, *Vindication*, 68.

37   Taylor, *Rights of Brutes*, 15, 19.

38   Anna Grear, "The Vulnerable Living Order: Human Rights and the Environment

described in these terms, nor has it been treated systematically. Contemporary readers are sometimes led astray because the English word "personhood" is of relatively recent vintage, essentially nonexistent until the 1970s; many languages still do not use such a term. Instead, the term "personality" incorporated both our contemporary idea of individual identity and distinctive characteristics (as in "personality traits") as well as that of philosophical and legal existence and status (as in "personhood"). This etymology needs to be kept in view when examining mid-twentieth century political theoretical critiques such as Simone Weil's and Hannah Arendt's, which typically use or are translated as using the term "personality" but, with that word, also incorporate philosophical and legal "personhood."

For those critical of legal personhood's dominance, Weil's essay "Human Personality" (1942–43) is foundational, with its account of the insufficiency of rights as an idea that could possibly capture the entirety of someone's personhood. "The notion of rights," she writes, "which was launched into the world in 1789, has proved unable, because of its intrinsic inadequacy, to fulfill the role assigned to it." For Weil, the idea of the rights-bearing person in the 1789 Rights of Man document is a degrading and inadequate inheritance from Roman law. It fails to capture what is sacred about human beings, an essential quality she describes as what is "impersonal" about them. Rather, the rights-based version of the person aligns with everything economic, collective, and mediocre: "The notion of rights is linked with the notion of sharing out, of exchange, of measured quantity; it has a commercial flavour, essentially evocative of legal claims and arguments." Such economic and legal concepts ultimately rely on force, which is always lurking in the background of the claim of rights, "or else it will be laughed at." You can see her point when reflecting on Taylor's *Vindication* for brutes' and vegetables' rights, taken as pure mockery, while Peter Singer's identical argument, financially supported by the Animal Liberation Front and PETA, and legislatively by various state-sponsored legal safeguards, is received as dead serious. To sum up, Weil deems the exclusive reliance on rights as a dangerous distraction from the real problem: a social drama (coercion into prostitution, for example) is "falsely assimilated" into an economic problem (the right to sell your body product at the best price).[39]

---

in a Critical and Philosophical Perspective," *Journal of Human Rights and the Environment* 2, no. 1 (2011): 32.

39   Simone Weil, "Human Personality" (1942–43) in *Simone Weil: An Anthology*, ed. Siân Miles (New York: Grove Press, 1986), 51, 61, 63.

A few decades later, Arendt's *On Revolution* (1963) tackles the inadequacy of personhood rights from a different direction, sketching out a story of how the activists of the French Revolution aimed to "tear off . . . the mask of hypocrisy" worn by the insincere role-players in society's games in order to "liberate the natural man in all men," giving him his entitled birthright of the Rights of Man. Their aim backfired, however. In the process of "unmasking society" and releasing people from a situation in which rights originate in the body politic, the activists inadvertently tore off that older fiction (from Roman law) of legal personhood. The Rights of Man was able to make men equal only because it left everyone, admittedly equally, without what she calls "the protecting mask of a legal personality."[40]

In *The Origins of Totalitarianism* (1951), Arendt explores what happens when this situation expands and devolves. It is the disastrous history from WWI through the Holocaust, leading to the nation-state's decline and "the End of the Rights of Man." Without the notion of a common world in which we all live, with our different legal personalities and statuses, people are forced to live, in a sense, outside the common world altogether. They find themselves "thrown back, in the midst of civilization, on their natural givenness, on their mere differentiation . . . they begin to belong to the human race in much the same way as animals belong to a specific animal species."[41] The Holocaust is obviously her target here. Yet, we are also starting to see Arendt warn us about a version of the model of personhood, albeit in an inverted and emergent form, that animal rights activists will seek to promote. It is a model that understands our species-centrism as a kind of racial difference ("mere differentiation") to be acknowledged and then overcome.

It is Arendt's version of this "thrown back" individual—the person legally unmasked, relying only on "natural givenness"—that Giorgio Agamben (via Walter Benjamin) appropriates as the notion of "bare life." For Agamben, "the inclusion of bare life in the political realm constitutes the original—if concealed—nucleus of sovereign power." And it is not just happenstance that causes him to note that the first time we see "bare life as the new political subject is . . . the 1679 writ of *habeas corpus*." As Agamben puts it, "democracy is born precisely" at the moment when it is an assertion and presentation of a "body" to show ("bare, anonymous

---

40   Hannah Arendt, *On Revolution* (1963; reprint, New York: Penguin, 1977), 107–8.

41   Hannah Arendt, *The Origins of Totalitarianism* (1951; reprint, New York: Harcourt Brace Jovanovich, 1973), 302.

life"), rather than a feudal subject or a future notion of citizen.[42] Roberto Esposito makes a similar point. Tracing the rejection of human beings as property from Immanuel Kant, to the French Civil Code (1804), to the current European Union's Charter of Fundamental Rights, Esposito describes "the paradox" this development inadvertently introduced: "By declaring the body to be a 'person,' such prohibitions have the unintended effect of sending it back to the status of *res* [a legal thing or matter, in contrast to person]," even if the body is understood as a kind of "thing" taken out of the circuit of commerce.[43]

I bring up these challenges to personhood and rights in part because, following Arendt's and later theorists' lead, a powerful and important critique of human rights has emerged from the left in political theory in recent decades. A critique from the right had long been familiar (since at least Edmund Burke and Taylor, ranging to contemporary scholars Alasdair MacIntyre and Mary Ann Glendon).[44] But the left's challenge to human rights has a different aim, whether emerging in Critical Legal and Critical Race Studies or in the progressive and sometimes Marxist-flavored legal history and political theory of Wendy Brown, Jessica Whyte, and Samuel Moyn.[45] One influential example, Moyn's *The Last Utopia: Human Rights in History* (2010), makes the case that human rights are a historical project of the neoliberal turn in the 1970s, "widely understood as a moral alternative to bankrupt political utopias."[46] The triumph of the discourse of human rights reflects the disappointment and failure of other political models, ones that found their authority in the state or nation. Other scholars, including Seyla Benhabib and Ayten Gündoğdu, consider the way actual practices of human rights fail to protect or serve migrants, exiles, and refugees.[47] Here, I simply want to acknowledge both

42   Giorgio Agamben, *Homo Sacer: Sovereign Power and Bare Life* (Redwood City, CA: Stanford University Press, 1998), 6, 123, 124.

43   Roberto Esposito, *Persons and Things: From the Body's Point of View* (Cambridge: Polity, 2015), 102.

44   Mary Ann Glendon, *Rights Talk: The Impoverishment of Political Discourse* (New York: Free Press, 1991); Alasdair C. MacIntyre, *After Virtue: A Study In Moral Theory* (University of Notre Dame Press, 1981).

45   Wendy Brown, "'The Most We Can Hope For . . .': Human Rights and the Politics of Fatalism," *South Atlantic Quarterly* 103, no. 2 (June 2004): 451–63; Jessica Whyte, *The Morals of the Market: Human Rights and the Rise of Neoliberalism* (London: Verso, 2019); Samuel Moyn, *Not Enough: Human Rights in an Unequal World* (Cambridge, MA: Harvard University Press, 2018).

46   Samuel Moyn, *The Last Utopia: Human Rights in History* (Cambridge, MA: Harvard University Press, 2010), 5.

47   Seyla Benhabib, *The Rights of Others: Aliens, Residents, and Citizens* (Cambridge

the significance and importance of human rights discourse, as well as the force of critiques pointing out their failures in contemporary practice. But my aims in this book are different. The legal discourses of expansive personhood often do not address *human* rights dilemmas at all, but focus on very different entities instead. To keep our view on target, critiques of human rights remain to the side in *The Problem of Personhood*.

In the chapters to follow, we will have opportunity to consider aspects of impoverished personhood both in theory and practice. But we can already start to see that expansive personhood needs one more element to at least temporarily fend off these critiques. In essence, that is the strategic move of *embracing* the inadequacy and hollowness as the entirety of what personhood means. We could put it as follows and say that the third requirement for expansive personhood is:

Thesis 3: Human personhood is positively equated with, and reduced to, artificial, legal personhood.

In other words, the totality of personhood—moral and legal—becomes reconceived as merely a tool, mask, legal device, or container of properties. This position tends to rely on a formalist view in which rights always correlate symmetrically with duties (the view Wesley Newcomb Hohfeld established over a century ago), and, consequently, personhood could be equated with standing and thus (say) with the right to sue and be sued. This theoretical position (or trend), later central to legal positivism, is trickier to track than some of the other elements, particularly when it seeps out of legal discourse and into the moral arguments of public discourse. But it is no less critical to expansive personhood's workings today.

A version of that reduction emerges already in Hans Kelsen's influential account in *The Pure Theory of Law* (1934):

> "To be a person" or "to have a legal personality" is identical with having legal obligations and subjective rights. The person as a holder of obligations and rights is not something that is different from the obligations and rights, as whose holder the person is presented—just as a tree which is said to have a trunk, branches, and blossoms, is not a substance different from trunk, branches, and blossoms, but merely the totality of these elements. The physical or juristic person who "has" obligations

University Press, 2004); Ayten Gündoğdu, *Rightlessness In an Age of Rights* (Oxford University Press, 2014).

and rights as their holder, is these obligations and rights—a complex of legal obligations and rights whose totality is expressed figuratively in the concept of "person." "Person" is merely the personification of this totality.[48]

From the very first clause to the last, Kelsen assumes that general personhood equates with legal personhood. "To be a person," he says, is interchangeable with "to have a legal personality." Personhood, on this account, is a kind of empty box ("the person as a holder"), a conventional, taxonomic container to be filled up with agreed-upon characteristics— by law, or moral rules, or social conventions. For a tree, its nominal characteristics are trunk, branches, and blossoms; for a person, they are some set of conventionally determined obligations and rights. We might use the figurative expression "person," Kelsen writes, but being a person is "merely"—and that "merely" is the primary, improbable gesture here—"the personification of this totality." And, once personhood is an empty box, becoming a person "merely" requires the law to authorize an act of box-filling: placing the characteristics of some kind of entity in the box.

Kelsen's pared-down, formalist account deliberately contrasts with that of slightly earlier natural law theorists such as John Chipman Gray, for whom the notion of human will is definitive and necessary to be a person.[49] Gray argues that legal personhood for nonhumans (say, for a corporation) is only possible by attribution, borrowing from a human being's will.[50] And, as Davies and Naffine note, his account of the legal person implies a "so-called 'normal' person—the adult of sound mind—who possesses a 'natural will.'"[51] Such normality is an onerous requirement that raises all sorts of objections for legal theorists today, not least because it shrinks rather than expands the pool of potential candidates for personhood. Kelsen's position would seem preferable for theories of expansive personhood, generating a seemingly enhanced view in which only rights are the necessary requirement for personhood, to be dealt out to all sorts of entities freely.

---

48   Hans Kelsen, *Pure Theory of Law*, trans. Max Knight (Oakland: University of California Press, 1967 [first edition 1934]), 172–3.

49   Davies and Naffine, *Are Persons Property?*, 55.

50   John Chipman Gray, *The Nature and Sources of the Law*, ed. David Campbell and Philip Thomas ([1909, 1997] New York: Routledge, 2019), 68.

51   Davies and Naffine, *Are Persons Property?*, 55.

Yet Kelsen's limited definition can be challenged in ways that do not necessarily need the apparatus of the natural law theorizing of someone like Gray. The baggage that comes with the label "person" has inherently personifying effects; corporate personhood theorists from the early twentieth century were already making versions of this point.[52] From that perspective, Kelsen's "merely" seems unrealistic and inaccurate. Once a "person" is in the picture, we will conceive, imagine, and interact with the personified entity in ways that we would not have otherwise—or else we will reject the label of "person" to begin with. In the philosopher Elizabeth Wolgast's words, the legal "fiction" of personhood does not enable us to simply erase or ignore the "moral import" of personhood because "other features of being a person, such as having rights and being entitled to respect and membership in the community . . . are connected with human capacities and with moral responsibility."[53] The idea that legal personhood can be conceptualized as purely instrumental, merely a totality of elements, seems at best wishful and at worst deeply misleading ("an anomaly," says Wolgast). Marxist legal theorists are particularly skeptical, arguing that Kelsen's theory "turns its back from the outset on the facts of reality," and thus is, "to put it bluntly, a waste of time."[54]

Mary Midgley is correct when she describes the problems with similarly reductive maneuvers in modern philosophy, focusing on the more capacious notions of moral personhood as well as its legal variant. For example: If you say that a person is only five pounds worth of chemicals, and deliver five pounds worth of chemicals instead of the person, and someone is unhappy with the result, then that "is because the word 'person' necessarily means a certain very highly organized, active item, and raw materials are not what it refers to at all."[55] We might say that, from Midgley's perspective, "merely the personification of this totality" of parts is not what we refer to at all when we say "person." Box-filling will not get us there.

Nonetheless, Kelsen's general approach has been useful for theorists of expansive personhood (some of whom I target throughout the book),

52   For a discussion, see Lisa Siraganian, *Modernism and the Meaning of Corporate Persons* (Oxford University Press, 2020), 115–22.

53   Elizabeth H. Wolgast, *Ethics of an Artificial Person: Lost Responsibility in Professions and Organizations* (Redwood City, CA: Stanford University Press, 1992), 88.

54   Evgeny B. Pashukanis, *The General Theory of Law and Marxism* (Piscataway, NJ: Transaction, 2003), 52, 53.

55   Mary Midgley, *Heart and Mind: The Varieties of Moral Experience* (New York: St. Martin's Press, 1981), 16.

who are responding to the challenges of Weil, Arendt, and Agamben, because it tacitly acknowledges the limits of legal personhood and its rights-centric account. Quite simply, he is not claiming more for personhood than what law agrees to. If a person is only a container or a legal device, then to make attributions of personhood we do not need to worry about rationality, will, or any of the other myriad conditions of natural persons. We just need to think about a person's rights and/or obligations. And because, as Kant saw, it is hard to envision how an entity without a will can have obligations (how could it meet them *as obligations*?), this requirement, too, is typically abandoned in expansive personhood theorizing.[56] For better or typically for worse, only rights remain.

Gaining an Object and Losing the Public

Summing up, the previous section suggested that the first three theses of expansive personhood are: (1) perfect equality; (2) an impoverished notion of personhood; (3) and, relatedly, an equation of all personhood, including moral, with artificial or legal personhood. Each of these three requirements of expansive personhood developed over centuries to give us the basic model we are working with today, whether fetal or nonhuman animal, environmental, or robotic.

The next chapter will explore, from a historical and theoretical perspective, one more essential claim of the book. This aspect of the expanding person's biography was initially most relevant in the US context but then traveled the globe. Specifically, the way to theorize artificial personhood has been through corporate personhood, which itself emerged out of theories of the state and legal conceptions of the commodity. A law scholar like Gray, writing in 1909, could already articulate aspects of this claim: "The usual form of a juristic person is a corporation. Indeed, corporations are the only juristic persons known to the Common Law."[57] Newly emerging forms of expansive personhood arise out of, and are variations on, this oldest version of fictional, juristic personhood: the corporate one. As the personification of capital, corporate personhood represents the flourishing of the commodity in structuring our conceptions of legal rights and personhood.

---

56   Immanuel Kant, *Lectures on Ethics*, trans. Louis Infield (Cambridge, MA: Hackett Publishing, 1963), 21.

57   Gray, *Sources of the Law*, 71.

These points will be expanded on. But already we have another thesis crystallizing, one to be tracked throughout the book:

Thesis 4: The developing model of expansive personhood forgoes the publicness of the moral person and replaces it with qualities of objecthood, thingness, or property.

The notion of expansive personhood, in other words, entails abandoning individuals' social situatedness, their place in a drama of humanity, and allowing the notion of person to take on, instead, some of the physical qualities of property. Persons begin looking and seeming more like things. Beyond what Taylor mocked in the eighteenth century (vegetables' dominion over the earth) and Singer contentiously championed half a century ago (animals' moral equality with humans), the notion of persons as objects has become, bizarrely, a welcome position. The next chapter will examine what this looks like in more detail.

This newly popular idea had been foreign to moral and legal theorizing after Kant's ethical philosophizing. As Esposito observes, the idea of the division between persons and things is "deeply rooted in our perception and in our moral conscience," so much so that it feels like a natural aspect, whatever its actual trajectory through history.[58] Firmly rejecting the Lockean notion that "every Man has a *Property* in his own *Person*" (including, notoriously, his labor), Kant claims that "a person cannot be a property and so cannot be a thing which can be owned, for it is impossible to be a person and a thing, the proprietor and the property."[59] And, as Hegel writes along similar lines, all defenses of slavery must regard "the human being simply as a *natural being*," rather than have "the *concept* of the human being as spirit, as something free *in itself.*"[60] Of course, more could be said about all these points, but we should note at least that expansive personhood is broadly rejecting these several ideas. It loosens the firm belief that person and thing are mutually exclusive, in part by making the person more natural (and less social) and more thing-like (and less constitutively free).

Yet this recent, fourth thesis of expansive personhood did not appear overnight; as feminist legal scholars have commented, there are all

---

58   Esposito, *Persons and Things*, 1.

59   John Locke, *The Second Treatise of Civil Government*, ed. John W. Gough (Oxford: Basil Blackwell, 1946), 15; Kant, *Ethics*, 165.

60   G. W. F. Hegel, *Elements of the Philosophy of Right*, ed. Allen W. Wood, trans. H. B. Nisbet (Cambridge University Press, 1991), §57, 87.

sorts of ways in which the property/personhood distinction was being fudged. For example, Davies and Naffine rightly note that Kelsen's positivist account of legal personality "bears a strong resemblance to his analysis of property" and thus, in certain respects, he ends up paralleling the two notions. More generally, they observe that in many important ways, "persons can still be rendered unfree and effectively reduced to something akin to the property of another in certain situations and under certain conditions," so much so that "it cannot be said that in the modern 'free world' persons are never the property of others."[61] Examples they explore include corpses, biotechnologies, and public personas, all of which have been understood as having property or quasi-property interests. From a somewhat different, Hegelian perspective, Margaret Jane Radin has argued that personal property is a right that must be recognized. As she explains, "If an object you now control is bound up in your future plans or in your anticipation of your future self, and it is partly these plans for your own continuity that make you a person, then your personhood depends on the realization of these expectations."[62] The person is importantly "bound up with the object" in a way that cannot simply be subsumed into commodity fetishism. In chapter 2, we will return to these and other feminist arguments about personhood and bodily or personal property in the difficult debates about abortion rights and fetal personhood.

Indubitably, there is something deeply counterintuitive and odd about the maneuvers of expansive personhood, which try to forsake the public and social aspects of personhood by incorporating more of what Kant would call "property" or "thing" and Hegel would call "natural being." These moves feel especially strange because legal property seems inherently societal, requiring that we accept a sovereign or institutional structure to make that property *legal*. And the person in law, historically at least, was by definition both public and social. We will track this transforming development in chapters to follow. Expansive personhood's progress also overlaps with certain recent theoretical trends, such as object-oriented ontology (OOO), speculative realism, new materialism, and posthumanism. Although this is not the place to examine such movements in detail, because of their technical specificity and the distinctions between them, it is worth glancing briefly

---

61   Davies and Naffine, *Are Persons Property?*, 53, 2–3.
62   Margaret Jane Radin, "Property and Personhood," *Stanford Law Review* 34, no. 5 (1982): 957–1015, 968.

at how these theoretical movements share many of the characteristics and principles of expansive personhood that we are pursuing and challenging.

Take the issue of equality between individuals, regardless of the type of individual under consideration. Many OOO and speculative realism theorists begin with this premise and develop the idea under the rubric of "flat ontology," which presumes, in Ian Bogost's words, "that there is no hierarchy of being, and we must thus conclude that being itself is an object no different from any other."[63] In rejecting hierarchies of being, locating all objects (capaciously, inclusively understood) on one plane of existence, theorists like Bogost develop a kind of phenomenological egalitarianism. "All objects must be given equal attention," declares Graham Harman, "whether they be human, non-human, natural, cultural, real or fictional."[64] The political implications are not far behind—*The Democracy of Objects* is the title of one book in the field.[65] David Wood makes explicit the connection to human political rights of self-determination, equality, and autonomy, prefacing his book *Thinking Plant Animal Human: Encounters with Communities of Difference* (2020) with a "Declaration of Interdependence": "We here highly resolve that these living beings, human and nonhuman—shall not have died in vain . . . and that the earth shall not perish by a myopic government of the people, by the people, for the people."[66] Riffing off Thomas Jefferson, and with the subtitle "encounter[ing] communities of difference," Wood's entreaty to liberal pluralism, albeit a better rendition of liberal pluralism, could not be clearer.

Another version of *The Problem of Personhood* might have concentrated its energy on challenging these recent theoretical trends of phenomenological egalitarianism. Theorists including Bogost, Harman, and Wood are certainly fellow travelers on the journey of expansive personhood and its logic. But law is not their focus. And because my aim, here, is explicitly to examine the legal and moral concept of expansive personhood, which less frequently engages with recent theoretical

63   Ian Bogost, *Alien Phenomenology, or What It's Like to Be a Thing* (Minneapolis: University of Minnesota Press, 2012), 22.

64   Graham Harman, *Object-Oriented Ontology: A New Theory of Everything* (London: Pelican Books, 2018).

65   Strangely, despite that title, Levi Bryant underplays the political stakes of his book, declaring that "the democracy of objects is not a political thesis . . . but an ontological one"; *The Democracy of Objects* (London: Open Humanities Press, 2011), 19.

66   David Wood, *Thinking Plant Animal Human: Encounters with Communities of Difference* (Minneapolis: University of Minnesota Press, 2020), xix.

trends, I am largely leaving a potential critique of OOO and similar ideas aside, a road glimpsed from afar yet not taken.

We can, however, start to envision how this critique might intersect with legal thinking. "Wherever nature is instituted as a subject, this is so thanks to the very act of this institution, which is a human act," notes Yan Thomas, writing on Roman law, suggesting a path forward. "In short, man is as much at the centre of the fiction that nature is a subject, as at that of the opposite fiction that nature is an object. Between these two fictions, the difference is ideological."[67] This is a very important point. Thomas is saying that the apparent objectivity of something like OOO's phenomenological egalitarianism, "the democracy of objects," is really an ideological sleight of hand. All these inclusive gestures are *human* gestures, human actions, and the result of human purposes and intentions—whatever we call them. That origin is inescapable. Wood's "encounters with communities of difference" could only make any sense to individuals (of whatever species or kind) who understand themselves as "encountering," already living in a community that can and does conceptualize cultural difference.

Harman devotes the bulk of one of his recent books to understanding the Dutch East India Company as the kind of "object" that only his OOO method can do justice to. And that is not really a surprise: Corporations, through the device of corporate personhood, are the clearest place to see the evasion of the public and its replacement by property.[68] It makes sense that a critical theory devoted to attending to objects equally would find an entity overcome with property to be its proof of concept. But the primary, state-sponsored, political-economic move remains; it is the origin of the corporate person, even if its state-sponsored workings have often been obscured. "Business incorporation is a social program for economic growth," writes David Ciepley, and while changes in the practice of incorporation have "obscured this government provenance," corporations today nonetheless remain "public-private hybrid[s]."[69] Even corporate personhood cannot entirely conceal the mechanism and process of using property in lieu of the public good. The erasure or loss of that good will be a refrain of the chapters to follow.

---

67   Yan Thomas, et al., *Legal Artifices: Ten Essays On Roman Law In the Present Tense* (Edinburgh University Press, 2021), 117.

68   Graham Harman, *Immaterialism: Objects and Social Theory* (Cambridge: Polity, 2016).

69   David Ciepley, "The Neoliberal Corporation," in *The Oxford Handbook of The Corporation*, ed. Thomas Clarke, Justin O'Brien, and Charles R. T. O'Kelley (Oxford University Press, 2019), 276–7.

Habeas Corpus, Redux: The Surrogate Person as Live Hologram

A person equal yet impoverished and radically reduced, without a public voice and with the qualities of objecthood or thingness, emerging strangely from the gargantuan yet hollowed out figure of the corporate giants. Where can we gaze on this figure, now realized? How can we see it?

Let us end by briefly returning to where we started, but with an illuminating difference: to habeas corpus and the plight of Guantánamo detainee Mohammed el Gharani, now portrayed as an art object. When the performance artist and avant-garde musician Laurie Anderson learned of El Gharani's story a few years after he was released, she began working with him on a project. He eventually became the subject of her multimedia installation *Habeas Corpus* (2015), at the expansive Park Avenue Armory in New York City.

Set in darkness, the show included live instrumental music, a sparkling disco ball, and luminous wall texts. One of these texts appeared in a handwritten script: "I have chosen to be here virtually because I am not allowed to come to this country and I have some things to say. Mohammed el Gharani." His virtual attendance dominated the cavernous room: A live video of El Gharani saying "some things" was projected

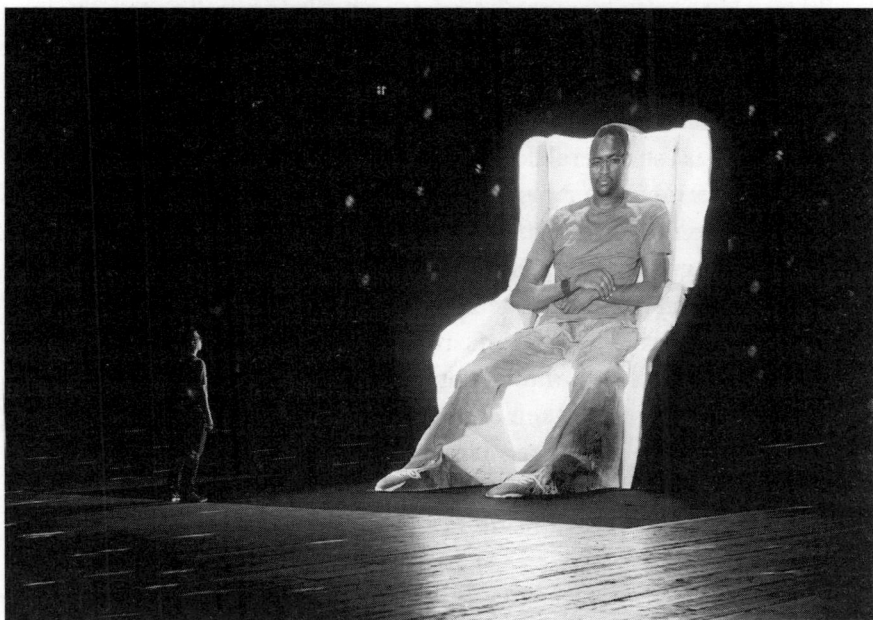

Fig. 1. Laurie Anderson, *Habeas Corpus* (2015), Park Avenue Armory (New York). Photo by James Ewing.

onto a monumental white foam sculpture, the size and shape of the statue of Abraham Lincoln at the Lincoln Memorial in Washington, DC.[70] At this time, El Gharani was living somewhere in West Africa and trying to heal his battered body and broken life. He agreed to sit in a chair in a Ghanaian studio every day for the many hours the exhibition was open, while video of himself was recorded and projected, via a live feed, to the New York exhibition space. As he watched the Armory spectators (he could not hear them) and they watched and listened to him, he told stories about his imprisonment and release.[71]

For the spectator of *Habeas Corpus*, the visual and auditory experience of El Gharani as a "live hologram" was, by turns, mesmerizing and haunting. To evoke a certain monumentality and presence, Anderson used a white foam substrate to render the projection not merely flat but somewhat three-dimensional. It resembled a glowing, animatronic marble statue from which, in my own experience, it was hard to look away. It demanded our attention and acknowledgment. That demand accorded with Anderson's aims. An apology, El Gharani told Anderson, was the one thing that he wanted from participating in her piece. By using the "war on terror" as pretext, Anderson writes, the "US government declared the detainees 'non-persons' and therefore ineligible for apologies or reparations."[72]

By invoking "non-persons," Anderson is likely alluding to decisions such as *Rasul v. Myers* (2009) and *Aamer v. Obama* (2014), both First Circuit Court of Appeals decisions holding that detainees at Guantánamo are *not* protected by the 1993 Religious Freedom Restoration Act (RFRA). This is the federal law that prohibits the US government "from substantially burdening a person's exercise of religion." The *Aamer* case involved several Muslim men—all of whom had already been cleared for release but were still being held at Guantánamo—who were engaging in a hunger strike in protest of their detention. The government instituted a force-feeding protocol that necessitated sedation, during which the men would be unable to conduct their prescribed prayers. They protested that this practice violated their constitutional rights, including their First Amendment rights to the free exercise of religion under the statute. In rejecting their arguments, the *Aamer* court reiterated its earlier holding in *Rasul*: "RFRA's protections do not extend to Guantánamo detainees,

---

70   Laurie Anderson, *All the Things I Lost in the Flood: Essays on Pictures, Language, and Code* (New York: Rizzoli Electa, 2018), 104.

71   For these and other recordings of El Gharani, see hirshhorn.si.edu.

72   Anderson, *Essays*, 105.

who, as nonresident aliens, do not qualify as protected 'person[s]' within the meaning of that statute."[73]

Four months later, the US Supreme Court held that corporate persons such as Hobby Lobby, a craft and supply store, *did* have such freedom of religion protections under RFRA. Justice Alito, writing for a narrow 5–4 majority, argued that Obamacare's contraceptive mandate violated the RFRA, and that requiring a corporation to provide women workers access to low-cost contraception substantially burdened the "free-exercise rights of corporations like Hobby Lobby."[74] The law had already determined that the word "'person' . . . include[s] corporations," and so "the person" known as Hobby Lobby, Inc. had the right to exercise its religion, a right that the *Aamer* detainees did not have. This situation led some outraged commentators to point out that the government was "prepared to argue that Guantánamo prisoners aren't people, while accepting that corporations are." How could President Obama complain about the scandal of Guantánamo "while his lawyers call detainees non-persons in court?"[75] Theorists have expanded on this complaint. As Joseph Pugliese writes, Guantánamo detainees are precluded "from embodying the figure of 'the human,' specifically the legal category of 'person.'"[76] They have become "illegible as legal subjects," suggests Jasbir Puar, and so perhaps are being conceptualized as "not human nor animal, but un-human."[77]

Anderson's piece rebuked that dehumanization and forced "non-person" status of detainees at Guantánamo, held without many basic rights, while also clearly alluding to the longer history of racial enslavement in the United States.[78] Enthroned at huge scale, echoing the famous monument of Abraham Lincoln, her live projection of El Gharani assisted him in graciously, firmly insisting on his personhood as well as an apology from all who came to gaze at him. Yet visitors to the work, like myself, walking around the sculpture, also experienced something beyond a demand for legal recognition. We perceived a distorted moving

---

73   *Aamer v. Obama*, 742 F.3d 1023, 1043 (D.C. Cir. 2014). See also *Rasul v. Myers* (2009).

74   *Burwell v. Hobby Lobby Stores, Inc.*, 573 US 682 (2014), 18.

75   Quoting attorney Cori Crider; Ryan J. Reilly, "Obama Lawyers: Corporations May Be People Under Law, but Actual Humans in Gitmo Are Not," *HuffPost.com*, July 9, 2014.

76   Joseph Pugliese, *Biopolitics of the More-than-Human: Forensic Ecologies of Violence* (Duke University Press, 2020), 129.

77   Jasbir K. Puar, *Terrorist Assemblages: Homonationalism in Queer Times*, Tenth anniversary expanded edition (Duke University Press, 2017), 158.

78   Muneer I. Ahmad, "Resisting Guantánamo: Rights at the Brink of Dehumanization," *Northwestern University Law Review* 103 (2009): 1683, 1687.

image, one that shifted into the eerie and uncanny. Seen in profile, the colossal image of El Gharani transforms from a compelling speaking person into a flattened, spectral projection cast onto an obviously artificial, even otherworldly object. Its form is exposed as the huge block figure that Anderson had carefully constructed "like a Cubist sculpture."[79] For Keith Feldman, these qualities of *Habeas Corpus* combine to "reveal the clichés at work in an aesthetics of recognition," even as the piece "also undercuts the liberal genre of a self-same autonomous body. The image flickers; it's noisy."[80] The images are indeed flickering and noisy, and Feldman is also right that something about liberalism and its relation to the body is being worked out here. But it might be more accurate to say that Anderson's piece perfectly captures a shifting, and shifty, quality of contemporary personhood broadly understood, even beyond its legal reality. Sometimes a person, whether El Gharani or one of us, feels like one whole, present person—let's call him a human being. And sometimes he seems separated into two parts: blocky awkward thing and weird speaking hologram—let us call it a representation of an expansive legal person.

From that perspective, *Habeas Corpus* should be understood as not only an artwork depicting the US government dehumanizing a vulnerable and stateless individual, violating El Gharani's liberty and human rights, but also a work that seems to represent personhood's complicated philosophy and history. By naming the work *Habeas Corpus*, Anderson has legal history in her sights too.[81] Her piece—projecting a colossal, object-like, yet existing person—captures the contemporary properties of expansive personhood that we have been examining. In portraying El Gharani's desperate situation, she explores that mysterious combination that is contemporary expansive personhood. It is something like an amalgamated foam corpus on which is shone a spectral, speaking, absent person. What Anderson represents is this combination of someone sympathetic yet strangely split, massively present yet hollowed out and alienated. It is the vision of expansive personhood that we have inherited today. And it is this version of the person that is being litigated and fought over in many different and surprising forms.

As readers will have noted, this book embraces and deliberately weaves together a number of different disciplinary fields: moral

---

79   Anderson, *Essays*, 105.
80   Keith Feldman, "You (Shall) Have the Body: Patterns of Life in the Shadow of Guantánamo," *The Comparatist* 42 (October 2018): 193.
81   Ibid., 189.

philosophy, legal history and case law, political theory, current political and ethical debates. Now contemporary art is folded in as well. That is because what I am calling "the problem of personhood" emerges in all these different realms of expertise and cannot quite be understood and summed up in any one of them alone. It dips and weaves in and out of philosophy and law, into politics and popular culture and art, and back into legal cases and ethical disputes. Along the way, historical realities, most pertinently the developing framework of corporate personhood in the late nineteenth century, add aspects to these conversations that call for understanding them contextually. Joseph Slaughter writes of the way the novel is able to do "some of the sociocultural work that [human rights] law cannot do for itself."[82] In *The Problem of Personhood*, we spy contemporary art doing a similar kind of "sociocultural work" that the law has not been able to think through, fully, for the expansive personhood of nonhuman animals and fetuses, or lakes and robots.

In the chapters to follow, we will see versions of this personhood problem explored not only in the contemporary visual art of Mary Kelly, Hew Locke, Ryan Gander, Nina Katchadourian, Wangechi Mutu, and others, but also in a Dr. Seuss book and the prestige television series *Westworld*. Much of this work, including Anderson's *Habeas Corpus*, relies on a phenomenon that the art historian and critic Michael Fried first noted in his paradigm-shattering essay, "Art and Objecthood" (1967). As Fried revealed, the Minimalist art objects then in vogue, created by Tony Smith, Dan Flavin, and Donald Judd (among others), derive their problematic power from a hidden anthropomorphism. One of those typically huge, empty, boxy objects faces the beholder in a gallery as if it were a "surrogate person," declares Fried, which even appears to possess "an inner, ever secret, life." In a sense, he writes, the ways a beholder usually communes with an art object, deploying all of her senses, is hijacked and transformed into a theatrical conflict with one of these works in a gallery. The Minimalist art object confronts the beholder, refusing to leave her alone, commanding her to acknowledge its presence rather than allowing her to engage with the work on her own terms.[83]

Fried's metaphor of physical threat underscores both how deceptive and successful an art object's surrogate personhood ruse can be.

---

82   Joseph R. Slaughter, *Human Rights, Inc: The World Novel, Narrative Form, and International Law* (New York: Fordham University Press, 2007), 30.

83   Michael Fried, *Art and Objecthood: Essays and Reviews* (University of Chicago Press, 1998), 156, 163–4. For a longer discussion of these issues, see Lisa Siraganian, "Art and Surrogate Personhood," *nonsite.org* 21 (Summer 2017).

The tactics of combativeness and coercion work on us because such art objects rely on a familiar scenario we know intimately. It is something like the experience of "being distanced, or crowded, by the silent presence of another *person*." (Clearly, he is using the word "person" not in a strict legal sense but in a more familiar everyday sense). Moreover, we understandably feel uneasy around such surrogate persons. Their "apparent hollowness," which "is almost blatantly anthropomorphic," leaves us with the impression that the art object before us possesses "an inner, even, secret, life."[84] But these art objects are not knowable in the way that people are—they are more like what we might imagine aliens would be, or entities exhibiting selective sentience. Or perhaps like an AI or a corporation.

In his essay, Fried explores how these surrogate-persons, as art objects, demand that their presence be acknowledged, a demand that—treacherously—resembles a moral imperative. Faced with one in a gallery, you feel as if this entity, this thing, is asking to be recognized, attended to, and respected. Even if that "person" is a proxy, what is being requested of us feels like a certain ethical stance, perhaps with a version of the rights, privileges, and respect that human beings demand and deserve. But, in a way that is clearer with art (and more disguised with legal theorizing), making this substitution is a dangerous error. There is a deception at work, one that relies on emotional tactics (like psychic distancing and intimidation) that we feel intuitively because we are social creatures. We experience these objects like persons because other persons are simply the closest equivalent we have to what is occurring in the aesthetic realm. But close to is not the same as.

Anderson's *Habeas Corpus* perfectly dramatizes this scenario—made all the more obvious by the fact that she is *also*, simultaneously, representing an actual human being whose rights have been trampled upon. She shows us, almost literally, what expansive legal personhood might look like—here, represented by the writ of habeas corpus—when it is detached from a real person, El Gharani. And, as we will see repeatedly throughout this book, treating objects or "non-persons" *as* persons has sometimes unforeseen consequences, whether in the domain of non-human animal or environmental rights or disputes over fetal, AI, or corporate personhood. The contemporary art I discuss in *The Problem of Personhood* grapples with all these types of artificial persons, and does so in the shadow of the minimalist art and the dynamic of surrogate

---

84   Fried, *Art and Objecthood*, 155–6.

personhood that Fried so memorably revealed. The best of this work recognizes and challenges the ethical demand of surrogate personhood. Rather than simply accepting the surrogate person for the real article, this contemporary art serves as a questioning guide for our explorations.

Finally, art is also included here because expansive personhood remains something of a baffling magic trick even to its experts—and this artifice fascinates artists, who represent it carefully in their own ways. In this instance, Anderson represents the legal concept of habeas corpus as her subject matter, and challenges her viewers with a disturbing vision of legal personhood detached from a human person's body. Expansive personhood is a notion that many struggle to perceive clearly, trying to understand how its different parts fit together and what the whole looks like. That struggle, too, is part of the story. "The jurists of the Middle Ages sometimes spoke of their own legal constructs as being 'chimeras,' calling those who elaborate them 'alchemists,'" observes Yan Thomas; "The 'person' that is constituted by a corporation, a city, a state, offers the example of a chimera."[85] Chimeras are mythological monsters in Greek lore, a grotesque combination of one animal's head on another's body: "an unreal creature of the imagination, a mere wild fancy; an unfounded conception," as defined by the *Oxford English Dictionary*. Works of art like Anderson's *Habeas Corpus*—a modern-day representation of a chimera if ever there was one—expose this legal alchemy. We grasp the constructed, expansive person with all the contradictory, shimmering, monstrous qualities it possesses. Quite simply, seeing the representation of a "non-person" as a "live hologram," as she aims to do, helps us see expansive personhood for what it is.

When Anderson made her "live hologram," El Gharani's location could not be disclosed. For the duration of the projection at the Armory he was in an unnamed country, attempting to secure his citizenship.[86] After Guantánamo, he had been sent to Chad, his parents' country of origin, but it was a country he had never even visited, having been born in Saudi Arabia. Meanwhile, Saudi Arabia refused to recognize him as a citizen because his parents were guest workers there and did not have Saudi citizenship. As of this writing, he remains a man without a country—a stateless person, demonstrating Samuel Moyn's point that "the alliance with state and nation was not some accident that tragically befell

---

85   Thomas, *Legal Artifices*, 138.
86   Esther Whitfield, "From Guantánamo to the Global South: Mohammed el-Gharani in Literature and Art," *Humanity: An International Journal of Human Rights, Humanitarianism, and Development* 13, no. 3 (2022): 371.

the rights of man: it was their very essence."[87] El Gharani has described his situation more recently, in a video from 2019: "I'm still searching for a country . . . I've been to, like, ten countries, to find where I can have my peace of mind . . . my life again."[88] Becoming a detainee at Guantánamo, losing so many of his rights as a person, and fighting for years for his release all added up to a status he could not undo. Finally, then, the undermining of the state's public power, and the ascendency of the physical, object-like, corporate person and its power, is also part of *The Problem of Personhood*'s larger story, as we move from chimerical, constructed persons to actual human beings.

87   Moyn, *Last Utopia*, 30.
88   "My Story," hirshhorn.si.edu.

1

Artificial, Inc.: Theorizing the Expansive Person

Not Naturally Civil

The US Supreme Court's decision *Citizens United v. FEC* (2010), uphold-ing the contentious claim that a corporation's "speech" has the same legal protections as a human being's, led to widespread outrage. Corporate entities are complicated and can be massive, usually with no single human being representing them. So the decision needed some contortions to turn a hallowed civil right—"free speech"—into a form that businesses could work with more easily. That form turned out to be *money*, specifi-cally campaign donations, which were equated with free speech. Casual observers could be forgiven for dismissing that equation as simply the weaponizing of law, enabling corporate capitalists to better "control the political superstructure."[1] As Karl Marx put it, has not society's ruling class always tried "to sanctify the existing situation as a law and to fix the limits . . . as legal ones?"[2] Is there anything more to say about this?

On some level, no. After *Citizens United*, businesses could pour unlimited amounts of cash into political campaigns, minus even the tri-fling speedbump of federal campaign finance rules. In roundabout ways, they did so. There has been "an explosion of outside, often-undisclosed money in elections" through super political action committees, as well

---

1   Hayden E. Pendergrass, "Corporate Capital and Legal Personality: A Marxist Account of *Citizens United* Ten Years Later," *Cardozo Journal of Equal Rights and Social Justice* 28, no. 2 (Winter 2022): 327–8.

2   Karl Marx, *Capital: A Critique of Political Economy*, vol. III, trans. David Fern-bach (Penguin, 1981), 929.

as evidence of foreign interference in US elections.[3] Only six years after the decision, corporate campaign spending increased by 900 percent.[4] Repeatedly upheld in subsequent years, the decision still reverberates politically. In August 2024, progressive Senator Bernie Sanders lambasted it at the Democratic National Convention: "For the sake of our democracy, we must overturn the disastrous *Citizens United* Supreme Court decision and move toward public funding of elections."[5] He is absolutely correct.

Nonetheless, I want to expose another damaging consequence of the decision. This corporate person with civil rights, granted free speech in *Citizens United*, is the powerful engine of expansive personhood today, helping to remove political issues from the political realm and bury them in legal technicalities. As the previous chapter introduced, that person, of which fetal, nonhuman animal, environmental, and AI persons are all varieties, has the characteristics captured in four theses: (1) perfect equality (all persons are equal), (2) an *impoverished* notion of personhood, (3) an equivalence of all forms of personhood (moral, religious, and so on) with its legal version, and (4) the replacement of the publicness of personhood with thingness or property. Now we will see that the common source for all these requirements is the mature, twenty-first-century corporate person with civil rights—the version assumed in *Citizens United*. Put slightly differently, contemporary corporate personhood is both the theory, and practical reality, that enables expansive legal personhood to thrive. Even more: the corporate person with civil rights—capital personified with legal standing and certain social protections—exemplifies the full flourishing of the commodity in structuring our conceptions of legal rights and personhood. Expansive legal personhood begins with the commodity and ends with the corporation.

This chapter reveals how and why these new types of legal personhood need the corporation—with its history and theory—to function. Quite simply, expansive personhood uses the mature corporate person as its default model because that is the only available legal form for "artificial" entities (ones that are not human beings). By splitting legal subjectivity from legal responsibility, corporate personhood became the primary tool to isolate and immunize legal subjects from the legal duties that would

---

3   Richard L. Hasen, "The Decade of *Citizens United*," slate.com, December 19, 2019.

4   Campaignlegal.org.

5   Jake Johnson, "In DNC Speech, Sanders Condemns 'Oligarchs' Buying Elections and Blocking Change," Common Dreams.org, August 21, 2024.

typically cling to them. To make any sense at all, each type of expansive personhood (whether fetal or tree, elephant or chatbot) needs that splitting and sequestering of persons from their responsibilities. Marx had started to observe aspects of this phenomenon, this separation in law of rights from duties, in the nineteenth century. But it was not fully grasped until Evgeny Pashukanis—the preeminent Soviet legal theorist until his execution in Stalin's purges of the late 1930s—worked it out in his *General Theory of Law and Marxism* (1924).

Already by that time, the corporate person had sloughed off its previous associations and theoretical alignment with the state, as well as its older history in Roman, Christian, and monarchical law, to become the consolidation of capital that we know today. At the end of the nineteenth century, when the very wealthy classes looked for even better returns on their investments, the modern corporate form developed general limited liability rules (and thus legalized irresponsibility) to serve financial desires.[6] (Limited liability is the now hallowed principle that shields individual shareholders, or a corporation's managers, from being obliged to pay back a corporation's debts.) Having emerged from antiquated notions of property, the corporation thus became "constituted as the legal subjectivity of capital," writes Mark Neocleous, a "legal subject [that] took to the stage as a fully-fledged persona."[7]

More recently, it also has been gaining something else: certain *civil* rights typically given only to human beings. *Citizens United* put those gains in the spotlight. In the process of releasing the full power of capital into US political campaigning, Justice Kennedy's majority opinion not only brought the older notion of corporate personhood back into public discourse. It also worked hard to erase the legal distinctions between corporations and human beings. He rejected the claim that a corporation's "political speech . . . should be treated differently under the First Amendment simply because such associations are not 'natural persons.'"[8] The basic point was clear. Corporations have free speech rights that should not be infringed upon by the government.

In his dissent, Justice Stevens challenges the operative presumption here: that corporations have special *human* rights and privileges. There is

---

6   Paddy Ireland, "Limited Liability, Shareholder Rights, and the Problem of Corporate Irresponsibility," *Cambridge Journal of Economics* 34, no. 5 (September 2010): 841–2.

7   Mark Neocleous, "Staging Power: Marx, Hobbes, and the Personification of Capital," *Law and Critique* 14 (2003): 154–7.

8   *Citizens United v. Federal Election Commission*, 558 US 310 (2010), J. Kennedy's opinion, 26.

"no evidence to support the notion that the Framers would have wanted corporations to have the same rights as natural persons in the electoral context." He explains that, while corporate "'personhood' often serves as a useful legal fiction," we should not be confused by this terminology. Corporations "are not themselves members of 'We the People' by whom and for whom our Constitution was established."[9] The majority of the Court, he felt, erred on this point. In a related decision from a decade earlier, Stevens spells out the mistake made in equating corporations with real people, money with speech: "Money is property; it is not speech." While the right "to fund 'speech by proxy'" merits some protection, "property rights . . . are not entitled to the same protection as the right to say what one pleases."[10] This gets to the core of the matter with expansive persons: *property* rights have become the anchor to demand *civil* rights.

The sections that follow provide a swift genealogical tour of the developing expansive person as a legal form and theory, illuminated by an artwork along the way. Beginning with the expansive person's ancestry as a so-called "artificial person" linked to the state (in sometimes vexed ways), we make our way to the civil protections for corporations in *Citizens United*. This "artificial" legal person gradually lost its earlier, albeit controversial, alignment with the state ("artificial person" typically refers to "a non-human legal entity"—not a single, live human being, but an organization, such as a colony or city, a corporation or university, "recognized by law as a fictitious person."[11]) The contemporary artist Hew Locke's *Ruined* series—of a graveyard for corporate persons—helps illustrate this process. We then turn to the maturing corporate form that Neocleous invokes: the corporate persona "as the legal subjectivity of capital," a version exported internationally. This corporate person becomes the model for fetal, nonhuman animal, environmental, and AI personhood, with consequences investigated throughout this book. Finally, we will discover how current understandings of expansive personhood have concealed this background. This obscuring supports a natural-seeming process. Power is removed from government and "the members of 'We the People'" (in Justice Stevens's words), transferred onto property and capital.

9   *Citizens United*, J. Stevens's dissent, 61, 76.
10   *Nixon, Attorney General of Missouri, et al. v. Shrink Missouri Government PAC et al.*, 528 US 377 (2000), 398–9; J. Stevens's concurrence.
11   "Artificial Person," Legal Information Institute: WEX, Cornell Law School, cornell.edu.

The State of, and as, the Artificial Person

In 2010, as the world was still in the midst of recovering from the 2008 global financial crisis, British Guyanese sculptor Hew Locke installed *Ruined*. The work consists of ten cast iron sculptures, up to five feet tall, mounted in the Brunswick Cemetery Gardens in Bristol, UK. A flyer explains that the cluster of apparent headstones marks "the passing of a company that no longer exists, for an area of the gardens adjacent to the existing graves . . . inspired by the ever-shifting economics and politics of international buying and selling, boom and bust."[12] One of the most striking sculptures presents the large "E" of the Enron symbol, the "Enron Corp" seal along with a man standing in a social realist pose. Adapting the image from an actual paper stock certificate of the infamous Enron Corporation, Locke adds eyes that are bleeding or crying profusely. Maybe those are salty tears (a natural, bodily product), or maybe they are liquified natural gas (an extracted resource as commodity).

Other memorial markers represent less familiar historical corporations, including the Persian Bank Mining Rights Corporation (a short-lived mining venture) and W. D. & H. O. Wills (a British tobacco company founded in Bristol). These stand next to markers for companies that were for a time indistinguishable from nation-states, such as the serpent-shaped memorial for a railway corporation of the Imperial Chinese government. Each portrays the human-like "lives" and "deaths" of influential and destructive corporations, some state-sponsored, that no longer exist as corporate entities. In the process, Locke's sculptures reflect on both the uncanniness and personifying force of corporate personhood. Although corporations could theoretically exist forever as legal entities, most do not; they are merely memorialized by their stock certificates, iconography, and brand imagery. Yet there is something else missing in this graveyard. No corpse rots below, buried in the earth. And exploitation is unrepresented; dispersed elsewhere, the harms businesses caused are felt far beyond the cities and countries in which they were incorporated.

Taking a step back, consider the longer story, admittedly largely from the Anglo-American common law perspective. Historically and conceptually, corporate personhood was a legal doctrine—often called a legal fiction—that allowed businesses to operate validly, particularly after the death of the company owners who had signed the original

---

12   Hew Locke, "Ruined," invitation, 2010. Aprb.co.uk.

Fig. 2. Hew Locke, *Ruined* (2010), close-up. Photo by Jamie Woodley, courtesy Bristol City Council and Situations © 2025 Artists Rights Society (ARS), New York / DACS, London.

contracts. Discussions of corporations date, in some form at least, to the early modern (medieval) period, with jurists glossing Roman law. By the eighteenth century, the legal treatise writer William Blackstone could forthrightly defend the necessity of the incorporation principle in his influential *Commentaries on the Laws of England* (1765). Because "all personal rights die with the person," and giving a series of individuals in the company those same rights "would be very inconvenient, if not impracticable," it made sense to constitute corporations as "artificial persons, who may maintain a perpetual succession, and enjoy a kind of legal immortality."[13] This artificial corporate personhood would permit

---

13   William Blackstone, "Of Corporations," in *Commentaries on the Laws of England (1765–69), Book 1. Of the Rights of Persons*, ed. David Lemmings and Wilfrid Prest (Oxford University Press, 2016), 303.

businesses to function more fluidly—and profitably—still within the ambit of English law.

However, when Blackstone writes that corporations can be understood as "artificial persons," he is mentioning only *one* of its original forms. "Artificial person" was originally a category used for describing various kinds of nonhuman legal entities. The phrase "corporations or bodies politic" identifies a broader category of entities that includes states, churches, universities, or governmental organizations designed to serve public society. Unlike "natural persons" (human beings formed by God), "artificial [persons] are such as created and devised by human laws for the purposes of society and government; which are called corporations or bodies politic." In *Trustees of Dartmouth College v. Woodward* (1819), a foundational US decision quoted in Stevens's *Citizens United* dissent, a corporation is described as "an artificial being, invisible, intangible, and existing only in contemplation of law." It is created for community purposes "such as the government wishes to promote. They are deemed beneficial to the country."[14] The commercial form was only one way to serve the public, and only one kind of artificial person.

To underscore this point, a view was being consolidated—although by no means in a uniform or undisputed way—that the *state* gave artificial entities their legal authority. This was known as the "concession" theory of the corporation. That is, the corporation would be given certain legal rights, expressly granted or delegated by the sovereign or state, as a privilege for undertaking expensive projects (like bridges or canals) that would benefit the public. Again, unlike our de facto vision of business as a private, for-profit arrangement between individuals, this notion of the corporation was understood as a public good licensed by the state. The German legal scholar Friedrich Karl von Savigny, with whom the young Marx studied, could simply assert the received wisdom that sovereign power is necessary to confer "the character of a Juristical Person," that is, artificial personhood.[15]

Over a century earlier, Hobbes was already underscoring a version of this point in *Leviathan* (1668), aspects of which Blackstone incorporated into *Commentaries*. When discussing "inanimate things, [such] as a church, a hospital, a bridge, [that] may be personated by a rector, master, or overseer," Hobbes notes that "such things cannot be personated before there be some state of civil government." All types of legal

---

14   *Trustees of Dartmouth College v. Woodward*, 17 US 518 (1819), 667–8, 636, 637.
15   Friedrich Karl von Savigny, *Jural Relations: Or, the Roman Law of Persons as Subjects of Jural Relations*, trans. W. H. Rattigan (Hyperion, 1884), 204.

"impersonation" need the state, and the "authority proceeded from the state."[16] Because Hobbes does not specify exactly what kind of person the state or civil government is, critics have debated it fiercely.[17] But, in either case, for Hobbes the state's authority precedes the corporation's. Most ominously, when parasitically overgrown and out of control, the corporation sucks the commonwealth of nutrients, "like worms in the entrails of a natural man," as Hobbes memorably puts it.[18]

The point to emphasize is that the state was coming into a privileged position of authority and power in relation to other kinds of artificial persons—even as, in a somewhat complicated maneuver, the state *itself* was understood to be a kind of artificial person too. For example, the early US Supreme Court decision *Chisholm v. Georgia* (1793), eventually ratified in the Eleventh Amendment, holds that the state of Georgia's conduct was subject to federal judicial review. This argument requires that the *state* be defined as "a complete body of free persons united together for their common benefit, to enjoy peaceably what is their own, and to do justice to others. It is an artificial person. It has its affairs and its interests: It has its rules: It has its rights: And it has its obligations."[19]

Because the state had those "obligations," it also had a more basic, fundamental form of personhood than the corporation, according to eighteenth-century political philosophers such as Emmerich de Vattel and Kant. For both, nations or states were considered "moral persons," which gave them both rights and duties, as well as the authority as legal actors internationally. "By the mid-eighteenth century," writes Quentin Skinner, "the idea of the sovereign state as a distinct *persona ficta* was firmly entrenched in English as well as continental theories of public and international law."[20] The world contained artificial persons in the form of both states and corporations. But, at this moment in time, the state was understood to be the more powerful person and the higher moral and political authority—with both rights *and* obligations. That moment, and those artificial persons with obligations, would not last.

---

16   Thomas Hobbes, *Leviathan, with Selected Variants*, ed. Edwin Curley (Cambridge, MA: Hackett Publishing, 1994), 100.

17   David Runciman debates Quentin Skinner on the personhood of the Hobbesian state; for an overview see Sean Fleming, *Leviathan on a Leash: A Theory of State Responsibility* (Princeton University Press, 2020), 46–51.

18   Hobbes, *Leviathan*, 218.

19   *Chisholm v. Georgia*, 2 US 419, 455–6, 1 L. Ed. 440 (1793).

20   Quentin Skinner, "The Sovereign State: A Genealogy," in *Sovereignty in Fragments: The Past, Present, and Future of a Contested Concept*, ed. Hent Kalmo and Quentin Skinner (Cambridge University Press, 2010), 26–46; 40.

Freeing the Venture-Colonial Corporation

At some point between the eighteenth century and *Citizens United*, the corporation liberated itself from both its subjugation to the state and the duties that came with it. How did this happen? The answer is a combination of state-sponsored colonialism, new legal tools to lock in capital, and the development of true limited liability.

Think again about Hew Locke's corporate cemetery in Bristol. Like graveyards everywhere, it includes markers for "persons" born in distant lands—not in Bristol, not even in England. Enron, originally a Texas energy corporation, swallowed up other businesses globally: fiber optics companies, power utilities, and pipelines, including Argentina's largest natural gas extraction company. Enron's collapse and fallout devastated communities around the world. By including corporations that were both Bristol-based and not, Locke offers the spectator a sense of how ubiquitous and far-reaching multinational companies are, but also how local, particular, and personal their damage can be. He reminds us that the systems of imperialism, colonialism, and capitalism together led to the importation and exportation of enslaved persons, raw materials, and commodities, as well as legal forms, such as corporate entities like Enron.

Fig. 3. Hew Locke, *Ruined* (2010), close-up. Photo by Jamie Woodley, courtesy Bristol City Council and Situations © 2025 Artists Rights Society (ARS), New York / DACS, London.

Locke's grave markers are thus depicting another important aspect of the entwined relationship between states and corporations. In a sense, this one almost directly reverses the terms we have seen, with the state delegating some power to the corporation. Instead, the (colonial) state was conceptualized *as* a corporation. Many of the corporations Locke represents participated directly in the colonial expansion of various empires into regions of Africa, the Middle East, the Americas, and Asia. For example, the West Indies Sugar Corporation was one of various corporations operating in Cuba and the Dominican Republic in the early twentieth century, yet it was originally incorporated in my home state of Maryland. Most explicitly, Locke depicts the grave marker for the colonial state, "Società Romana di Colonizzazione in Somalia." In the early twentieth century, Italy developed this corporation in Somalia—"Italian Somaliland"—to exploit the East African region.

Both of these companies are prime examples of what the historian Philip Stern calls "venture colonialism, a particularly prolific, if controversial, brand of overseas expansion" that operated on the principle that private companies were the best ones to take on public empire-building. Famous examples, such as the East India Company or Hudson's Bay Company, ruled over millions of people in vast territories around the globe, in what Stern and others have named "company-states."[21] The company-state "needs to be approached as a form of political community and polity" on its own terms.[22] And, on this point, we might further recall that what became the United States began, essentially, as various corporate venture colonies.

From its founding, the American colonies were governed by English law, and many of the original colonies, such as Virginia, were originally organized as English joint-stock companies (the Virginia Company, for example) chartered by the Crown. England was cash poor in the early seventeenth century. The Crown had an incentive to create arrangements that would help them develop colonies without a direct investment of public funds. By chartering private individual or corporate investors with legal title and governance, they could do just that.[23] For example, the colonies of Massachusetts (until 1684), Connecticut, and Rhode Island

21   Philip J. Stern, *Empire, Incorporated: The Corporations That Built British Colonialism* (Harvard University Press, 2023), 1, 11.

22   Philip J. Stern, *The Company-State: Corporate Sovereignty and the Early Modern Foundations of the British Empire in India* (Oxford University Press, 2011), 10.

23   Alan Taylor, *American Revolutions: A Continental History, 1750–1804* (Norton, 2016), 31.

were corporations according to Crown charters.[24] This also meant that, in certain situations, England effectively granted these companies nearly total authority over local matters, without having to request permission from the Crown. The state governor and the company or corporation had enormous power to create and uphold law, as long as they did not defy the laws of England.[25]

Revolting and winning independence from England did not entirely change this company-state formation. Even the US Constitution (1787) itself "should be seen as a popularly issued corporate charter," writes David Ciepley, in part because the terms "constitution" and "charter" were used interchangeably during this time.[26] More broadly, Ciepley suggests that the liberal democratic state developed out of the corporate principles and practices that we have already been considering. US jurists in the first decades of the new nation took seriously this "corporate" notion of the United States government, a term that was more capacious then and could include unions, universities, and towns in addition to all types of businesses.[27] In cases such as *Chisholm* (1793), *Dixon et al. v. United States* (1811), and *United States v. Maurice* (1823), the justices identified the state, and particularly the American state, as a corporation. This point is repeated bluntly: "All states whatever are corporations" (*Chisholm*); "'The United States of America' is the true name of that grand corporation which the American people have formed" (*Dixon*, J. Marshall); and the United States is a "great corporation" (*Maurice*).[28]

But as the US grew throughout the nineteenth century, many more corporations had to be chartered to finance bridges, utilities, railroads, and other expensive enterprises. More capital, and thus greater financial risk, was needed. To facilitate investment, US states in the second half of the nineteenth century made it easier to incorporate through "free incorporation" laws. These laws dropped the requirement that incorporating necessitated special acts of legislation for each company. Instead,

---

24   Joseph Stancliffe Davis, *Essays in the Earlier History of American Corporations*, vol. 1 (Harvard University Press, 1917), 20.

25   Mary Sarah Bilder, *The Transatlantic Constitution: Colonial Legal Culture and the Empire* (Harvard University Press, 2004), 48.

26   David Ciepley, "Is the US Government a Corporation? The Corporate Origins of Modern Constitutionalism," *American Political Science Review* 111, no. 2 (2017): 419.

27   For a longer discussion, see Lisa Siraganian, *Modernism and the Meaning of Corporate Persons* (Oxford University Press, 2020), 14–30.

28   *Chisholm v. Georgia*, 2 US (2 Dall.) (1793); *Dixon et al. v United States*, case No. 3934, Circuit Court D. Virginia (1811); *United States v. Maurice*, 26 F. Cas. 1211 (C.C.D. Va. 1823).

investors could incorporate easily through standardized form-filling methods. Essentially, these are still in use today.[29]

Businesses also started experimenting with different kinds of organizations and legal structures. Joint-stock companies began using "trust law, in combination with partnership law, to lock in business assets, yet provide liquidity to the investors," Margaret Blair explains. Ready cash today, capital locked in for tomorrow—this was an enormously powerful combination. Assets were sheltered for centuries, effectively binding community wealth in perpetuity.[30] These new, more available corporate and trust forms enabled additional capital to be securely dedicated to financial endeavors. And the individual investor had far less to risk than in earlier types of business, such as partnerships.

Added to this, by the end of the nineteenth century, true limited liability became the norm globally, in all commercial regions. Creditors could only tap the assets of the company, and not the wealth of the shareholders, to recoup their losses. It is at this point that "the modern doctrine of separate corporate personality, with its reified corporations and 'complete separation' of shareholders and company, crystallized out."[31] The doctrine of corporate personhood blooms all over the legal record. In the US, the Supreme Court decision *Santa Clara County v. Southern Pacific Railroad* (1886) became notorious for (supposedly) confirming the personhood of corporations under the Fourteenth Amendment, giving corporations basic civil rights promised (and not fully delivered) to formerly enslaved persons.[32] In the decades to follow, the idea continued to develop that the corporation was a so-called "natural" or "real entity," one conceptually distinct from the shareholders owning it, or the directors running it. English legal scholar Frederic Maitland describes this view of the corporation as that of "a living organism and a real person, with body and members and a will of its own."[33] In the United States, extreme versions of this idea will not last much beyond the first decades of the twentieth century. But, in other ways, the conception of the corporation as a separate real entity with rights, a legal person, has never left us.

---

29   David Millon, "Theories of the Corporation," *Duke Law Journal* 39, no. 2 (1990): 206.

30   Margaret M. Blair, "Locking in Capital: What Corporate Law Achieved for Business Organizers in the Nineteenth Century," *UCLA Law Review* 51, no. 2 (December 2003): 395; 389–90.

31   Ireland, "Limited Liability," 847.

32   *Santa Clara County v. Southern Pacific Railroad Co*, 118 US 394 (1886).

33   Frederic Maitland, "Translators Introduction," in Otto Gierke, *Political Theories of the Middle Age* (Cambridge University Press, 1900), xxvi.

Critically, as the corporation became more of "a real person," the emphasis on its state-sponsorship disappeared from the story. The idea of the corporation as a special gift from the state started to look quaint and erroneous—although, of course, state intervention never goes away, since "free-incorporation laws" are legislative acts. Simultaneously, the corporation emerged as *the* exemplary version of artificial legal person-hood. By 1909, the Harvard law professor John Chipman Gray could declare offhandedly that the "usual form of a juristic person is a corpo-ration."[34] And a powerful person it was. "*Ir*responsibility was now firmly built into the corporate legal form," Paddy Ireland observes.[35] Whereas the eighteenth-century state as artificial person was understood to have both rights *and* obligations, the early twentieth-century corporation was rarely hampered by anything more burdensome than its own financial liabilities. Often, those duties, too, could be cleverly shrugged off. The corporate person continued to rise in status as supposedly abstracted, unembodied, and largely free from responsibility to the public—even though its material effects remained everywhere apparent.

This evolving Anglo-American model of the corporation as a legal person also spread widely. First, in the United States, the corporate laws of the tiny state of Delaware began to dominate; to this day, Delaware remains a popular state in which to incorporate because of its corporate-friendly law. Then, the world converged toward the "shareholder-oriented model" in the law of business corporations, still following the Anglo-American lead. Across the globe, identical features appeared, as "large-scale business enterprise in every major commercial jurisdiction had come to be organized in the corporate form."[36] This model further consolidated its dominance over the course of the twentieth century.

Finally, a consequence of Anglo-American corporate law's devel-opmental dominance is the elaboration of a relatively new, emergent legal phenomenon that Kevin Crow calls "International Corporate Personhood." A post–WWII form that still retains its Anglo-American pedigree, this legal entity is "composed of persons, transnationally fluid in form and in ownership, transcending states yet receiving form from states—a person that overlaps at times with the individual and at times with the state, yet accrues rights available to neither." Unlike other judicial

34   John Chipman Gray, *The Nature and Sources of the Law* (1909), ed. David Campbell and Philip Thomas ([1909, 1997] New York: Routledge, 2019), 71.

35   Ireland, "Limited Liability," 845.

36   Henry Hansmann and Reinier Kraakman, "The End of History for Corporate Law," *Georgetown Law Journal* 89, no. 2 (2001): 439–68, 439.

subjects, international corporate persons can be legally bound by states only in disjointed, partial ways. This has enabled ad hoc international law, such as it is, to support corporations *against* the power of states. As Crow also puts it, "through the fluidity of its legal form, [International Corporate Personhood] can retain alternatively or simultaneously elements of both personhood and thinghood," a flexibility that turns out to be formidably useful to business.[37] In the process, the role of the state as *the* delegating artificial person—along with its corporate-colonial history and its public responsibilities—is neglected or forgotten.

Monsieur le Capital, from Marx to Pashukanis

We have been exploring the broad theoretical transformation of the corporate legal person: from an ancillary legal fiction of the state (in the eighteenth century) to its "real personhood" status (in the twentieth and beyond). Something can feel a bit magical or mysterious about this development, a quality that Hew Locke's sculptures play with. Perhaps we walk up to one of his grave markers respectfully, expecting to learn something about the deceased human individual honored there. Instead, we discover a memorial for a defunct entity—not for a single human being, or even for a group of human beings, but for a gigantic corporation. Rather than responding reverently, we are prompted to wonder why entities like the West Indies Sugar Corporation were given the power, status, and right to operate in the world the way they did. How did the corporation manage this maneuver?

The remainder of this chapter looks more closely at law's *micro level*, to understand the uniqueness and usefulness of the corporation functioning as "a special legal subjectivity for capital."[38] To do so, we will consider the mystification of corporate personhood's development, in what Marx described as our "bewitched, distorted and upside-down world, haunted by Monsieur le Capital and Madame la Terre, who are at the same time social characters and mere things."[39] In other words, the aim now is to make better sense of the corporation "as the personification of capital: Monsieur le Capital," by considering how it is created

---

37   Kevin Crow, *International Corporate Personhood: Business and the Bodyless In International Law* (New York: Routledge, 2021), 26, 4, 181, 175.

38   Geoffrey Kay and James Mott, *Political Order and the Law of Labour* (London: Macmillan, 1982), 9.

39   Marx, *Capital*, vol. III, 969.

as both a haunting social character and a mere thing.[40] Marx and the Soviet legal theorist Evgeny Pashukanis will help us see how expansive personhood relies on the innovations of the corporation in capitalism. Put most simply: the expansive person, whether considered in the form of fetuses, rivers, or AI, has been established on the corporate legal form, that subjectivity of capital.

An early paragraph in the first volume of *Capital* is a germinating seed for this idea. At the beginning of chapter 2 on "Exchange," Marx makes the seemingly obvious point that "commodities cannot go to market and make exchanges" on their own; these manufactured things need to rely on their "guardians, who are also their owners."[41] Apparently, commodities strangely blend aspects of underage *persons* who need guardians and *things* that are owned. Commodities cannot resist someone simply snatching them; they need their owner-guardians to act on their behalf to protect them. We might note, already, that this relation resembles that of recent forms of expansive persons (fetuses, nonhuman animals, trees, AI) that need individual human beings to speak for them in a court of law.

Marx's analysis of capitalist exchange continues. These objects can only relate to one another as commodities if their owner-guardians "mutually recognize" the rights of other commodity owners as "private proprietors" and thus "as persons whose will resides in those objects." Their existence *as* commodities requires some kind of understanding and reciprocity between individual people. Put slightly differently, "exchange" does not mean people approaching a stockpile of things in a marketplace to loot with abandon. "Exchange" means buyers and sellers understanding commodities that, having taken on their owner-guardians' will, may be exchanged only with the "mutual consent" of other owner-guardians.[42]

What is Marx getting at in this passage? His point is that, logically, there *already* must be some mutual understanding and agreement— what he calls a "juridical relation"—between the two owner-guardians. It is the germ of a legal contract. That mutual understanding imbues the commodity, and the buying and selling of it, with legal standing in the marketplace.[43] This "is a relation between two wills, and is but the reflex of the real economical relation" between a buyer and seller. Economic

---

40   Grietje Baars, *The Corporation, Law, and Capitalism: A Radical Perspective on the Role of Law in the Global Political Economy* (Leiden: Brill, 2019), 31.

41   Marx, *Capital*, vol. 1, 56.

42   Ibid.

43   Alan Norrie, "Pashukanis and the 'Commodity Form Theory': A Reply to Warrington," *International Journal of the Sociology of Law* 10 (1982): 423.

processes cannot exist without being mediated by the law, explains Étienne Balibar in his reading of this passage. "Without the juridical form, the economic process *does not work*." There is, instead, "a kind of *chiasmatic relationship* between the juridical form and the value form," with each relying on and mediating the other.[44]

Through this process of mutual reliance, writes Marx, the status of the owner-guardians also transforms: "The persons exist for one another merely as representatives of, and, therefore, as owners of, commodities . . . the characters who appear on the economic stage are but the person-ifications of the economical relations that exist between them."[45] Here is another powerful yet subtle point. Marx is suggesting that their economic relationship essentially undermines the full agency and relationality of buyers and sellers. Although the will of buyers and sellers resides in the objects they exchange, the commodity enacts a transformation in which individual people play second fiddle to their goods. Individuals become "representatives" of their commodities, "personifications" rather than persons. And this will be the key to expansive personhood.

Of course, *Capital* is not overtly a critique of law but of political economy; the commodity is its analytical focus. Scholars took decades to create a Marxist jurisprudence. But law was Marx's first serious study at university, and jurisprudence had "a kind of temporal priority" in his intellectual thought.[46] Not only was he extremely knowledgeable about legal philosophy and history, he also studied with major legal scholars of the era, including the aforementioned Von Savigny, who had developed an important theory of the corporation as an artificial entity sanctioned by the state. Marx himself acknowledged that his early work had a legal flavor before the economic became dominant. When he developed a critique of Hegel's legal philosophy, he was coming to see that judicial relations were "rooted in the material relations" of bour-geois society and had to be investigated via political economy.[47] This legal heritage appears throughout his work, although it is not always made explicit.

---

44   Étienne Balibar, "Hegel, Marx, Pashukanis, and the Idea of Abstract Right as Bourgeois Form," in *Institutions: Critical History of Law*, ed. Cooper Francis and Daniel Gottlieb (London: Centre for Research in Modern European Philosophy, 2023), 82, 91.

45   Marx, *Capital*, vol. 1, 56–7.

46   Donald R. Kelley, "The Metaphysics of Law: An Essay on the Very Young Marx," *American Historical Review* 83, no. 2 (1978): 352, 367.

47   Karl Marx, "'Preface' to A Contribution to the Critique of Political Economy," in *Marx: Later Political Writings*, ed. Terrell Carver (Càmbridge University Press, 1996), 159.

This is the motivation for Evgeny Pashukanis's *General Theory of Law and Marxism* (1924), which mines the implicit logical and legal assumptions in *Capital*'s theory of exchange, extrapolating what China Miéville terms "the deep grammar of the law." Writing in the world-shattering moment after the October Revolution, Pashukanis understands his project as clarifying "a theory already-existent, although not rigorously formulated" in *Capital*, continues Miéville, a theory examining how legal form maps onto the logic of the commodity.[48] Rather than envisioning law as *merely* mystifying or ideological (part of the superstructure), Pashukanis *also* sees law as part of our material conditions (the base), and understands the relation between law and exchange as one of "mutual entailment."[49] For him, in other words, the principles of legal personhood are not only instruments of bourgeois "deceit" and "hypocrisy." They are also concrete, real, and embodied in every legal contact, part of an actual, material process.[50]

Pashukanis explains his central idea as follows: "At the same time . . . that the product of labour becomes a commodity and a bearer of value, man acquires the capacity to be a legal subject and a bearer of rights." He is saying that having labor value or having legal rights are two sides of the same coin—and the coin, to be clear, is money. Simultaneously, as the commodity comes to bear value, "social life disintegrates" and splits into two. On the one hand, into economic relations, "in which people have no greater significance than objects," and on the other, into relations between legal subjects with the capacity to have rights. In other words, the same economic forces and conditions that put the commodity to work in a scenario of market exchange, the same forces and conditions that make people into legal subjects, are *also* the forces and conditions that destroy complex social relationships. Once the social world has collapsed, individuals are spit out: either as object-like commodities, valuable for their alienable labor, or as legal subjects with valuable rights. Or as both, since any individual could take on these different positions at different moments and in various ways. The individual is then "slavishly dependent on economic relations" while also being compensated by "a rare gift" of being "absolutely free and equal to other owners of commodities."[51]

---

48   China Miéville, *Between Equal Rights: A Marxist Theory of International Law* (Leiden: Brill, 2005), 114, 77, 78.

49   Norrie, "Pashukanis and the 'Commodity Form Theory,'" 424.

50   Evgeny B. Pashukanis, *The General Theory of Law and Marxism* (Piscataway, NJ: Transaction, 2003), 40.

51   Ibid., 112–14.

By expanding on Marx, Pashukanis is aligning the moment of commodity exchange with the moment when legal personhood comes on the scene in its full maturity; the two phenomena are too deeply interconnected to be disentangled. The difference between them, he suggests, is just a matter of a diverging focus. Whereas Marx begins by analyzing the commodity, Pashukanis foregrounds the legal subject becoming the abstract legal person.[52] In Lon Fuller's paraphrase, "The legal subject is . . . merely the economic trader seen in his juristic aspect."[53] Just as a commodity's market value is merely a hollow "shell," masking the true variety of uses an object might have, so, says Pashukanis, a legal subject with rights functions like an abstract covering over the real individual, dissolving "all concrete peculiarities" that differentiate individuals from one another. Mature capitalism achieves this dissolution of an individual's concrete particulars. Those are the conditions in which "every person becomes man in the abstract, every subject becomes an abstract legal subject." That is, under certain "real conditions" of capitalism, individuals will "be transformed from a zoological individual into an abstract, impersonal legal subject, into the legal person."[54] And it is precisely this split, between your body's concrete particulars and your shell-like legal subjectivity, which also allows you to be separated—alienated—from your legal personhood.

Although corporations are not his target, Pashukanis is helping us make sense of something critical about them. The rise of the corporation as a discrete, real entity—that is, as a corporate person—works hand in hand with the rise of *alienated* legal subjectivity or personality (what we call legal personhood).[55] As capitalism develops, he notes, "the capacity to be a legal subject" will separate from actual individual people and become instead "a purely social function." This is another description of artificial (corporate) personhood. Even the "capacity to act" will be "itself abstracted from the capacity to possess rights." Capitalist property

---

52   Carl Wilén, "Why Pashukanis Was Right: Abstraction and Form in *The General Theory of Law and Marxism*," *Capital and Class* (December 14, 2023).

53   Lon Fuller, "Pashukanis and Vyshinsky: A Study in the Development of Marxian Legal Theory," *Michigan Law Review* 47, no. 8 (1949): 1157–66; 1160.

54   Pashukanis, *General Theory*, 113, 120–1, 115.

55   Pashukanis's terminology can be a little tricky: He more often uses the terms "legal subject" or "legal subjectivity" to describe real individuals (in the marketplace), and reserves "legal personhood" for the full legal abstraction. Legal subjectivity is the necessary starting point for what we call "legal personhood": "The principle of legal subjectivity (which we take to mean the formal principle of freedom and equality, the autonomy of the personality, and so forth)." Preface to the second Russian edition, *General Theory*, 40.

becomes abstracted in the process and "is transformed into an absolute, fixed right" wherever it goes, expanding its dominion "to encompass the whole globe" while protected by international law.[56] Although he does not utter the phrase "joint-stock company" or "corporation" at this point, he is headed there (it comes up a few pages later). Multinational corporations partaking in "venture colonialism," as Stern terms it, exploiting resources widely and indiscriminately, acting on their own without worrying about duties or consequences—these are the quintessential active, abstracted entities with property rights.

Indeed, Matthew Dimick draws out Pashukanis's argument about legal subjectivity, abstract legal personhood, and the commodity to support an analysis of corporate capitalism. Because capitalist law generates "a society of autonomous legal subjects, law is linked with a certain kind of individualism." For that reason, the notion of a "corporation acquir[ing] legal personality is not a refutation of Pashukanis's theory but, in fact, a striking confirmation of it."[57] When the differences between any abstract legal subject—human, corporate, or other—have been dissolved away, corporations can then function like individual legal subjects as easily as can any human being. The corporation has become fully personified in law, hiding its thing-like, commodity-based nature by haunting the globe as a social character.

Expansive Personhood as the Privilege of Speaking Property

As powerful as his theory was, there are limits to Pashukanis's Marxist account; he cannot provide us with the final verdict on legal personhood in liberal capitalist societies. His focus was on legal form in the 1920s, not on its sociological or technical developments since then. He simply does not fathom the way expanding capitalist societies *also* would support more types of social justice for more diverse categories of people (for example, the ongoing revolutions of racial, disability, queer, trans, or women's rights). But the reason to question commodified legal subjectivity is not to diminish the diverse people it manages to serve. It is to emphasize all those it simply cannot value—those ever-increasing numbers without capital. Anticipating the full blossoming of artificial

---

56   Ibid., 115.
57   Matthew Dimick, "Evgeny Pashukanis' Commodity-Form Theory of Law," in *Research Handbook on Law and Marxism*, ed. Paul O'Connell and Umut Ozsu (Northampton, MA: Edward Elgar Publishing, 2021), 121.

personhood as a legal and technocratic tool in capitalism, his analysis remains unmatched.

As both he and Marx might have predicted, evidence suggests that the corporate person is becoming the prevailing account of legal personhood, full stop. Imagining this situation artistically, Hew Locke mounts Enron's tombstone in a human cemetery. Far more dangerously, *Citizens United* gives corporate money free speech protections in US elections. Or think of specimens once limited to the realm of science fiction, such as surgical creations of human-animal hybrids ("cybrids"), or genetically fertilized three-parent babies. Considering such examples, Britta van Beers suggests that "the natural person seems to be hemorrhaging into the artificial person . . . [and is] now adopting certain traits of the artificial person." She details how this legal trend comes with damaging consequences, rendering biomedical law unable to protect our complex embodied nature. And, critically, she reminds us that "artificial legal persons such as corporations clearly offer the best example in contemporary law of this legal category's bodiless character."[58] Although its biotech is probably corporately patented, these biological "cybrids" are not corporations. Yet, legally, we might think of them as a kind of adapted corporate form, artificial persons made manifest.

All this is to suggest that the alienated legal personhood that Pashukanis theorizes, the one that was developing a century ago, is coming to full fruition now in the form of the expansive person we know today. Personhood for other entities, whether cybrids, trees, or AI, relies on this interwoven cultural and legal story of the artificial person, while it has not, yet, transcended its limitations. Just recall the four theses of expansive personhood we investigated in the introduction. Each one maps onto the alienated legal subjectivity Pashukanis develops as a feature of capitalism:

(1) *Perfect formal equality.* Sameness for all is necessary, of course, and Pashukanis clearly establishes it as a necessary element of legal subjectivity. Abstract, formal equality is a requirement to enter into contractual agreements of buying and selling, hence all the emphasis on mutuality and reciprocity in the passage from *Capital* that Pashukanis expands on. Pashukanis underscores that "the capacity to be a legal subject is a purely formal capacity"—which is also to say that being someone who can

---

58 Britta van Beers, "The Changing Nature of Law's Natural Person: The Impact of Emerging Technologies on the Legal Concept of the Person," *German Law Journal* 18, no. 3 (2017): 564, 574.

theoretically buy and sell property does not make you a property owner. In fact, the capacity to freely dispose of capitalist property, in order to maximize profit, requires "the existence of propertyless individuals." As he quips, echoing Marx, "the fundamental principle of bourgeois society is 'the equal opportunity to attain inequality.'"[59] That is just to reiterate, as Paul Hirst has written: The equivalence between legal subjects is "formal not ethical."[60] This observation leads us to:

(2) *The thinness of personhood in theories of expansive personhood.* For Pashukanis, the total absence of an ethical component to legal subjectivity already implies the basic impoverishment of the form. We already notice instances of this stripping away of other potential elements of personhood when Pashukanis writes that "all concrete peculiarities which distinguish one representative of the *genus homo sapiens* from another dissolve into the abstraction of man in general, man as a legal subject."[61] The "peculiarities" that make you who you are, including the roles you play in society, or your unique capacities to reflect and think about yourself in the world—all these qualities are irrelevant to the legal subject in capitalism. As noted in the previous chapter, reducing the features that will *count* to make you a person (to give you standing in a court, to make you matter to the law) is a crucial strategy in expanding the circle of who or what matters. More and different entities can then be incorporated into the personhood category.

As with expansive personhood, Pashukanis sees a similar kind of hard pruning back of legal personality in commodity relations, such that there is:

(3) *An equivalence of all forms of personhood (moral, religious, and so on) with the legal version.* We sense this when he writes that "the moral personality is nothing but the [legal] subject in commodity-producing society" or that "moral being is a necessary complement of legal being; they are both modes of intercourse utilized by commodity-producers." Social life has already reduced to either economic relations or legal ones; there is no room for anything else (morality, religion, ethics) except as it can be accommodated to that reality. The kind of morality that liberal capitalism preaches is, accordingly, morally bankrupt. The worker's personhood might be equal to a capitalist's, in principle. "But all that comes out of this 'materialized freedom' . . . is the freedom to die of starvation— without any interference." Moral fetishism is like commodity fetishism

---

59   Pashukanis, *General Theory*, 127, 123.
60   Paul Hirst, *On Law and Ideology* (London: MacMillan, 1979), 117.
61   Pashukanis, *General Theory*, 113.

and legal fetishism, observes Pashukanis: They are all ideological constructions that need to be exposed for what they truly are.[62]

Finally, as we explored in the previous chapter:

(4) *The developing model of expansive personhood forgoes the publicness of the moral person and replaces it with qualities of objecthood, thingness, or property.* Most simply, we might say that expansive personhood could so easily emerge out of artificial corporate personhood because the corporation stipulated that economic relationships, and thus private property, trump all other kinds of values. This empowering of possessions and economics alters our sense of self. John Rodman, an early, radical environmentalist, understood this problem of expanding moral rights for nature and animals: "If the project of redeeming nature from objecthood is also a project for humanity, it must mean that . . . we have come to suspect that *we* are really objects or things," ones that, if we are lucky, can acquire some market value.[63] It is precisely this privileging of property values that has made it far easier for liberal, mainstream legal theorists to imagine how objects or entities with no will, agency, or intention could still be considered persons. Again, often this means reimagining our physical bodies as property—or, at least, as having property-like qualities.

On this point, it is worth underscoring the influence of a different Locke: John Locke, and his notions of the person as property. Although the earth and all its "inferior creatures" are held in common, he writes, "yet every Man has a Property in his own Person."[64] Ideas building upon Locke's commitment to one's labor as one's alienable property were incorporated directly into the US Constitution. Private property, particularly of enslaved persons, ends up distorting the country's founding principles, as Jennifer Nedelsky brilliantly shows: "Inequality became both a presumption and an object of protection" in the US Constitution, skewing and stunting the functions of democracy to this day.[65] This becomes a feature, not a bug, of advanced capitalism. And historical conceptions of legal persons and corporations are an inescapable part of this story.

When, in 1972, Christopher D. Stone asks "Should Trees Have Standing?" in what would become a historic law review article, his argument

---

62   Ibid., 154, 155, 157, 158.

63   John Rodman, "The Liberation of Nature?," *Inquiry* 20 (1977): 108.

64   John Locke, *Second Treatise of Government*, ed. C. B. Macpherson (Cambridge, MA: Hackett Publishing, 1980), 19.

65   Jennifer Nedelsky, *Private Property and the Limits of American Constitutionalism: The Madisonian Framework and Its Legacy* (University of Chicago Press, 1990), 1.

on behalf of the trees explicitly relies on the long-standing normality of artificial corporate personhood:

> It is no answer to say that streams and forests cannot have standing because streams and forests cannot speak. Corporations cannot speak either . . . Lawyers speak for them, . . . the legal problems of natural objects [should be handled] as one does the problems of legal incompetents—human beings who have become vegetable.[66]

We will consider Stone's arguments on behalf of trees and other natural entities at length in chapter 4. But, for now, note that Stone uses corporate *speech* (or, more accurately, incapacity for direct speech) as a wedge for expansive personhood, in order to counter arguments that a lack of voice, agency, or will might impair the status of trees' standing.

For Stone, human beings that have become object-like—"who have become vegetable"—are like natural things that have always been that way: the streams and forests that "cannot speak." Since the publication of Stone's article, nonhuman animals have also been gaining personhood in the same way, with rights "exercised on their behalf by third parties."[67] Stone accepts that human beings can, in certain important instances, start to take on more of the attributes of thinghood or property rather than those of willful, conscious, morally responsible persons. That is what happens when people "become vegetable." It is as if personhood works on a kind of sliding scale, rather than an on/off switch: at the one pole, being fully alive with a will, and at the other, being a corpse-like object with the characteristics of property.

This sliding scale is critical to expansive personhood claims. Personhood, singular or collective, becomes a category with permeable boundaries and a low barrier for admission. The ascendency of corporations as legal, civil persons, albeit as artificial persons, has made it easier to recast as a soft continuum what had been a stiff binary in Roman law through (at least) Blackstone, and into the nineteenth century—the law of persons versus the law of things. Whether we understand that flowing continuum as supporting the legal standing of trees and animals or juridical corporate personhood, the principle is the same. That is, rather than see persons as opposed to things, they are understood as continuous: person becoming thing or property, legal subject blending with commodity.

---

66   Christopher D. Stone, *Should Trees Have Standing? Law, Morality, and the Environment*, third edition (Oxford University Press, 2010), 8.

67   Crow, *International Corporate Personhood*, 183.

Crowding Out the Public with Artificial Persons

This chapter has explored the historical and theoretical development of the concept of the artificial person in law: the nonhuman being as a legal subject or person. At the macro level, we have seen a process spreading globally from its start in Europe, the United States, and other colonies. The corporate person becomes the de facto artificial legal person, losing its previous association with the state. Nation-states, meanwhile, take on a corporate guise, via venture colonialism, while corporations eventually free themselves from virtually all this legislative grounding and limitations, becoming "real entities" that can spread more widely and move more freely. Meanwhile, at the micro level, we have considered (following Marx and Pashukanis) how legal personhood in capitalism could easily develop into what became corporate personhood: first, because being a legal subject and being a market actor are two sides of the same coin, and second, because "the need for a special legal subjectivity for capital arises from the nature of capital as such."[68] Despite the corporate person's supposedly "abstract" nature, private property became a substantial and eventually preeminent aspect of its existence. Altogether, the expansive person repeats the corporate form.

When corporations started exercising their new powers over a century ago, some legal theorists objected to the shape that they were taking. English legal scholar Thomas Baty provided an intriguing example. He also wrote and portrayed himself, sometimes, as "Irene Clyde" and is considered an important transgender pioneer. Baty argued that we should be very clear about what is happening in scenarios that give rise to corporate persons. When a country permits a business to incorporate, that is, "to establish a new entity, an 'artificial person,'" it has done nothing more than "clothe the persons who are carrying out the idea with certain powers, liabilities, and immunities" that ordinarily they would not possess. The country in question "has not created a person" that other countries are obligated to receive and treat as a human being. Rather, the incorporating country is just setting up a costumed example:

> It might just as well enact that horses and donkeys were to be regarded as "subhuman persons," if duly admitted to registration and managed by committee—and then demand that they should be received everywhere on the footing of citizens, and admitted to sue and to acquire property.[69]

---

68   Kay and Mott, *Political Order*, 9.
69   Thomas Baty, "The Rights of Ideas—and of Corporations," *Harvard Law Review* 33 (1920): 364–5.

Baty leaps from artificial personhood for corporations to artificial personhood for "horses and donkeys" to clarify the strategic moves being made here. For him, both are a disguised, unreal form of personhood. In referencing nonhuman animals (the topic of chapter 3), Baty also spies our contemporary forms of expansive personhood on the horizon.

One of Baty's larger claims is that it is countries, in the end, that allow corporations to exist. In making this point, he is weighing in on a vigorous dispute whose outlines we have already seen. During the early twentieth century, the debate took the form of asking whether a corporation should be understood as a person with a "will that [had] become unified" through its single-minded purpose (as Harold Laski contended), or if, in contrast, a corporation's personhood should be regarded "as a figure of speech," as Justice Oliver Wendell Holmes Jr. argued.[70] Holmes's view reiterates Hobbes's point in *Leviathan*: that artificial persons, inanimate things that are "being represented by a fiction," borrow their authority from the state.[71] But this was a contentious debate over a century ago, not so much resolved as abandoned as unresolvable.

More recently, some legal theorists have built on aspects of Baty's and Holmes's positions, proposing that understanding a corporation as, in effect, "a little government" or a "public-private hybrid" offers the most apt description for what corporations truly are. These phrases are David Ciepley's, who implies that there is a kind of elaborate public relations deception at work with corporate personhood today. As he puts it, "a corporate economy is not a 'free-enterprise, private property system,' but a state-sponsored, socialized property system," a "social program for economic growth" designed to support businesses and protect them from risk. Even to this day, the state is the governing authority delegating power to the corporation. In fact, every corporation that has *ever* existed "has operated on the authority of a government-issued charter that grants these privileges."[72] Looking at another view of this process, Joshua Barkan suggests that, by the 1890s, lawmakers saw public welfare in terms of the economy (a view utterly familiar to us in the neoliberal present), and admitted "a legal embodiment of capital into the political community as a juristic person with *rights held against the state*." In other words, the corporate person's standing in the community was justified in

---

70   Harold Laski, "The Personality of Associations," *Harvard Law Review* 29, no. 4 (1916): 424; Oliver Wendell Holmes Jr. to Felix Frankfurter, August 6, 1916, in *Holmes and Frankfurter: Their Correspondence, 1912–1934*, ed. Robert M. Mennel and Christine L. Compston (Hanover: University of New Hampshire, 1996), 53–4.

71   Hobbes, *Leviathan*, 100.

72   David Ciepley, "Neoliberal Corporation," 276–7, 285, 276.

terms of economic security.[73] In the process of legally embodying capital and taking on various attributes of government, corporations have undermined the very public values they were supposed to help support.

Contemporary legal theorists of corporations have also articulated the way that corporate personhood has undermined the authority of the state itself, damaging human rights in the process. They have shown how the international form of corporate persons has gained political power without political community and thus, also, without political responsibility.[74] Others have made the case that the right to property works to the advantage of corporations rather than individual human beings, enabling corporations to subvert human rights law.[75] Turkuler Isiksel describes a nefarious "dehumanization of human rights" in progress in international law, in which private economic actors are acquiring rights and "eroding states' ability to control commercial and financial flows across their borders."[76] Years ago, Susan Strange suggested that such phenomena are an unintended consequences of capitalism itself, with the state failing to uphold its basic duties: "At the heart of the international political economy, there is a vacuum . . . a yawning hole of non-authority, ungovernance it might be called."[77]

In contrast to the sophisticated analysis of corporate personhood's history, contemporary arguments for expansive legal personhood for fetuses, animals, or rivers have largely obscured its legal origins or these "ungovernance" effects. That is surely a smart practical tactic, since immediate legal precedents matter most to convince courts of one's rightness. But it has damaging consequences. The unacknowledged legal and economic origin of the corporation as artificial person, which we have been piecing together and theorizing in this chapter, is precisely what permits expansive persons to function legally. It is the corporate form that separates the legal subject from its potential liabilities and duties, and it is that fundamental division that every new form of personhood reactivates. Subjects and rights proliferate, while liability and duties languish unaddressed. Furthermore, the alignment of artificial personhood with

---

73   Joshua Barkan, *Corporate Sovereignty: Law and Government Under Capitalism* (Minneapolis: University of Minnesota Press, 2013), 44.

74   Crow, *International Corporate Personhood*, 19.

75   Anna Grear, "Human Rights—Human Bodies? Some Reflections on Corporate Human Rights Distortion, the Legal Subject, Embodiment and Human Rights Theory," *Law and Critique* 17 (2006): 196.

76   Turkuler Isiksel, "The Rights of Man and the Rights of the Man-Made: Corporations and Human Rights," *Human Rights Quarterly* 38 (2016): 299.

77   Susan Strange, *The Retreat of the State: The Diffusion of Power in the World Economy* (Cambridge University Press, 1996).

property, via the corporation, supports a seemingly natural process of relinquishing government control and oversight. It also tends to depreciate the public more generally. Capital has adopted the artificial person as its own (Monsieur le Capital), and wresting control away from it is made more difficult by how stealthy that adoption process has been.

This chapter has aimed to expose the tools of this process at work. Expansive personhood was a development of the corporation first; this is where we see the withdrawal of the public realm and the triumph of property rights. Creating more legal persons without legal duties is a perfect formula to produce more property rights. And that is also why all forms of artificial personhood today entail the removal or degradation of a robust public sphere. That effect is the other half of privileging property. The two phenomena move in tandem, a duet of inverse relationships. As Pashukanis laments, the economic forces that make commodities, and make legal subjects, *also* make us more object-like, and *also* cause social life to disintegrate. We see it today, and we will follow its path in each of the chapters to follow.

That degradation impacts us as individuals, too. Hannah Arendt observes that the "personal element in a man can only appear where a public space exists."[78] Following a similar line of thought, Meir Dan-Cohen writes that "contemplating what I take at the outset to be the content of my inner life turns out upon reflection to imply a public space."[79] The corporation's version of being "a person" tempts us to forget this point, the way that blending property with personhood subtly but irrevocably alters our understandings of who we are.

Entities and objects without duties, without an obvious right to the social realm, might seem to gain a lot by following in corporations' footsteps. But, again, we should be absolutely clear about what is going on here. As *Citizens United* made absurdly literal, property is being offered a speaking role on the public stage, property that is always ultimately owned (through however many shell companies) by someone—a human being. We might enjoy, while watching science fiction or looking at contemporary art, the surprise of nonhuman things acting in human ways, with human characteristics. But we should not confuse our delight at that pretense with our obligation, if not always our desire, to attend to and act for the people in our world.

---

78   Hannah Arendt, "Karl Jaspers; a Laudation," *Men In Dark Times* (New York: Harcourt Brace Jovanovich, 1968), 73.

79   Meir Dan-Cohen, *Normative Subjects: Self and Collectivity in Morality and the Law* (Oxford University Press, 2016), 188–9.

The chapters to follow explore expansive personhood as it is now playing out: from corporations to fetuses, nonhuman animals, trees and other natural entities to, most recently, AI. Mostly we depart from the longer historical and theoretical story in order to keep our focus on this group of expansive persons. But each chapter will also replay aspects of this older pattern, including the turn toward property rights and, with it, a transformation in the notion of the public sphere, or what might count as a public sphere. The engagement of nation-states is often unmentioned or forgotten, as their legal systems become simply a kind of apparatus of capitalism. Yet recovering that story also offers the potential for hope. The corporation as a product of the state and fashioned by its laws reminds us that property is also a creation and tool of the state. These are creations that we could change, tools whose shape and form could be modified and be put to radically different ends. Artists like Hew Locke remind us that, when it comes to personhood, the real people living and suffering in them should not be underestimated.

2

Unborn Fictions: Fetal Persons and Their Women Containers

The fetus thus becomes an incorporation of the woman, a business fiction.
—Patricia Williams[1]

Becoming No Person

In a devastating decision, *Dobbs v. Jackson Women's Health Organization* (2022), the US Supreme Court negated nearly fifty years of precedent supporting reproductive justice, health, and women's autonomy to overturn *Roe v. Wade* (1973). Simultaneously, the decision gave new life to a strange entity whose recent history has been less closely studied: "the unborn." *Dobbs* reviewed Mississippi's Gestational Age Act (2018), a state law ordering that "a person shall not intentionally or knowingly perform . . . or induce an abortion of an unborn human being" after fifteen weeks of gestation, except in extreme medical emergencies. The Mississippi law thus outlaws non-lifesaving abortion after the first trimester; because, in the act, gestational age is defined as beginning at the first day of a woman's last menstrual period, the law effectively makes abortion illegal in Mississippi roughly thirteen weeks after conception or twelve weeks after fertilization. As the *Dobbs* opinion quotes, the Mississippi law repeatedly uses the language of "unborn human being" or "unborn child." Sometimes "unborn" is simply left adrift, transformed

---

1   Patricia J. Williams, "Fetal Fictions: An Exploration of Property Archetypes in Racial and Gendered Contexts," *Florida Law Review* 42, no. 1 (1990): 93.

from an adjective into a noun (as in "protecting the life of the unborn"). *Dobbs*'s lengthy and inaccurate historical survey of nineteenth-century state laws found various centuries' old uses of "unborn child" to support its claims. Justice Roberts's concurrence even accepts the phrase "unborn child" without quotation marks: for him, this phrase is not an historical artifact but a present-day reality.[2]

By overturning *Roe*, and holding that abortion would no longer be protected by the federal government, *Dobbs* returned abortion decisions to individual states, many of which had or soon tried to pass laws like Mississippi's. These laws end abortion protections sometimes as early as the moment of conception. They also tend to use similar rhetoric, such as references not to embryos or fetuses but to an "unborn human individual," "persons, born and unborn," "unborn children," or "unborn persons."[3] As the organization Pregnancy Justice observes, "The idea of a fetus as a legal person has gone from a fringe idea . . . to the ascendant framework of anti-abortion states."[4] Although Ohio voters rejected a broad fetal personhood bill in November 2023, over half of US states still include personhood-related language in their anti-abortion laws, laws which suddenly became alive—like unborn persons—when *Dobbs* was decided.[5] "Proudly stand[ing] for families and Life," the 2024 Republican platform incorporated support for these laws as part of its vague anti-abortion stance: "We believe that the 14th Amendment to the Constitution of the United States guarantees that no person can be denied Life or Liberty without Due Process, and that the States are, therefore, free to pass Laws protecting those Rights."[6] Although avoiding reference to the Equal Protection clause (no equality for women here), the platform's mention of the Fourteenth Amendment and persons clearly signals support for state fetal personhood laws. And that amendment, of course, is the same constitutional source for corporate and all forms of expansive personhood.

---

2   *Dobbs v. Jackson Women's Health Organization*, 597 US___(2022), 6, 7, 68; Roberts' concurrence, 3.

3   For ease of reference, I generally follow the amendments in using the term "fetus" throughout this chapter. A biologically accurate account would distinguish between the developmental sequence of zygote, blastocyst, embryo, and fetus.

4   Pregnancy Justice, "When Fetuses Gain Personhood: Understanding the Impact on IVF, Contraception, Medical Treatment, Criminal Law, Child Support, and Beyond" (August 17, 2022), 1. Pregnancyjusticeus.org.

5   Julie Carr Smyth, "Ohio Voters Enshrine Abortion Access in Constitution in Latest Statewide Win for Reproductive Rights," APnews.com, November 7, 2023.

6   *2024 GOP Platform: Make America Great Again!*, 14.

These state fetal personhood laws create new, quasi-legal entities whose true qualities often remain unexamined: the "unborn child," "unborn person," "unborn human being," or simply, in Justice Roberts's words, "the unborn." Each of these "unborn" individuals is understood as deserving and possessing the various rights and privileges of living human beings. Of course, there is a much longer history here. The National Right to Life Committee (NRLC), founded in 1968 by the National Conference of Catholic Bishops, deployed the topical language of civil rights to make its assertions, arguing that "abortion denied the personhood and most basic rights of unborn children."[7] But what exactly do anti-abortion proponents need to claim to make these entities, these "unborn children," come alive as legal persons with rights and standing? Furthermore, what do they need in order to grant these quasi-legal entities a legal standing in active conflict with, even favored over, that of women?[8] And, most pertinently, in relation to the subject of this book, what do these so-called "unborn persons" have to do with corporate or artificial personhood?

This chapter aims to answer these questions, arguing that "fetal personhood" claims share the premises of corporate, artificial personhood, while adding (or adapting) some patriarchal premises of their own. Artificial corporate personhood became part of a powerful set of strategies that attempted to secure the ground for fetal rights. That fetal personhood emerged roughly at the moment of the late 1960s and early 1970s, when civil rights for corporations was also reemerging with new life (eventually culminating in *Citizens United*), is no mere happenstance but part of the same story. These so-called fetal persons are some of the most impoverished, reductive versions of artificial legal persons we will see. As theorized by anti-abortion activists, they are rendered perfectly equal to the women who must bear them, while necessarily lacking status or publicness; given the moniker of "unborn child" or simply "life," they are reduced nearly to genetic code. They barely exist yet possess the rights of persons. In the process, these fetal persons evoke the Court's

---

7   Mary Ziegler, *Reproduction and the Constitution in the United States* (New York: Routledge, 2022), 33–4.

8   The issue of gendered language for pregnancy is complex; any choice arguably has both positive and negative health and social consequences. While I generally accept the current NIH Style Guide by using both "pregnant women" and "pregnant person" interchangeably, for ease of reference I will often use the term "women" as a shorthand for the majority of pregnant persons, with the understanding that the term also includes pregnant people who are trans or non-binary, or do not identify as women.

language for the corporation from over two centuries ago: "an artificial being, invisible, intangible."[9] In the half century after *Roe*, a tacit theory of artificial fetal personhood was carefully constructed out of corporate personhood's building blocks.

Of course, artificial or corporate personhood, on its own, would not be a sufficient support for arguments that fetuses are persons. Such claims also rely on a basic sexist commitment to reducing and confining women to the roles conventionally ascribed to their natural bodies. Simone de Beauvoir captures that misogynist notion on the first page of *The Second Sex* (1949): "What is a woman? . . . 'She is a womb,' some say."[10] To this day, ethical and legal thinking on pregnancy remains shockingly dated and patriarchal: Aristotle gave us the basic trimester formulation, which, despite scientific advances that complicate it, was codified and retained as a legal standard in *Roe*.[11] Roman law had a concept of the "unborn"—rather than a biological term, it was a category in paternalistic inheritance law.[12] Along with a firm commitment to patriarchy, a related set of claims and arguments is being put to work in contemporary fetal personhood arguments. These claims are rhetorical, true, but not merely rhetorical. There is a perverse and insidious logic to these fetal personhood arguments; it is those tools and that logic that need to be challenged, however fraught and contentious these arguments might be, however different from our usual ways of making the case for reproductive justice.

Exposing that toolkit is one of this chapter's larger aims: to show these arguments at work in order to think about how to contest them. These ideological premises and arguments supporting fetal personhood do not stand on their own; they are interrelated with one another, even as I present them sequentially here. We should understand their overarching aim as creating, or performing, the culminating fiction of "unborn life." This is a pseudo-entity that would possess standing in *our* community, as one of all human beings alive today. Generated in ways remarkably similar to the creation of corporate personhood, it also functions like corporate personhood once established, giving a dubious abstraction power over actual people. And, also in the case of that legal fiction, we

---

9   *Trustees of Dartmouth College v. Woodward*, 17 US 518 (1819), 636.

10   Simone de Beauvoir, *The Second Sex*, trans. Constance Borde and Sheila Malovany-Chevallier (New York: Random House, 2011), 3.

11   Jean Reith Schroedel, *Is the Fetus a Person?: A Comparison of Policies across the Fifty States* (Ithaca: Cornell University Press, 2000), 55.

12   Yan Thomas, "L'enfant à naître et l'héritier sien': Sujet de pouvoir et sujet de vie en droit romain," *Annales: Histoire, Sciences Sociales* 62 (2007): 29–68.

have evidence available to us, at every moment, that corporations are not people and so should not be given the rights and privileges of human beings. But, regardless, these substitutions of corporations for persons, as with fetuses for persons, are legally made and acted upon in the world. And because they are made and acted upon, they are then assumed as a given, like a fact in the world, by many more people. In other words, the tools we are examining attempt, often successfully, to convince us that reality is not what it appears to be, that the pseudo-creature in front of us is other than what it looks like. All of this is to underscore that what we are seeing are not strictly legal or philosophical arguments but just as often the deceptive workings of ideology.

Each section below explores one of these rhetorical and analytical tools, showing how each works individually while also building upon one another. First, we see how, from the very beginning, arguments for fetal personhood rely on its alignment with corporate personhood lurking in the background. Anti-abortion activists mentioned these corporate arguments warily, not wanting to put this point too much in the foreground for fear it would expose the basic artificiality and arbitrariness of their claims. This section sets up the other claims to follow. We first see women theorized as merely property—as containers—reduced to their bodily and natural destiny. It is the oldest story, but one that remains surprisingly persistent. A more recent development is the move of reframing human DNA as the evidence of ensoulment, a way of making legal, moral persons out of unique genetic material. This rhetorical technique provides anti-abortion thinkers a way to bypass the long-standing religious and legal tradition of "quickening" as the moment when the fetus gains its soul and thus becomes a person ("quickening" refers to the moment when a pregnant woman can feel the fetus moving inside her uterus, a moment that can vary drastically but usually begins at some point in the second trimester). Once the conceived embryo has become ensouled, the penultimate, crucial step is erasing the placenta's role and importance in pregnancy. The placenta is a novel, transitory organ embedded in the pregnant woman's uterine wall to keep the fetus alive; it is an organ whose existence refuses any attempt to separate woman and fetus into two autonomous individuals. Finally, with all these tools in place, that new quasi-legal entity can be rhetorically, performatively "born": the so-called "unborn" child.

Perversely, this entire rhetorical process of mystically creating a quasi-legal entity mimics the gestation and birth of actual babies, even while it relies on making human persons look and act more like artificial ones. The chief perversion is the way pregnant persons are, in a step-by-step process, erased along the way—perpetuating a phenomenon already apparent by the nineteenth century, when scientists struggled against "the opacity of the mother's body [which] withdrew the unborn from the scientific grasp."[13] The mothers' legal personhood is now reduced to the objecthood of containers for genetic souls, their experiences of pregnancy (feeling the fetus inside them at quickening) rendered irrelevant, and their symbiotic, entwined process of producing another organ (the placenta) with the growing fetus is literally ignored in virtually every cultural representation of pregnancy and birth. The chapter breaks down this procedure into steps, because this whole process is hard to perceive on its own. Like the other chapters, this one also relies on contemporary visual art to explore the ideological operations of fetal personhood at work, with Damien Hirst's recent sculpture series of embryonic and fetal development, *The Miraculous Journey* (2013), as a convenient example.

But rather than Hirst's series, it would be better to keep in mind another, more important and intriguing work of art, created the same year that *Roe* was decided. Mary Kelly's video performance *Antepartum* (1973) is a radical challenge to the rhetorical, legal, and ideological operations of producing the unborn person. In a ninety-second loop transferred from black and white Super 8 silent film (an early form of home movie technology), the viewer witnesses a very pregnant person running her hands lightly over her midsection. Shot from a startlingly low angle on a stationary tripod, the video frame is entirely filled up with what is actually Kelly's abdomen at full term—she called it "an extreme close-up"—with only her hands floating in and out of view, presumably as she is palpably tracing the fetal movements inside her. If they watch closely, observers can see gentle swells and pulsations on her abdomen. But, from our disorienting viewing position, we are more generally placed in the spot of having to trust her experience and response to whatever she is feeling inside her uterus. "Her perception of the subtle shifts of body within body is referenced in her gesture," notes Siona Wilson, "although of course it cannot be made visible."[14] Kelly is the one who chose to turn the camera on, for us, at the moment when the fetus was moving vivaciously enough that we too could see it from the outside. We

---

13   Caroline Arni, *Of Human Born: Fetal Lives, 1800–1950*, trans. Kate Sturge (New York: Zone Books, 2024), 242.

14   Siona Wilson, *Art Labor, Sex Politics: Feminist Effects in 1970s British Art and Performance* (Minneapolis: University of Minnesota Press, 2015), 82.

are following the lead of her hands feeling that movement, and we are dependent on her actions.

Watching this video today, we might be tempted to see Kelly's work as refiguring the pregnant Madonna image (classically, "Our Lady of Parturition," with Mary laying protective hands around her womb). It would then be an iconic version of motherhood modified for the twentieth century. But, while the performance piece surely, and deliberately, invokes that Catholic religious imagery, it would be a real mistake to read this work as disconnected from the feminist abortion rights debates of the early 1970s. And it also would be a mistake to see its extreme self-framing of the artist's belly as her rejection of reproductive justice or of feminist political movements such as Wages for Housework. Kelly was an active participant in the second wave feminist movement, co-directed the labor protest documentary *Nightcleaners* (1972–5) with the Berwick Street Film Collective, and raised the son she soon gave birth to on a commune. In *Antepartum*, she deliberately omits anything like the Madonna's loving maternal gaze, as well as a potential pornographic view of a woman's body (her pubis and breasts are mostly cropped out

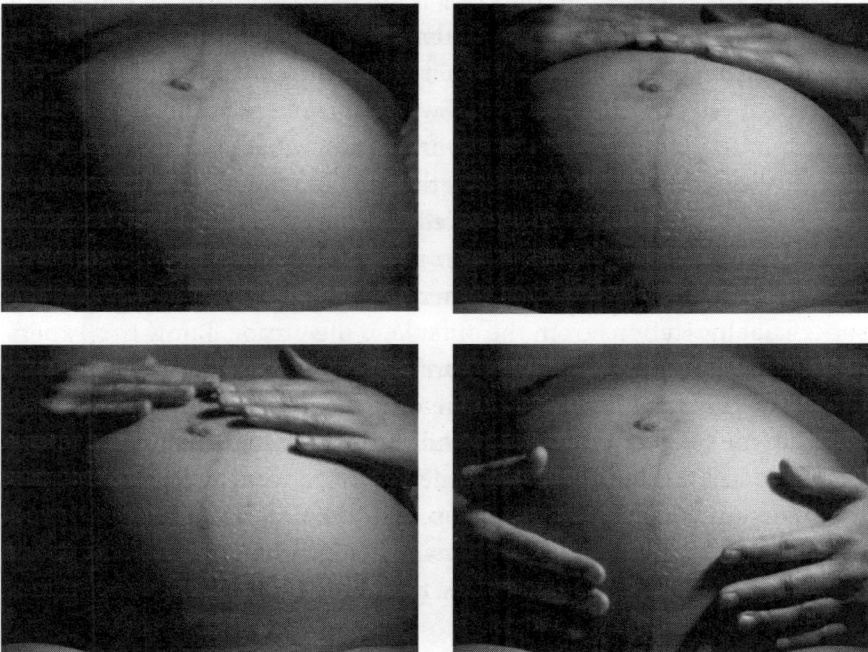

Fig. 4. Mary Kelly, *Antepartum* (1973). Screenshots of video loop transferred from Super 8 film, black and white, 1:30 minute duration. Courtesy of Mary Kelly and Mitchell-Innes & Nash, New York © Mary Kelly © 2025 Artists Rights Society (ARS), New York / IVARO, Dublin.

of the shot). In fact, when the film was first exhibited in 1974, Kelly ran it side by side with another video: a close up of a female factory worker operating an industrial machine, also repeated in a continuous film loop. Although Kelly abandoned that version of *Antepartum* in later exhibitions, the early dual-screening of mother and laborer bares the coolly Marxist critique at its heart, the contrast between "reproductive labor with productive wage-labor."[15] Rather than an anti-choice paean to idealized maternity, it is a protest work determined to rethink long-standing fantasies of pregnancy and motherhood.

In the process, Kelly's simple yet brilliant *Antepartum* makes entirely obvious why we cannot do without her, the mother's, personhood, and everything that it entails. There is no escaping her body, her perspective of this pregnancy, or her agency—here presented by Kelly herself turning on the camera at a certain moment, and by her roving hands, mediating her experience of pregnancy for the viewer. Often, talking in this way about how the pregnant person feels and thinks about the pregnancy "makes many people nervous," observes the philosopher Margaret Olivia Little; "it can sound as though we are ceding far too much power to her subjective experience." But the point is not that a woman has "some absolute dominion" over the fetus's status, but rather that her perspective is "the only thing we have, other than mere biology, to tell whether there is a personal relationship extant and what its textures are like." Gestation is "first-order" intimacy, and we cannot know what kind of relationship it is for the gestating person unless they tell us.[16]

Or show us with an artwork. Kelly is everywhere, while the spectator is always outside and trying to make sense of the undulations we see. Watching Kelly experiencing her pregnancy fully, while we only see superficial indications from the outside, *is* the way we know and experience fetuses we are not currently carrying to term. In this representation of post-quickening, we witness the only way fetuses are actually seen without medical interventions and intrusive technologies. The film camera is still, a static observer, while the entire scene is projected on the wall (currently, at the Whitney Museum of American Art). Deceptively simple, Kelly's ninety-second cinematic work undoes, in its own way, the mystifying tools that work to create the unborn person.

---

15   Ibid., 72, 74.

16   Margaret Olivia Little, "Abortion, Intimacy, and the Duty to Gestate," *Ethical Theory and Moral Practice* 2, no. 3 (1999): 311, 309, 296.

From Corporate Personhood to Performative Fetal Personhood

The fetal personhood movement seems, at first glance, like a very recent development. But it actually began in the 1960s as a reaction to progressive trends in US law. During this period, the American Law Institute, a century-old nonprofit dedicated to modernizing and improving American laws to make them more just, recommended the decriminalization of abortion. States began to act on those suggestions by modifying their criminal codes. In a conservative reaction to these liberalizing efforts, the National Right to Life Committee (NRLC) sought strategies to assert the supposed rights of fetuses and to fortify criminal penalties for abortion providers. Personhood was key to this effort. The NRLC's arguments used the same amendments we have already seen invoked, in this and in previous chapters, in demands for equal rights: the Fourteenth Amendment of the Constitution. "Abortion foes insisted that the drafters of the Fourteenth Amendment intended to include unborn children in the category of [rights-bearing] 'persons,'" Mary Ziegler explains, and "fetal personhood" captured this idea.[17]

The alignment between fetal personhood and corporate personhood always lurked in these arguments, whether or not it was activated. Consider one high-profile case from 1972, when the Fordham University law professor and anti-abortion activist Robert Byrn attempted to have a court appoint him as legal guardian for all the potentially aborted fetuses in New York, during a period when the state was in the process of liberalizing its abortion laws. His argument was that the embryo or fetus "is a person protected by the Fifth and Fourteenth Amendments of the Federal Constitution and, as such, cannot be deprived of life without due process or denied the equal protection of New York's laws."[18] His guardianship was temporarily granted but eventually invalidated, and a year later his entire strategy upended by *Roe*. He objected to this development in a law review article that made clear the alignment with corporate personhood, entitled "An American Tragedy: The Supreme Court on Abortion": "It is too late in the evolution of human rights to label a whole class of live human beings as non-persons, while at the same time extending the equal protection of the laws to corporations." Neither live birth nor human citizenship determined whether or not someone was considered a person in law: "a corporation is not 'born'

---

17   Ziegler, *Reproduction*, 34.
18   *Byrn v. New York City Health and Hospital Corporation*, 38 A.D.2d 316, 321, 329 N.Y.S.2d 722, 726–7, aff'd, 31 N.Y.2d 194, 286 N.E.2d 887 (1972).

but it is protected as a person by the equal protection clause." There-fore, he reasoned, if never-born corporations could be considered legal persons under the Fifth and Fourteenth Amendments, then so could "an unborn child."[19]

For Byrn and the lawyers, judges, and public who agreed with him, employing corporate personhood to strengthen the case for fetal person-hood must have seemed an enticing strategy. True, it posed risks: It could make any form of legal personhood appear artificial and arbitrary. But by aligning the notion of fetal personhood with the corporate version, which already had a long and established history from at least the 1880s, proponents might avoid arguments that there was something radically new or unusual about fetal personhood. Rather, they could say that it was an American tradition to give more and more non-persons person-hood, and, arguably, fetuses were just following the corporation's path. One anti-abortion legal theorist has made a related argument, claiming that the Fourteenth Amendment really offers fetuses *more* standing than corporations: "The unborn have a stronger case than corporations for personhood, and yet have not attained the same degree of protection that corporations enjoy."[20]

There was also another, rhetorically powerful alignment between corporate persons and fetal ones that helped to strengthen fetal person-hood arguments. Both are crucially dependent on live human beings. At least legally, if not in fact, corporations are supposed to relate to us passively: They cannot act for themselves. They (like fetuses) need human beings to perform and act for them, since human beings are corporations' authorized agents. Yet, as the previous chapter explored, once corporations are treated as legal persons, they subtly influence and transform our conception of what personhood really is. That is, their remoteness from what human persons seem to be and look like makes *all* forms of personhood look a little more corporate, a little more like the situation of being a thing that cannot act on its own. Some conservative philosophers have taken this notion a step further, arguing that, histor-ically and theoretically, "human individuals derive their personality in part from corporations." The idea is that in some sense corporations are the more original or larger category of persons, and human beings are

---

19   Robert M. Byrn, "An American Tragedy: The Supreme Court on Abortion," *Fordham Law Review* 41 (1973): 853, 856.

20   Charles I. Lugosi, "Conforming to the Rule of Law: When Person and Human Being Finally Mean the Same Thing in Fourteenth Amendment Jurisprudence," *Issues in Law & Medicine* 22, no. 2–3 (2006): 187.

merely a subset.[21] This is not a widely accepted opinion, suffice it to say. But there are antecedents for it. Aspects of corporate personhood had been becoming a model for personhood more generally. For supporters of fetal personhood, the advantage of this development was that they could use this artificial, object-like personhood to attempt to defeat the rights of the pregnant person growing, nurturing, and living with the fetus, women whose rights rather obviously supersede something living in and by their own bodies.

Regardless of these seemingly odd emerging ideas, by 1973 Roe effectively shut down this entire avenue of legal reasoning, at least as an argument to be debated in American courts. In a famous (or, depending on your perspective, notorious) sentence, Justice Blackmun's majority opinion in Roe declared that "if this suggestion of [fetal] personhood is established, the appellant's [Roe's] case, of course, collapses, for the fetus' right to life would then be guaranteed specifically by the [Fourteenth] Amendment."[22] This sentence really is somewhat peculiar. On the one hand, fetal personhood had not been "established," he underscored, and so the fetus had no "right to life." But, on the other hand, Blackmun's language suggested, rather ominously, that if fetal personhood *could have been* established, then the situation would have turned out very differently for women and their right to abortion. If fetal personhood had been established, then the "fetus' right to life would then be guaranteed" under the Fourteenth Amendment.

After Roe legalized abortion rights across the US, conservative activists, distressed that personhood was not yet available to fetuses, began to look for new legal paths to outlaw abortion. One clear way forward was to restrict abortion access to as many women as possible by cutting off sources of public funding. The Hyde Amendment (1976) did just that, prohibiting the use of federal funds for abortion for anyone enrolled in Medicaid, Medicare, or the Children's Health Insurance Program (CHIP). Congress has since expanded this regressive legislation to more potential federal beneficiaries, cutting off abortion services to members of the military, for example. It has been stretched globally as well, to restrict abortions in countries receiving US financial support. In the following decades, other restrictions included mandatory waiting periods, non-medically necessary ultrasounds, the national (and then global) gag rule, and restricted contraception and abortion services for minors without

---

21   Roger Scruton [and John Finnis], "Corporate Persons," *Proceedings of the Aristotelian Society, Supplementary Volumes* 63 (1989): 240.

22   *Roe v. Wade*, 410 US 113 (1973), 146–7.

parental authorization. Until 2022, *Roe* held despite these restrictions, and abortion remained legal throughout the United States, at least on paper, to women who could afford it and could find their increasingly lengthy way to access it through ever more tortuous obstacles.

Yet Justice Blackmun's personhood sentence, in *Roe*, also began to change its guise. It started to look more like a hopeful roadmap rather than a stop sign for anti-abortion activists. Through their lawyers, these activists started to strategize, recognizing the potential value of legal notions and rules that assumed *certain* aspects, qualities, and rights of fetuses as persons, even if courts refrained from making a full attribution of personhood. If laws and decisions incrementally established that vague phrase, "sanctity of life," it would, over time, require courts to see and treat embryos and fetuses more and more like legal persons. Fetal personhood might not be defined at one legislative or judicial stroke, but with millions of them, painstakingly built out of its disparate component rights. That is, fetal persons would become an artificial performative composite through an identical process that corporations used to become legal persons: step by step, assumption by assumption, right by right. And Blackmun's sentence in *Roe* was the beginning. Even today, the webpage of the Georgia Right to Life organization (tagline: "Advancing Personhood—The Paramount Right to Life") quotes and then misinterprets Blackmun's famous sentence in *Roe* to support its refrain.[23]

Although there is a much larger story to be told here, the contentious but also enormously powerful interpretive doctrine of originalism has been part of this process too. "Originalism is not only a method of interpreting the Constitution," legal scholar Reva Siegel argues; "originalism is also a politics whose long-standing goal has been reversing *Roe*." This interpretive theory is so useful to anti-abortion justices and legal thinkers, suggests Siegel, because it "locates democratic authority in *imagined communities of the past*" and reasons using outdated, inegalitarian legal stories, norms, and traditions.[24] *Dobbs* is the specific focus of Siegel's analysis, but we can also note how originalist methods enabled anti-abortion legal and moral philosophers to situate their fetal personhood arguments in selective quotations from eighteenth-century authorities or fragments of nineteenth-century congressional debates. In their amicus brief on *Dobbs*, John Finnis and Robert P. George, for example, use

---

23   grtl.org.

24   Reva B. Siegel, "Memory Games: *Dobbs*'s Originalism as Anti-Democratic Living Constitutionalism—and Some Pathways for Resistance," *Texas Law Review* 101 (2023): 1127, 1134.

these sources to determine that, regarding the Fourteenth Amendment, "the originalist case for including the unborn is much stronger than for corporations."[25]

Like originalism, the other rhetorical and legal tools discussed in the following sections are all designed as strategies that have one apparent goal but furtively aim at another. That other goal always aims at making proposed traits of assumed fetal personhood function as *actual* legal personhood. Anti-abortion legal thinkers and activists adopt a theory of artificial personhood—in this case, artificial fetal personhood—without necessarily stating it as such, and its aspects have been put it into place, in a piecemeal way, over the fifty years following *Roe*. Doing so has warranted a public relations campaign that relies strongly on visual imagery of fetuses, suggests Rosalind Petchesky, "mak[ing] fetal personhood a self-fulfilling prophecy by making the fetus a *public presence*."[26] In the process, anti-abortion activists have made *Roe*'s claims defending abortion rights on privacy grounds seem outlandish, or inaccurate, or simply disconnected from what "we" think pregnant persons and fetuses are. In combination, all these strategies have paved the way for *Dobbs* and the fetal personhood amendments and restrictions that are flourishing now in many American states; these laws foreshadow what anti-abortion activists hope a federal, nation-wide fetal personhood amendment will look like.

Uncontainable Containers

"Lo, children are an heritage of the Lord: and the fruit of the womb is his reward" (Psalm 127:3). Women go unmentioned in this biblical lyric on pregnancy, except as they exist as physical wombs growing fetal fruit. God receives the reward of children, his heritage, like a harvest from the fecund earth, and women's bodies are the submissive vessel of this process. This myth of woman as a passive container, reduced to the functions of her reproductive biology, is a very old story, so old we might presume it had been long since discredited and forgotten. But no. In the "Myths" section of *The Second Sex*, de Beauvoir recounts, repeatedly, all the ways in which women and their roles and life possibilities have been

---

25   John Finnis and Robert P. George, "Equal Protection and the Unborn Child: A *Dobbs* Brief," *Harvard Journal of Law and Public Policy* 45, no. 3 (2022): 931.

26   Rosalind Petchesky, "Fetal Images: The Power of Visual Culture in the Politics of Reproduction," *Feminist Studies* 13, no. 2 (1987): 264.

reduced to "the female womb." "In the human world, woman transposes the female animal's functions: she maintains life . . . she transports the warmth and intimacy of the womb into the home." Women's identity is collapsed into and conflated with their material bodies, and women's fate has been their alleged inability to transcend this body. "Woman appears to us as *flesh* . . . thus, woman is akin to *nature*, she embodies it."[27]

On some level, it is not surprising to see obsolete, unscientific myths and rhetorical language reappearing in anti-abortion arguments, state laws, or in proposed fetal personhood amendments. These amendments, as well as the related state codes that trend toward full personhood for fetuses, typically omit any mention of pregnant persons' rights, interests, or even of women's bodies other than their "womb." Legal scholar April L. Cherry notes that such rhetoric makes it very hard to see "pregnant women as self-governing persons," a situation that undermines social justice and women's dignity. The effect is to "marginalize pregnant women by encouraging the view of pregnant women as fetal containers."[28] Consider the Georgia state law, passed in 2019, that defines an "unborn child" as "a member of the species Homo sapiens at any stage of development who is carried in the womb" (Alaska and Wyoming have identical language in their state laws too). The Georgia code continues, taking this point a step further: "An unborn child with a detectable human heartbeat" will be considered to be a "natural person" and member of the "population."[29] According to this "heartbeat" law, and all the laws like it, pregnant persons are reduced to womb carriers for the embryonic population of "natural persons" inside them.

For at least a half century, if not longer, reproductive justice advocates have pointed out that reducing women to vessels—to walking wombs—dehumanizes them. In Margaret Atwood's dystopian novel *The Handmaid's Tale* (1985), a pregnant woman trapped in oppressive Gilead is considered "a sacred chalice"; in the recent sequel, *The Testaments* (2019), the operative phrase has been updated to "precious containers," a more secular, but no less patriarchic, coinage closer to state laws like Georgia's.[30] Atwood's language tracks academic accounts. Examining criminal indictments of pregnant women in the 1980s, scholars show

---

27   De Beauvoir, *Second Sex*, 194, 261–2.

28   April L. Cherry, "Shifting Our Focus from Retribution to Social Justice: An Alternative Vision for the Treatment of Pregnant Women Who Harm Their Fetuses," *Journal of Law and Health* 28, no. 1 (2015): 8.

29   Georgia Code Ann. § 1-2-1 (2022).

30   Margaret Atwood, *The Handmaid's Tale* (New York: Houghton Mifflin, 1985), and *The Testaments* (New York: Nan A. Talese, 2019), 159.

how a policy that favors the fetus over pregnant women drastically debases women in the process, "treat[ing] her like an inert incubator, or a culture medium for the fetus." Women are thus "relegated to the role of containers," with their own rights and protections subordinated to the fetal contents inside. The pregnant woman "container may be opened to gain access to the fetus, even when the container may be damaged."[31] Such objectification of women is of a piece with oppression: It works in combination with others to undermine solidarity between women of different classes, increase surveillance of working-class women, and gouge funding for the public sector.[32]

Even those writing in support of reproductive justice struggle to put the confounding scenario of pregnancy and abortion into the contemporary language of personhood or equal protection. *Roe*'s defense of privacy simply and problematically avoided the more complicated claims of equal protection for women. Progressive thinkers have sometimes found themselves caught in "container" metaphors too, suggesting just how tempting these models are for everyone. Consider Sophie Lewis's controversial recasting of surrogacy and pregnancy "as work under capitalism," part of her effort to envision "a horizon of gestational communism." Although Lewis rebuts critics who see her as a neoliberal advocating for women's alienation of their bodies, it is hard to make sense of pregnancy-as-work without metaphors of laboring vessels.[33] As Margaret Olivia Little sums up, "Abortion asks us to face the morality and politics of intertwinement and enmeshment with a conceptual framework that is, to say the least, poorly suited to the task."[34]

Another repercussion is the difficulty of finding terms and assigning value (whether emotional or pecuniary) for the myriad experiences of pregnancy—including the difficult yet very common scenario of pregnancy loss. The failure to accurately articulate pregnancy as a situation *and* an intimate relationship leads to real legal harms that are simply unaddressed. "When wrongful misconduct is to blame [for pregnancy loss], the legal system lacks coherent answers to basic questions: What is the nature of that injury? What makes it more harmful or less? And how much is owed to these victims of reproductive misconduct?" As Dov

---

31 George J. Annas, "At Law: Pregnant Women as Fetal Containers," *Hastings Center Report* 16 (1986): 14.

32 Faith Agostinone-Wilson, *Enough Already! A Socialist Feminist Response to the Re-emergence of Right Wing Populism and Fascism in Media* (Leiden: Brill, 2020).

33 Sophie Lewis, *Full Surrogacy Now: Feminism Against Family* (New York: Verso, 2019), 9, 21, 33.

34 Little, "Abortion, Intimacy, and the Duty to Gestate," 297.

Fox and Jill Wieber Lens ponder, although there is a "wealth of abortion scholarship about the legal treatment of nascent life," there is a "virtual absence of literature" about how to legally value wanted pregnancies that end in miscarriage.[35]

And yet another repercussion appears in one of the most famous thought experiments defending abortion. In 1971, the philosopher Judith Jarvis Thomson proposed a scenario likely designed for male readers who might struggle to imagine the experience of themselves becoming pregnant:

> You wake up in the morning and find yourself back-to-back in bed with an unconscious violinist. A famous unconscious violinist. He has been found to have a fatal kidney ailment, and the Society of Music Lovers has canvassed all the available medical records and found that you alone have the right blood type to help. They have therefore kidnapped you, and last night the violinist's circulatory system was plugged into yours, so that your kidneys can be used to extract poisons from his blood as well as your own. The director of the hospital now tells you . . . "To unplug you would be to kill him. But never mind, it's only for nine months. By then he will have recovered from his ailment, and can safely be unplugged from you." Is it morally incumbent on you to accede to this situation?[36]

In this scenario, "you" have no sex or gender, no reproductive organs to worry about, no womb: the organ at stake is your kidneys, and just about everyone born alive is born with those. Moreover, for the sake of argument, Thomson's thought experiment temporarily accepts the premise of fetal personhood. That is why her example proposes saving a male, adult (and famous!) violinist, someone whose personhood no one could reasonably think of contesting since his value in and to the world has already been secured. Her point in doing so is to show how and why, even in this scenario of accepting fetal personhood, you are not morally obligated to accept the hospital director's and Society of Music Lovers' plans for your nine-month imprisonment in a hospital bed. You may refuse to be plugged in to the unconscious violinist and still be on morally safe ground. To think otherwise would be to withhold the status

---

35   Dov Fox and Jill Wieber Lens, "Valuing Reproductive Loss," *Georgetown Law Journal* 112 (2023): 90, 64.

36   Judith Jarvis Thomson, "A Defense of Abortion" (1971), in *Rights and Wrongs of Abortion: A Philosophy and Public Affairs Reader*, ed. Marshall Cohen (Princeton University Press, 2021), 4.

of personhood from you—a pregnant person—a personhood that the fetus supposedly has.

No doubt Thomson's analogy helped male philosophers, and perhaps the nine men (and zero women) on the US Supreme Court a half century ago, think a little more carefully about how abortion restrictions impact women. It was a powerful intervention that still resonates, and it did the trick at the time. Yet her imaginative scenario starts looking more peculiar as the thought experiment and its metaphorical permutations continue. Explaining her argument by way of another analogy, Thomson points out that "the mother and the unborn child are not like two tenants in a small house which has, by an unfortunate mistake, been rented to both: the mother owns the house." The idea is that the mother has seized the house first—she is the first tenant of her body and so has first dibs. Echoing the familiar language of Lockean liberalism, Thomson explains that a (male) human being has "a just, prior claim to his own body."[37] For that reason, even were we to grant the fetus personhood, that still would not give the fetus the right to claim and to use a woman's body against her desires and consent. Pregnant persons have a property interest in their body that overrides that of the fetus's interests.

But other thinkers rejected this entire way of thinking about pregnancy as inadequate. The issues of pregnancy, they felt, are not dispatched by resorting to bodily self-possession and private property interests. Mary Anne Warren was one of Thomson's earliest critics on this point, noting that owning property does not simply give someone the right to kill people on it; nor is it clear that I have a "moral right to expel an innocent person from my property when I know that doing so will result in his death."[38] And, for Drucilla Cornell, the violinist thought experiment already gives too much away by analogizing feminine sexual difference to "a relationship between two already independent persons." It succumbs to a way of thinking about the womb and the fetus as separate from and "other to the woman rather than a part of her body." For Cornell, such thought experiments reproduce the same kind of imaginary projection of the womb as a vessel, one that reduces the pregnant woman to "a *what*, a thing, a container, an environment, not *a who*, a self." Transforming someone into a "what" is what physicians, the state, and private organizations, like the Society of Music Lovers or Georgia Right to Life, seek to control. The alternative Cornell offers instead is to think of the

---

37   Thomson, "Defense of Abortion," 9, 10.

38   Mary Anne Warren, "On the Moral and Legal Status of Abortion," *The Monist* 57, no. 1 (1973): 44.

womb as it really is, as Mary Kelly showed the world in *Antepartum*: entirely integrated with all of a woman. This means respecting her body "as opaque," as having an inside that "cannot be forcibly 'exposed' as an outside" without destroying the very idea of a woman's person and her personhood rights.[39]

In briefly rehearsing this debate, my point here, more generally, is that the pregnancy container metaphor (and its rhetoric) is seductive, tantalizing, and ubiquitous. It is also an instance of the broader phenomenon of the impoverishment of personhood that we have been tracking. Surveying her discipline's literature a few years ago, the philosopher Elselijn Kingma found that the "*containment view* of pregnancy" remains widely assumed even though it is under-defended and implausible in reality.[40] It is also a perspective and metaphorical rhetoric that remains crucial to fetal personhood arguments, part of establishing a political movement in which ova, embryos, and fetuses are all given moral and legal precedence over adult women.[41] And, so, a certain amount of vigilance is necessary to keep this containment view from seeping into even the most well-meaning of arguments, like Thomson's. Other feminist philosophers, such as Little, have suggested potential tweaks to the containment metaphor that might make it more accurate, such as the experience of being dwelt in, potentially against one's will: "To be pregnant is to be *inhabited*. It is to be *occupied*. It is to be in a state of physical *intimacy* of a particularly thorough-going nature . . . To mandate continuation of gestation is, quite simply, to force continuation of such occupation."[42]

Alternatively, reducing women to their bodies, to property, and to their biological fate means making them more object-like and less person-like (as Cornell puts it, "a *what*, a thing" rather than "a *who*, a self"). Barbara Katz-Rothman describes the estrangement built into this process: "It is not the rights of one autonomous being set against the rights of another, but the profound alienation of the woman set against part of herself."[43] In its reliance on alienation, fetal personhood also galvanizes the dynamics and history of commodity relations, legal subjectivity, and corporate personhood lurking in the background, put to work to make these ideas a

39   Drucilla Cornell, *The Imaginary Domain: Abortion, Pornography, and Sexual Harassment* (New York: Routledge, 1995), 47, 50, 49.

40   Elselijn Kingma, "Were You a Part of Your Mother?," *Mind* 128, no. 511 (July 2019): 609–10.

41   Agostinone-Wilson, *Enough Already*, 159.

42   Little, "Abortion, Intimacy, and the Duty to Gestate," 301.

43   Barbara Katz-Rothman, *Recreating Motherhood: Ideology and Technology in a Patriarchal Society* (New York: W. W. Norton & Co., 1989), 109.

little less shocking. Turning wombs into physical containers, and women into passive vessels, manages a similar kind of incapacitation of women's personhood. Women are reduced to carriers for artificial persons—their agency dismissed and undermined, and their personhood devalued, not even equal to the fetuses they carry. The next related hurdle for anti-abortion activists is how to render fetuses as artificial persons as early as possible, starting at conception, tying the hands of the people carrying these fetuses before they even realize their situation.

A DNA Soul

Perhaps surprisingly, contemporary fetal personhood amendments do not necessarily use the terms "person" or "personhood" in making their explicit case for fetal personhood. A few states do: Montana's law "extend[s] to unborn persons the inalienable right to defend their lives and liberties," and Tennessee's defines "'person' [to] include a human being from the moment of fertilization and implantation." But these are outliers. More often, such laws avoid using the word "person" to portray the fetus, as in Kentucky's definition: "'Human being' means any member of the species homo sapiens from fertilization until death." Instead of "personhood," these laws discuss *species* membership, as we have already seen with Georgia's: "'Unborn child' means a member of the species Homo sapiens at any stage of development who is carried in the womb." Typically, they use or imply the language of "from conception until birth" (Arkansas), as in "the life of each human being begins at conception" (Missouri), or "the life of each human being begins at fertilization" (Kansas).[44] Yet personhood is clearly implied in all these definitions and all these laws, even when the term is not explicitly mentioned or invoked.

Why do these amendments avoid using the language of personhood, especially when making the case for fetal rights beginning at conception or fertilization? Most obviously, because there is *no* settled bioethical, moral, or religious argument for doing so. Up through the early modern period, quickening was understood (in the West) as the initiation of personhood, but the progression of institutional Christianity, the Enlightenment, and modern medicine complicated this story in different ways. There remains a great deal of variation and controversy on when precisely to date a moral person's start. For Western philosophers

---

44   Pregnancy Justice, "When Fetuses Gain Personhood," appendix.

and Catholic theologians—the primary influences for US legal developments—the questions that arose centered on the difficulty of timing the precise moment of "ensoulment": when the soul was understood to enter the body of the fetus. Determining the moral personhood of embryos and fetuses, therefore, is not a question that can be empirically answered through more scientific studies of fetal biology, writes Bertha Alvarez Manninen, in her helpful summarizing of the dilemma. It "is a metaphysical, philosophical, and theological one."[45] And it is a question, suffice it to say, that has been answered very differently by various thinkers representing different traditions.

For a Catholic jurist in 1968, the answer was clear: "Everyone is human who is conceived by human beings," writes John T. Noonan, who later became Judge Noonan on a US appeals court. Therefore, fetuses should be "properly classified with babies," through an argument of their further potential: "If a fetus is destroyed, one destroys a being already possessed of the genetic code, organs, and sensitivity to pain, and one which had an 80% chance of developing further into a baby outside the womb who, in time, would reason."[46] According to this rationale, fetuses are categorized as persons due to their prospective genetic capacity to become people somewhere down the causal chain of growth and development. The argument combines that belief with some dubious statistical invocation of what typically happens to fetuses, as if a pregnant person's agency were wholly irrelevant to fetal development. In Noonan's later directing of the National Right to Life Committee, he worked tirelessly to turn this classification and argument into law.

On the other hand, for philosophers supporting reproductive justice, such an argument for fetal personhood simply did not hold up. Mary Anne Warren's influential position, first published the same year as *Roe*, offered five criteria for personhood and argued that "a fetus, whatever its stage of development, satisfies none of the basic criteria of personhood, and is not even enough like a person to be accorded even some of the same rights on the basis of this resemblance." For these reasons, she wrote, there is no argument in support of the idea that the fetus be considered a member of our moral community. Warren also made the important critique that anti-abortion claims like Noonan's, particularly in their argument for potentiality, conflate two ways of referring to

---

45   Bertha Alvarez Manninen, "Beyond Abortion: The Implications of Human Life Amendments," *Journal of Social Philosophy* 43, no. 2 (2012): 140.

46   John T. Noonan, "Deciding Who is Human," *American Journal of Jurisprudence* 13, no. 1 (1968): 134, 135, 136.

"humanity": genetic humanity and moral humanity.[47] One is biological, the other is moral and religious, but they are not determined in the same way, and it is profoundly misleading to use them interchangeably.

This dispute over "humanity," as highlighted by Warren, is important. It flags a significant expansion of the fetal personhood toolkit, one that puts cutting-edge scientific discoveries to ideological uses. From the perspective of those arguing on behalf of fetal rights, the problem was how to make *conception* the single, bright-line, person-making event of pregnancy. As we have already started to see, thinking on the establishment of personhood has always been muddier—a problem for anyone desiring a precise moment of personhood creation. Why not pinpoint the moment at fertilization, or gastrulation (around fourteen days post-conception), or the start of the second trimester, or quickening, or when human EEG patterns emerge, or viability, or birth, or some other point in fetal development?[48] All those distinct moments have been suggested as a feasible start date for personhood. Other contentious moments have been suggested too, and more recently legislated by US states, such as the particular moment when fetal cardiac activity of some kind can be picked up on an ultrasound monitor or when a fetus might perceive pain. Even the Catholic Church, historically, has not spoken with one voice on this topic, with some arguing that ensoulment varied with the fetus's sex. According to St. Thomas, a female fetus was not "animated" until the eightieth day after conception, while a male fetus was animated at forty days.[49] Apparently, the male sex was more intrinsically ready to be soulful.

Eventually, the anti-abortion solution proposed an unholy combination of DNA and ensouled bodies, now imagined as a new source of selfhood. Again, this is an old strategy that has been newly weaponized with updated scientific research. Decades ago, Rosalind Petchesky observed that, when anti-abortionists presented evidence of fetal personhood, they were not even bothering to identify "its alleged possession of a soul but its possession of a human body and genotype." The self or person was being confused with a human being's genetic basis, and women were demeaned and objectified in this process, rendered "as the physical vessels for genetic messages rather than responsible moral

---

47   Warren, "Abortion," 48, 54.

48   Scott F. Gilbert, "Pseudo-embryology and Personhood: How Embryological Pseudoscience Helps Structure the American Abortion Debate," *Natural Sciences* 3, no. 1 (2023): 2–4.

49   De Beauvoir, *Second Sex*, 138.

agents."[50] That same strategy is entirely entrenched today. Over the intervening years, soul and genotype have blended together seamlessly, constructing a supposedly whole fetal person out of religious doctrine and DNA. It is this strategy that produces arguments, from anti-abortion activists, that "science, history, and tradition establish that unborn humans are, from the time of conception, both persons and human beings, thus strongly supporting an interpretation that the unborn meet the definition of 'person' under the Fourteenth Amendment."[51] Science, history, and tradition have not established anything of the kind.

The idea that one's unique DNA is the sole ingredient for personhood or selfhood has become so common—and unquestioned—that it can be hard to feel its strangeness at work. Consider that it is the basic, unstated premise of Henry Louis Gates Jr.'s popular public television series *Finding Your Roots* (currently in its eleventh season), which explores celebrities' DNA profiles deeply, as a kind of supplemental biography, in order to help "expand America's sense of itself." Actual human DNA, human biography, and a metaphorical story of America are collapsed together, with DNA as the soul-generating (or soul-replaceable) material. Esteemed scientists have castigated such cultural manipulation of genetic research as pseudoscience, but to little effect. "The American public is being informed continuously that DNA is our essence, our soul, and the basis of our selfhoods," writes embryologist Scott Gilbert, "but this is not science. This is ideology." As Gilbert meticulously shows, biologists have reached no consensus about when something like an independent human life might begin, and they do not think the question of when ensoulment or selfhood might occur is something that embryology can answer. What scientists do know is that genes do not reveal our selfhood or soul, which is the opposite of what *Finding Your Roots* believes about DNA. For scientists, all genes can do is "give us the parameters to become many different things in various contexts."[52]

Proving that human reproductive cells, such as sperm, eggs, and embryos, have the DNA of homo sapiens is a straightforward, if technically involved, task: Cells are genetically analyzed and statistically compared to cells with DNA known and accepted to be from members of the human species. A certain percentage reveals the answer. Perhaps it feels seductive to use these laboratory techniques to try to establish

50   Rosalind P. Petchesky, *Abortion and Woman's Choice: The State, Sexuality, and Reproductive Freedom*, revised edition (Northeastern University Press, 1990), 338, 345.

51   Lugosi, "Conforming to the Rule of Law," 119.

52   Gilbert, "Pseudo-embryology," 5, 9, 6.

something else, something actually impossible to prove through genetic analysis: that, at some point, these clusters of cells possess a soul and, therefore, should be treated as a person.

But it also might be worth pondering why such substitutions—like seeing cells as forming a soul, and DNA as personified—are so common, so easy, for everyone to believe, even those skeptical about fetal rights. To revisit a point from the previous chapter, I would speculate that the answer is hidden in the dynamic of capitalism itself, that process by which our ideas appear to us outside our minds as autonomous and strange figures, ideas with agency over their own lives. We are used to objects—commodities—personifying themselves, Marx writes, taking on voices and roles that they could never have without us (like the table that, when it emerges as a commodity, "evolves out of its wooden brain grotesque ideas" beyond mere animation).[53] Or "Monsieur le Capital," haunting us as both a social character and a thing. For Marx, this process is part of the drama of capital as social relation. When we let our DNA speak for us as distinct from us, this process of commodification has already been at work. We let our genes take on grand ideas too.

Disposing of the Placenta

Let us take stock of the aspects of legal fetal personhood we have been describing before considering the final strategy or tool. Here is what the composite looks like so far: The fetus has been reimagined as "an incorporation of the woman, a business fiction" (as Patricia Williams writes), as well as, paradoxically, a DNA soul created at conception.[54] The pregnant person, meanwhile, has been transformed into a precious (but ultimately expendable) container for the fetus's genetic information. There are two entities envisioned here, a fetus-soul and a woman-container, and two legal persons, both artificial in various senses, both in conflict. One tends to be endowed with the quality of soul (the fetus), the other merely has the qualities of the fleshy body (the pregnant person). This division sounds familiar—not only because it obviously riffs on basic Christian theological assumptions, but because those assumptions (abstract soul with a corpus) were being built into corporate person-hood theorizing by the nineteenth century. You might complain that

---

53   Marx, *Capital*, vol. I, 163–4.
54   Williams, "Fetal Fictions," 93.

this composite looks nothing like anyone's experience of pregnancy and childbirth. Yet that is the state of legal fetal personhood today.

There is at least one more strategy in the fetal personhood toolkit before the "unborn person" can come to "life." This strategy is something like a disappearing act, in that it entails disposing of the most important organ in a pregnancy, before you even see it. The vanishing organ is the placenta, also called the afterbirth, a term that alludes to its history and destiny of being disposed of as medical waste. An absolutely essential yet transitory structure, the placenta grows by embedding itself in the wall of the uterus and remodels the women's blood vessels in the process. Jointly created and sustained by the pregnant person and the fetus, the placenta contains the cells of both, intermingled together. It serves its life-giving function of delivering oxygen and nutrients, and removing carbon dioxide and waste, until the baby has been fully delivered; only at that point are vital functions fully taken over by the baby's lungs, heart, and other organs, some of them transformed instantaneously with a first breath. The placenta's essential vascular functions explain why it resembles a thick purplish frisbee with many branching blood vessels, networked like a tree and connected to the umbilical cord. The whole meaty organ is heftier than an adult's heart and even more critical to the fetus.

Maybe you are struggling to visualize the placenta except on a plate (sautéed) or ground into a pill, rendered as some bizarre, post-pregnancy foodstuff. If so, likely it is because the placenta is shockingly absent from cultural, not to mention legal, representations. Even before it appears in the moments after delivery, it has been erased from the story of pregnancy and childbirth. It is nearly impossible to see on television shows or films of childbirth unless a bad ending is forecast for mother or child. Yet anyone who has given birth vaginally, or who has attended such a birth—and manages to remain attentive during the elation of the new baby wailing away—knows that the critical work is not yet finished. There is a "third stage" of labor in which the placenta disentangles itself from the uterine wall and, with some additional contractions and pushing, is delivered, usually several minutes after the baby. Midwives and doctors sometimes speed that process along if the placenta lingers inside. They press firmly on the women's abdomen and administer hormones to urge the swollen uterus to snap back to its pre-pregnancy, plum-like size, in the process sheering off the placenta and expelling it in one piece. Vigilance is necessary because a placenta that breaks apart and is incompletely delivered causes an extremely dangerous situation, to this day often leading to profuse, life-threatening hemorrhaging and subsequent, and often fatal, infections.

After I learned about placenta delivery, fictionalized television depictions of birthing scenes became unwatchable. Waiting anxiously for the third stage of labor that never arrived, I imagined all those suffering women with undelivered placentas, bleeding to death outside the frame while the camera cuts to the squirming newborn. That is an extreme reaction, admittedly. Yet to become attuned to this part of labor means acknowledging its disturbing absence everywhere. It bespeaks a larger problem of how we have become habituated to understanding pregnancy and childbirth. Analogizing the pregnant person as a vessel for fetal DNA, or as simply hooked up to the fetus like a mechanical device (as in Thomson's ill-violinist scenario), bears little resemblance to the situation of pregnancy once we understand that a whole other organ has been created to transform and mediate between both fetal and maternal bodies. And obliterating our vision and potential understanding of this organ is, in part, what enables all the other tools of legal personhood to function unopposed. The existence of the placenta, in other words, contradicts all the other tools of fetal personhood we have been examining, tools that have become so common that we see them, in combination, simply as the performance of the fiction of the fetal person, now realized.

Fig. 5. Damien Hirst, *The Miraculous Journey* (2013). Installation view, Sidra Medical and Research Center, Doha, Qatar. © Damien Hirst and Science Ltd. All rights reserved / DACS, London / ARS, NY 2025. B. O'Kane / Alamy.

No wonder proponents of fetal personhood choose not to see this veiny organ at all.

The sculpture sequence *The Miraculous Journey* (2013), by the contemporary British shock artist Damien Hirst, vividly dramatizes this scenario. Commissioned and designed as public art, and installed outside a maternity hospital in Doha, Qatar, the huge work is meant to be viewed from the street and by people strolling around the hospital grounds. A series of fourteen monumental sculptures, all of roughly similar size, is rendered in exquisite bronze and lined up in a long row atop a shallow, black pool. Together, the sculptures purport to represent different stages of embryonic and fetal development, from conception to baby boy. But we quickly realize something strange about this depiction. Early stages in this temporal process, when the fertilized zygote, blastocyst, and embryo would actually be tiny specks, barely visible without a microscope, are portrayed at nearly the same colossal scale as the full-term baby at the series' end. In this representational mode, Hirst is following in a long tradition of Western scientific imaging of embryos and fetuses, of which modern 2-D and 3-D ("sneak-peak") sonogram technology is a late development. The scalar effect makes even the earliest zygote and blastocyst seem as grand as a full-grown infant, both far larger than life. And, as monuments, each on their own, they appear singular and autonomous, telling a heroic story of individual self-creation—a journey that really would be miraculous if it were even remotely accurate.

Many anatomical and embryonic details are absent here. But what is most obviously left out of this representation is the woman in whom, to whom, with whom, all of this is happening. The uterus is included but only as "a kind of decorative flourish," stylized like a gilt framing device; her cervix is nonexistent, along with the rest of her body.[55] The rendering of the placenta is particularly misleading, undermining the basic union of pregnant person and fetus. Rather than represent the interrelated way that the embryo and placenta develop and grow together throughout pregnancy in order to sustain the fetus, Hirst snips the organ out for many of the stages. At others, the placenta is obscured or radically mispresented. For example, it is hard to know exactly what he is attempting to represent in the third sculpture with its four free-floating cell clumps, presumably depicting a moment in the blastocyst stage. But one thing obfuscated is that a majority of blastocyst cells would develop not into

---

55   Beck Wise, "Fetal Positions: Fetal Visualization, Public Art, and Abortion Politics," *Rhetoric of Health and Medicine* 1, no. 3 (2018): 307.

Fig. 6. Damien Hirst, *The Miraculous Journey* (close-up installation view). Sixth sculpture. This is the clearest rendering of the placenta in the entire sequence (it appears as the large saucer-halo behind the fetus), but it is also deeply misleading because the placenta is shown as if free of the uterus in which it would be entangled and embedded (the uterus is entirely absent here). © Damien Hirst and Science Ltd. All rights reserved / DACS, London / ARS, NY 2025. B. O'Kane / Alamy.

the fetus but into the placenta and membranes supporting the fetus. The placenta itself only begins to appear in the fourth sculpture as part of the embryo's decorative frame; the life-sustaining organ then disappears entirely from the fifth sculpture before reappearing in the sixth, where it is represented like Christ's halo, entirely removed from the uterus wall that would sustain it. Scientific imaging is deployed when it might afford a striking scene, and ignored or misused when it muddies the fantasy of autonomous fetal selfhood.

Hirst's refusal to adequately or accurately represent the placenta in these sculptures is not merely an aesthetic or decorous choice. Like the erasure of placental delivery in contemporary television and film, it is a decision that directly reflects how pregnant persons and fetuses are typically and inaccurately conceptualized as distinct and autonomous entities. Hirst's sculptures represent an ideological belief, one that cannot make sense of an organ that combines fetal and uterine tissue together. The placenta actually grows into and out from the uterine wall, writes Kingma, "just as a tail grows out of the cat."[56] As Gilbert puts it, "The cells interact to make this organ, and no clear anatomical line separates them," no boundary or cavity separates fetal from maternally derived tissue. Fetal stem cells mix and flow together with maternal blood cells, circulating back and forth such that "anatomically the fetus forms a part of the mother."[57] The work of philosophers, bioethicists, and legal schol-ars, when assembled together, shouts a chorus protesting the vision that Hirst creates here. Seeing the mother and the fetus as separate entities, whether biological, moral, or legal, does not follow from reality. Rather, they should be understood and conceptualized together as one entity, in which rights would, like maternal blood cells, "'flow through' the woman to her fetus."[58]

The routine use of enhanced medical devices helps normalize the view Hirst creates. Imaging technology like sonography promises to show us the fetus more clearly, autonomously, as well as earlier than ever before, but it actually facilitates the illusion that the fetus can be discretely separated from the pregnant person. Early in the cultural wars on abortion, Rosalind Petchesky pointed out the mechanism at work. All the images of fetuses that we see are viewed from the perspective of the camera, rendering the fetus into a kind of fetish—a thing alienated and unreal. Hirst's imagery, too, functions like the microscopic and sonogram images he relies on to create his sculpture. The parts of women's anatomy that he does include, like the stylized uterus, are transformed, rendered superfluous to the event of the fetus's miraculous journey in freeing itself from its uterine frame. Sometimes both the placenta and women's bodies are absent from the sculptures entirely, not even functioning as a site or

---

56   Elselijn Kingma, "Lady Parts: The Metaphysics of Pregnancy," *Royal Institute of Philosophy Supplement* 82 (2018): 173.

57   Gilbert, "Pseudo-embryology," 8.

58   Amanda Gvozden, "Fetal Protection Laws and the 'Personhood' Problem: Toward a Relational Theory of Fetal Life and Reproductive Responsibility," *Journal of Criminal Law and Criminology* 112, no. 2 (2022): 412.

environment for the fetus. All these representational choices are consistent with medical imaging and the effects it produces, as Petchesky describes them: displacing and discrediting a woman's *"felt* evidence" of pregnancy "in favor of the more 'objective' data" on screen.[59] That data helps fill out our view, the flesh and bones, of the imagined fetal person.

Disposing of the placenta—whether literally as medical waste, or figuratively in representations of childbirth—has long been a part of this process. Hirst's sculptures are as good an example as any of the erasure of the placenta and the related reduction of women to a physical container for the fetal DNA soul. His sculptures enact, at scale, what Catherine Mills describes as the sonagram's performative force. It is public art that does not simply represent the fetus but "constitutes the fetus as an embodied, social being toward whom we bear a particular ethical relationship."[60] Moreover, it is an ethical relationship introduced from far away. Situated in Qatar, a Muslim country with a historically multidimensional relationship to abortion, *Miraculous Journey* makes a bewildering, colonizing journey of its own.[61] Western conceptions of fetuses, pregnancy, and childbirth, with all the technological and visual trappings included, have been exported across the globe. The new legal conceptions of fetuses are not far behind. Elements of US fetal personhood laws have already started trickling into the judicial systems of other countries.[62]

Unborn Fictions

We have been sketching out a series of tools and strategies that anti-abortion activists have developed, over the past half century, to create a new legal entity: the fetal person. It is an artificial entity understood to exist in direct conflict with a pregnant woman, even though a fetus's actual relationship to the pregnant person can in no way be summed up

---

59   Petchesky, "Fetal Images," 269, 277.

60   Catherine Mills, "Making Foetal Persons: Foetal Homicide, Ultrasound, and the Normative Significance of Birth," *philoSOPHIA* 4, no. 1 (2014): 95.

61   Zahra Ayubi, "There is No One Islamic Interpretation on Ethics of Abortion, but the Belief in God's Mercy and Compassion is a Crucial Part of any Consideration," *The Conversation*, July 8, 2022, theconversation.com.

62   Anne O'Rourke, "A Legal and Political Assessment of Challenges to Abortion Laws by Anti-Choice Activists in Australia and the Progression of Abortion Law in Australia and the United States," *American Journal of Comparative Law* 70, no. 1 (2022): 162–204.

as simply antagonistic—or, for that matter, as simply spatial, as with the proverbial "bun in the oven." And we have seen all the different kinds of strategies that must be put to active use to make this confabulation seem convincing. Human personhood of any type must be increasingly conceptualized as artificial and corporate. Women must become sacred bodily vessels—womb containers. DNA has to be transubstantiated into souls, while placentas are disposed of as disregarded medical waste. If it sounds like a horror show, that is because it shares horror's favorite tricks. The undead thing looking and acting alive; fetish-like dolls becoming animated and terrifying; the dejected half-being returning with vengeance in its dead eyes. But rather than "the undead," fetal personhood demands a final related idea or fantasy: "unborn life" or the "unborn child." The "unborn" thus returns us to the start of this chapter, and to the recent past, with Justice Roberts's concurring opinion in *Dobbs*.

When Roberts writes about the moment "when the unborn child can live outside the womb," what exactly does he mean?[63] The *Oxford English Dictionary* (*OED*) provides some guidance that indicates why the term "unborn" is so fruitful for antiabortion activists. When used as an adjective, "unborn" can refer to a person "not yet born or delivered"—as in a fetus "gestating in the womb." Presumably this is what Roberts means. Yet this usage of "unborn" also deploys the language of potential, of a future life that might (or might not) be forthcoming. All of the *OED*'s definitions emphasize this prospective, theoretical quality: "with reference to notional or hypothetical children or generation" or those "to be born in the (distant) future." The *OED* helpfully notes, at the end of each of these adjectival uses, that the term is used in "figurative contexts" and "figurative and . . . extended use." That is, "unborn life" might not be referring to an actual fetus that has not yet been delivered; it might, rather, be referring to something far removed and still to arrive, hypothetically, or something "never born." And when "unborn" is used as a noun, the *OED* tells us, it is "now chiefly used in expression or description of anti-abortion or pro-life views."[64] As bioethicists have observed, anti-abortion activists are taking *descriptive* uses of "unborn" and applying them *normatively* to assert the moral and legal status of fetuses.[65]

---

63   *Dobbs v. Jackson Women's Health Organization*, 597 US ___ (2022); Roberts's concurrence, 3.
64   "unborn"; OED.com.
65   Laurence B. McCullough and Frank A. Chervenak, "A Critical Analysis of the Concept and Discourse of 'Unborn Child,'" *American Journal of Bioethics* 8, no. 7 (2008): 34–9.

Transforming an envisaged figure into a real one, with moral and legal standing, has always been the goal of the fetal personhood amendments and laws. "Unborn," whether adjective or noun, is a word that performs and actualizes this aim with eerie perfection. Folded into a thick batter of metaphor is a tiny pinch of literal usage. The slippery combination can then be whatever is needed in any given rhetorical situation—specifically medical, technically legal, or loftily spiritual. "Unborn" also trades on law's predilection for crisp binaries, those familiar terms and oppositions like "reasonable" or "unreasonable," "just" or "unjust," "lawful" or "unlawful." But unlike those abstract conceptual terms, "unborn" also functions in a more ordinary and daily register, like legal terms such as "unrecorded" (for something not officially recorded), "unsworn" (for testimony by someone never sworn in officially), or "untimely" (for an event proceeding either too soon or too late). In this way, "unborn" resembles legal procedural terms that indicate minor bureaucratic or practical slipups. Appropriating all this legal terminology, the word's true purpose, today, is very different, so much so that "unborn" really shares little in common with any of those words. It is a far more radical term, one that creates a whole new category of person.

Quite simply, performing the phrase "unborn child" (or "unborn life," or simply "the unborn") aims to contort women and their entire experience of pregnancy into the rigid shape of existing law. To do so, the interwoven developmental histories of fetus and woman, throughout pregnancy and childbirth and beyond, must be reduced to a fantastical on or off switch: the fetus is unconceived or conceived, unborn or born. It is as if a legal contract had been signed at conception and the "unborn child" has just been awaiting clear passage out of the pregnant person—the moment of birth—for the eventual performance of the contract. Artificial personhood (with its corporate flavor), women as container, DNA as soul, erased placentas—all those conceptual strategies that we have seen worked out in this chapter add up to make this fantastical contract of pregnancy supposedly plausible.

The process of turning an act of figuration into a real figure, a metaphor into a person, is the process of artificial personhood performed. With fetal personhood, something person-like is crafted into a real person, a new legal entity. All these tools, strategies, and conceptualizations are deliberately designed to make fetal personhood feel like a fact in the world, something *already* always there, that we can seek out a new instance of by spying an image on a sonagram. But the point of this chapter has been to show how fetal personhood—like corporate personhood, and like all the other forms of expansive personhood at work in this book—is actually an ongoing process and performance that requires an enormous amount of rhetorical, analytical, and theoretical work in the shadows. It is something that abortion activists and the law *make* happen, something we are allowing to come into being every day and to continue to be created. That does not necessarily make it less powerful. Like corporate personhood, which the US Supreme Court off-handedly declared to be an obvious reality more than a century ago with *Santa Clara County v. Southern Pacific Railroad* (1886), fetal personhood too has been functioning for decades as a *fait accompli*, even while arguments on its behalf were half-formed.

Nonetheless, fetal personhood laws and arguments must work very hard to deflect a reality that was also already perceived long ago (which is, again, why these laws must be understood as ideological). Two years before the Supreme Court clarified that corporate personhood was the law of the land, another heralded judge, then sitting on the highest state court of Massachusetts, explained that a fetus should not be considered a person when a pregnant woman is injured if the fetus cannot live outside its mother. In *Dietrich v. Northampton* (1884), Judge Oliver Wendell Holmes Jr. ruled that since "the unborn child was a part of the mother at the time of the injury, any damage to it . . . was recoverable by her."[66] In other words, in such wrongful death cases, because the pregnant woman received the injury, and because the fetus was "part of the mother" at that time (and not yet viable), the mother should be the person to recover any damages. (Wrongful death statutes now provide critical remedies when people suffer pregnancy loss due to negligence.) To be sure, Holmes's decision-making on reproductive justice, in this case and others, was far from perfect (see the notorious *Buck v. Bell*, in which he upheld a Virginia state law authorizing sterilization for some institutionalized women).[67] Despite his limitations, decades earlier, Holmes could see clearly enough on this issue of a woman's personhood versus that of a fetus. As contemporary scientists and theorists now argue, separating the mother and the fetus into distinct biological or legal entities does not make sense.

Sometimes it seems as if the technological sophistication and development of more reproductive technologies (not just sonograms but also IVF, fetal genetic testing, and in vitro surgical interventions) will require

---

66   *Dietrich v. Northampton*, 138 Mass. 14 (1884).
67   *Buck v. Bell*, 274 US 200 (1927).

our laws also to become more and more complex. Perhaps the terminology must shift as the technology does. But if the development of fetal personhood tells us anything, it is that it might instead be the case that we need a simpler perspective on this issue. Justice Ruth Bader Ginsburg reminded us that also hanging "in the balance" when considering the issue of abortion "is a woman's autonomous charge of her life's full course . . . her ability to stand in relation to man, society, and the state as an independent, self-sustaining, equal citizen."[68] As in Mary Kelly's *Antepartum*, what a pregnant person chooses to do, with both her hands feeling her belly and the fetus within, is what it means for her to be a person like anyone else.

---

68   Ruth Bader Ginsburg, "Some Thoughts on Autonomy and Equality in Relation to *Roe v. Wade*," *North Carolina Law Review* 63, no. 2 (January 1985): 383.

3

Animals: The Majority Group
to Which We Belong

Fig. 7. Ryan Gander, *The End* (2020). Close-up installation view. Animatronic mouse, audio. Dimensions variable; duration 15:36. © Ryan Gander; Courtesy the artist and Lisson Gallery. Photograph by George Darrell © 2025 Artists Rights Society (ARS), New York / DACS, London.

Equality Before Personhood

"I've spent my whole life being tolerant of differences," observes Ryan Gander's imitation mouse. Specifically, this is an animatronic black mouse in the art installation *The End* (2020), peeping out of a hole in a museum wall it seems to have chewed through. In an English child's voice, and despite tripping over some of the difficult words, the mouse explains her predicament: "I happen to have been born with a great difference to most, and one that is visually recognizable at that. A curse to some, a blessing to others. To me, it is neither." In an almost seventeen-minute monologue directed to museumgoers "towering above me in an otherwise empty room that is colossal to me," she reflects on the "differences between a human and an animal" and suggests that the real differences are not particularly physical ("It's not like I've got six heads and you've got one") but linguistic and cultural. Through language, humans can tell and learn stories from the entirety of human history, and they can imagine themselves in different worlds, exploring "para-possible versions of reality." Despite these gifts, says the mouse, humans can't answer the most basic question of what happens after they die, and they distract themselves from "this unanswerable worry" with all sorts of substitutes: drugs, alcohol, the internet. "It does, however, seem to calm you all. I was once asked by a small white mouse, 'if you had ten days to live, would you spend it looking at Instagram?'"[1]

Gander's philosophical rodent is arresting and a bit uncanny—it is hard to look away from her peephole near the floor. She bobs her head expressively in sync with her narration, a speech read by Gander's then six-year-old daughter. But, if you lean in, you can detect the whirring of the object's mechanical gears. The child's occasional throat clearing and garbled pronunciation also resist attempts to envision this creature as an imaginary, Disney-like anthropomorphized animal. Rather, the ornate syntax recalls the speech of the ape in Kafka's "A Report for an Academy," dismally observing humanity's degradations without being fully at home with them.

Particularly intriguing is that the mouse discusses her situation in terms of difference—the language, familiar to our ears, of DEI (diversity, equity, and inclusion) and anti-discrimination. She explains that she long ago chose "not to identify with my difference . . . in the hope that being different would not consume my time and energy that would

---

1   Ryan Gander, *The End* (2020), lissongallery.com.

be better spent doing all the good stuff in the world." Whereas we might have expected that an articulate spokes-animal for the animal rights movement might rely on arguments against physical cruelty, the mouse's advice is quite different. She proposes that we should endeavor to live alongside those with differences, and she invokes the oppositional terms of racism, sexism, and other forms of social inequality to make her case. The surprising move here, in other words, is the way in which these arguments are being made: that nonhuman animals, despite their dis-similarities from us, should not be discriminated against, but abided and treated as equals, just as liberal societies accept human differences. This is the language of toleration.

In fact, some version of this basic argument has been familiar in the animal rights literature since Peter Singer's *Animal Liberation* a half century ago. "Speciesism," Singer declares, is "a prejudice or attitude of bias in favor of the interests of members of one's own species and against those of members of other species."[2] The moral wrongness of species-ism, for Singer, emerges by analogy with the moral wrongness of racism and sexism. If speciesism is just another version of discrimination, along the lines of racism and sexism, then we must do everything we can to eliminate it. Utilitarian Jeremy Bentham's well-known challenge—"The question is not, Can they reason? nor Can they talk? but, Can they suffer?"—is Singer's guiding premise, demanding that, if we continue to discriminate against animals, we identify a principle for doing so. For Singer, the critical unit of value is the individual animal—whether human or nonhuman—that feels pain, and (as in a democracy) every individual animal is formally, morally equivalent. The sheer number of animals on the planet means that preventing nonhuman animal suffer-ing would cause the greatest "reduction in the total sum of suffering in the universe."[3] The challenge is to identify the line of demarcation that permits us to devalue the pain felt by a nonhuman animal compared to that of a human being.

Posing versions of this question, Singer delays discussing the ques-tion of personhood for nonhuman animals. But by beginning with the wrongs of illegal discrimination (speciesism), he effectively accepts the moral truth of animal personhood without explicitly asserting it. He describes how various groups—women, Black people, Native peoples—were denied their personhood status historically and had to struggle to

---

2   Peter Singer, *Animal Liberation: A New Ethics for Our Treatment of Animals* (New York: Random House, 1975), 8.
3   Peter Singer, *Practical Ethics*, third ed. (Cambridge University Press, 2011), 61.

attain it. As we have noted in previous chapters, being a person has traditionally required certain attributes as well as a certain social standing, all of which shifts over time. Traditionally, personhood entailed having and participating in public culture, and being created by and as a person by that culture, both through the roles one inhabited and the rational, reflective selfhood with which one performed those roles. This is a more difficult claim to make for many nonhuman animals. But viewing nonhuman animals as the victims of discrimination elides that problem. If their equality is being contested due to their innate differences, the fact of the contestation itself already presumes their innate equivalence to human beings. Toleration and anti-discrimination sneak in personhood through the back door.

As this brief example on anti-discrimination suggests, debates and terms about personhood seem to undergo some set of transformations before they can be applied to all nonhuman animals. This chapter looks at these transformations more carefully, to explore what is happening with animal legal personhood in claims (developed from Singer's) for animal liberation. I start from the intuition, which I share with Singer and others, that the horror of billions of nonhuman animals' lives and deaths today is a global wrong. Despite that premise, for myself as well as for some other sympathetic thinkers, there is the sense that something almost undefinable is missing in utilitarian arguments for animal liberation, and also that something is going wrong in legal activists' arguments for animal legal personhood. Different suggestions have been offered as to what is awry. Perhaps social-cultural realities are being ignored or something about animal personhood demands conceptual distortions to the notion of person. That is where we begin.

The next several sections explore this debate with the help of two contemporary artists—Gander and Nina Katchadourian—whose work advances the concept of "bio-art": art objects of various types that incorporate animals. Over the last forty years, bio-art has included (among others) Joseph Beuys's infamous performance piece in which he photographed his cohabitation with a wild coyote for three days in a New York Gallery; Damien Hirst's tiger shark preserved in a formaldehyde tank; and Eduardo Kac's genetically modified rabbit that glowed in the dark. Often, bio-art work elevates animals "to the status of collaborators, even if their participation is unwanted or unconscious."[4] Undesired, nonconsensual participation raises obvious ethical questions. When

---

4   Nina Amstutz, "The Avian Sense for Beauty: A Posthumanist Perspective on the Bowerbird," *Art History* 44, no. 5 (Nov 2021), 1045; 1045–6.

sculptor Richard Serra incorporated live and taxidermized animals into *Live Animal Habitat* (1966), his artistic justification was "that any material was as good as any other material." Nonhuman animals functioned as simply part of the cornucopia of natural resources available to him, another object to be acquisitioned, as private property, for the artist's larger aim.[5] For the philosopher Elizabeth Grosz, art has historically possessed this quality: "The human capitalization on the inhuman . . . the submission of these materials to other requirements than the instinctive."[6]

More recently, contemporary artists have deliberately challenged the "human capitalization" of nonhuman animals, often by forcing the viewer to consider the anthropomorphizing disguises we force on other species. Pierre Huyghe's short film *Human Mask* (2014), set in the no-man's land of a post-nuclear-catastrophe Fukushima, Japan, follows a trained monkey wearing the mask of a young woman as the monkey wanders through its "home." The work, writes Anne Stenne, "presents a residual image of human presence carried by an unconscious actor and sole mediator."[7] The result is disconcerting and mesmerizing, like so many representations of artificial personhood. The art discussed in this chapter often focuses on another type of anthropomorphic mask: human language use, traditionally the bright line that divides animals who deserve moral and legal concern (human beings) and those who do not. For example, Nina Katchadourian's "uninvited collaborations with nature" include her inserting English words in spiderwebs with glued threads and writing messages with live (albeit reluctant) caterpillars. In doing so, Katchadourian presents an impish challenge to our sense of ourselves and others when we interact with—or try to assist—entities in the natural world.

Ryan Gander, too, helps us see the limitations of claims to speciesism via language, through the artificiality implied. His animatronic mouse is obviously not a live mouse; its voice is clearly that of an English child, and his installation does not aim for perfect realism. He makes certain we can see both the desire to understand the mouse as different merely on a racial or gender level and the impossibility of doing so without flattening out the differences between her world and the encultured world

5   Richard Serra quoted in Giovanni Aloi, *Art and Animals* (New York: I. B. Tauris, 2012), 7.

6   Elizabeth A. Grosz, *Becoming Undone: Darwinian Reflections on Life, Politics, and Art* (Duke University Press, 2011), 170.

7   Anne Stenne, "Exhibition Guide," Pierre Huyghe, *Liminal*, Pinault Collection (Venice, Italy, 2024), 9.

of speaking human beings. And, in a certain way, by invoking the terminology of difference, Gander seems also to be cannily referring to his own very human identity here. Although he has used a wheelchair since childhood, he entirely rejects the disability label.[8] The work thus seems to be more invested in making a broader point. Rather than preoccupying ourselves with the superficial differences between human beings, or between human animals and nonhuman ones, we should focus on what the human species is *doing*, and why.[9] "You should choose how to spend your time," the mouse advises (enough with the Instagram already). Toleration is merely a minimal standard, and perhaps an inapt one. What really matters is everything else we are doing even if we manage not to discriminate against one another based on our identities.

Works by Katchadourian and Gander also help reveal something that has gone entirely unexamined, which this chapter starts to redress: the way arguments for animal legal personhood, like other forms of expansive personhood, inevitably rely on artificial corporate personhood. This is the impoverished version of personhood that we have been exploring in previous chapters—the person of perfect equality, thinned out and legalized, taking on more of the characteristics of things, developed from theories of other artificial persons, and detached from the public sphere. All these characteristics fittingly work for the notion of animal legal personhood, which is one of the earliest and clearest instances of all the features of expansive personhood in action. Animal personhood, too, follows the path that corporate persons have laid down. And figuring out a way to glimpse that path, in order to imagine a different one, is the ultimate goal of this chapter.

On Personhood for Nonhuman Animals

Note, at the outset, that mainstream animal rights and protection organizations have not fully embraced the animal personhood effort, the major premise of the Nonhumans Rights Project's (NhRP) habeas corpus suits on behalf of chimpanzees as well as for Happy, the Bronx Zoo elephant discussed in the introduction. For example, the Animal Legal Defense Fund (ALDF), which describes itself as "the legal voice for all animals"

---

8   royalacademy.org.uk.

9   I use "animals" and "nonhuman animals" interchangeably throughout this chapter, for ease of reference and because the phrase "nonhuman animals" is of relatively recent vintage. Many of the earlier thinkers on this topic whom I cite did not use it.

and which attorney Steven Wise helmed before starting NhRP, is cautious about the necessity of animal legal personhood to reach its aims of protecting animals from harm, supporting prosecutors battling animal cruelty, and promoting animal protection legislation.[10] Personhood, they note on their website, "is not an all or nothing concept." Animal personhood advocates, for their part, sometimes dismiss protectionist, anti-cruelty goals like ALDF's as inadequate and as failing to alter the basic legal relationships in play for millennia. Without the stature of persons, nonhuman animals can only attain the legal status of things, of property.[11] We will look at these arguments for and against nonhuman animal legal personhood more carefully in this and the next section, to understand the stakes of the debate as well as to consider what is not being considered in them.

To understand what personhood advocates want, and what they hope personhood will do for animals, consider *Naruto v. Slater* (2018), popularly known as the Monkey Selfie case. In 2011, wildlife photographer David Slater set up a camera in Indonesia's Tangkoko Reserve, where a community of crested macaques could play with it. After Slater observed that one of the monkeys—Naruto—had noticed his own reflection in the lens and was curious about the camera, Slater set up the device to self-focus and be tripped by Naruto, activating a remote shutter press.[12] While Slater was absent, Naruto proceeded to make faces, including smiles; he pressed the shutter and generated "monkey selfies." After Slater licensed the resulting photographs to various newspapers, a user uploaded the images to Wikimedia Commons. Slater demanded that they be removed but Wikipedia refused on the grounds that because the image was not created by a human being, no one—not even Slater—held copyright to it. Shortly thereafter, PETA became involved, filing a lawsuit in federal court on behalf of Naruto as the selfie's creator and author: "Naruto has the right to own and benefit from the copyright" of the images, just as would "any other author."[13] According to PETA, Slater, by licensing

---

10   Consider ALDF's entry on "Animals Legal Status": "Obviously, animals can have standing or be legal persons without having identical rights to humans or upending animals' legal property status"; aldf.org.

11   See Gary L. Francione and Robert Garner, *The Animal Rights Debate: Abolition or Regulation?* (New York: Columbia University Press, 2010).

12   Nathan Hakimi, "Monkey Business: Copyright, Stunt Litigation, and New Visions in Animal Law," *Journal of Animal and Environmental Law* 9, no. 1 (Fall 2017): 3.

13   Complaint for Copyright Infringement, Case No.: 15-cv-4324, *Naruto, et al. v. David John Slater, et al.*, in United States District Court, Northern District of California (September 21, 2015), 2.

Fig. 8. Self-portrait of Naruto, triggered by Naruto using photographer David Slater's camera (2011). From wikicommons.

images of the selfies, improperly infringed on Naruto's intellectual property; Naruto owned this property, those charming images of himself.

District Court Judge William Orrick rejected PETA's argument, dismissing the case not on the grounds that Naruto had not authored the image, but, more fundamentally, on the grounds that Naruto lacked legal standing to sue for damages under the Copyright Act. When the US Congress passed the Copyright Act, it did not give nonhuman animals the right to sue for copyright infringement—to stand at, address the law, and have their copyright complaints heard. But, as PETA pointed out, the act does not explicitly limit what it means by "owners" of copyrightable property. PETA contended that legal standing was available to anyone creating "an original work of authorship." In response to this argument, Judge Orrick admitted that "the Copyright Act defines neither 'works of authorship' nor 'author.'"[14] However, he continued, "there is no mention of animals anywhere in the Act," and courts "repeatedly referred

---

14   *Naruto v. Slater*, No. 15-CV-04324-WHO, 2016 WL 362231, 2 (N.D. Cal. January 28, 2016), *aff'd*, 888 F.3d 418 (9th Cir. 2018).

to 'persons' or 'human beings' when analyzing authorship under the Act."[15] The Judge could not find any precedential cases that expanded authorship from human persons to nonhuman animals. Reviewing the trial court decision, the Ninth Circuit Appeals Court affirmed all these points: "We conclude that this monkey—and all animals, since they are not human—lacks statutory standing under the Copyright Act."[16] They also added (in a footnote) that "any argument that animals are akin to 'artificial persons' such as corporations, which are allowed to sue . . . makes no sense" for issues of, say, habeas corpus relief; "persons" in that instance means "natural persons."[17]

We will return in more depth to the Ninth Circuit's reasoning and this mentioning of artificial corporate personhood. But, already, these discussions reveal the emerging problem that animal personhood is supposed to solve. Most basically, the problem is how to get nonhuman animals through the courtroom door as individual *litigants*. Here, the courts simply dismissed the more nuanced question of whether Naruto was the author of the selfie (versus Slater authoring it, or no one) because Naruto did not count as a person the court had to listen to and respond to. Wise, the founder of the NhRP, puts animals' situation this way: "Without legal personhood, one is invisible to civil law. One has no civil rights. One might as well be dead."[18] Although that somewhat overstates the situation, since there are other ways besides personhood to be visible to civil law, Wise does have a point. In this case, the courts refused to recognize Naruto, and did not even accept PETA's legal designation of themselves as Naruto's "next friend" (a guardian or representative) suing on the monkey's behalf: "An animal cannot be represented, under our laws, by a 'next friend.'"[19]

Gary Francione describes this as the plight of what it means to be an animal as *property* according to the law, as animals generally remain in Anglo-American jurisprudence: "It is a fundamental premise of our property law that property cannot itself have rights as against human owners and that, as property, animals are objects of the exercise of human property rights."[20] Even were we to grant animals certain rights

---

15   Ibid., 3.

16   *Naruto v. Slater*, 888 F.3d 418 (9th Cir. 2018), 420.

17   Ibid., 431.

18   Steven M. Wise, *Rattling the Cage: Toward Legal Rights for Animals* (Cambridge, MA: Perseus, 2000), 4.

19   *Naruto* (2018), 421.

20   Gary L. Francione, *Animals, Property, and the Law* (Philadelphia: Temple University Press, 1995), 4.

while still considering them legal property, they would remain stuck in the same limbo, because property cannot have interests "that transcend the rights of property owners to use their property."[21] This was precisely the situation that Naruto found himself in. Without the status of personhood, he was relegated to the condition of property, and as property, he could not hold copyright. More generally, he could not own intellectual property or any other kind of property. Under these conditions, legal personhood for Naruto clearly looks like the escape route out of the subjection of property-hood.

Besides these arguments, advocates for animal legal personhood often make two additional points. First, they note that legal personhood is just a term of art anyway, one that can be defined quite differently in different contexts and in various statutes. From that perspective, there is no justifiable reason why animals could not be considered persons in the law. "If corporations, ships, and natural resources have legal personhood protections," writes Randall Abate, then some "wildlife should enjoy similar protections."[22] Likewise, NhRP argues in their various legal petitions that law "has never made 'person' a synonym for 'human'"; "person" has been a more variable term designating an entity that can have legal rights, whether or not that entity also has duties.[23] Other commentators note that courts inconsistently apply various definitions of personhood, and reach judgments that confusingly equivocate "between these different meanings of personhood."[24] We see an instance of this when the Ninth Circuit adamantly rejected the comparison between animals and other legal, nonhuman persons (like corporations). On the one hand, they accept the concept of artificial legal personhood (for corporations), and on the other hand, they reject it (for nonhuman animals).

Perhaps the most influential argument on behalf of legal personhood for nonhuman animals is not a legal one at all. Creative deployments of the law, like NhRP's on behalf of Happy, or PETA's on behalf of Naruto, "can be a tool to raise awareness" and might lead to legislative reforms.[25] Both Happy's and Naruto's lawsuits were covered extensively in the media, even though the plaintiffs failed to convince the judges of the

---

21   Francione, *Animals, Property, and the Law*, 14.

22   Randall Abate, *Climate Change and the Voiceless: Protecting Future Generations, Wildlife, and Natural Resources* (Cambridge University Press, 2020), 97.

23   Reply Memorandum of Law, *NhRP, on behalf of Happy v. James J. Breheny, et al.*, Index No.: 18-45164, State of New York Supreme Court, County of Orleans (December 10, 2018), 20.

24   Kristin Andrews, et al., *Chimpanzee Rights: The Philosophers' Brief* (New York: Routledge, 2018), 3.

25   Abate, *Climate Change and the Voiceless*, 97.

merits of their arguments. Just the act of formally demanding legal personhood for certain animals functions as public consciousness raising, helping more people see the possibilities, flaws, and injustices of our current stark division between persons and animal-property. Starting this crusade with social mammals (such as chimps, monkeys, elephants, dolphins) who exhibit sentience, intelligence, linguistic capacity, and other human-like qualities makes both rhetorical and legal sense. These campaigners assume that legal change will be piecemeal and will involve many tiny victories first. But someone has to take the first step.

How to "Quit Using" Them

Since the nineteenth century, emotional visual imagery was used by animal rights activists and reformers to challenge conventions about nonhuman animals, in part because, as Keri Cronin writes, imagery can "draw attention to that which is *culturally invisible*."[26] Nina Katchadourian explicitly invokes this activist legacy in a staged photograph that also, disarmingly, raises many of these kinds of arguments for animal legal personhood. Part of her *Uninvited Collaborations with Nature* series, in one photograph Katchadourian "arranged, with some difficulty," about twenty-five "conscripted" caterpillars into a political statement that is also the title of the piece: *Quit Using Us* (2002). She printed the photograph in a large and long format, "at a size reminiscent of a political banner," supporting her simultaneously cheeky and dogmatic point.[27] That is, while we can make arguments about why animals are not property, until we really "quit using" them and thinking about them as ours to exploit, they will find themselves in the same situation as Katchadourian's conscripts: being used.

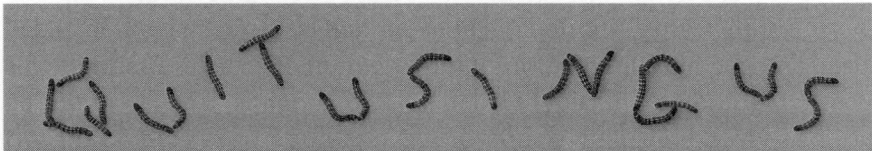

Fig. 9. Nina Katchadourian, *Quit Using Us* (2002). C-print mounted on aluminum. © Nina Katchadourian, courtesy of the artist, Catharine Clark Gallery, and Pace Gallery.

---

26   Keri J. Cronin, *Art for Animals: Visual Culture and Animal Advocacy, 1870–1914* (University Park: Penn State University Press, 2018), 6.

27   ninakatchadourian.com.

Katchadourian's reluctant collaborators seem uninterested in being in her arrangement of letters, their movements enacting what they unknowingly spell out. That is clear from the "Q" caterpillars already attempting to crawl away from their assigned formation at the very moment the photograph was taken. In that way, the photograph forces us to confront the long-standing argument that animals cannot have the protections of personhood because they lack human language to express their desires. Here, their interests are simultaneously represented (in English) *and* legally trumped by the human person who wants to use them, and who can and does so. With that offhand, culturally specific expression (not "stop" but "quit"), the photograph also reminds us that we are encultured as *human* persons with particular linguistic dialects that exist at specific moments of time and place. Simultaneously, we know relatively little about the interests of those creatures (such as caterpillars) not so encultured, and who do not express their intentions the way we do, if at all. Capturing all these facets of acting for and compelling, Katchadourian's slogan-photograph slyly undercuts a straightforward equivalence of human political autonomy with that of nonhuman animals. Quitting the use of nonhuman animals is not so easy.

In addition to art like Gander's and Katchadourian's, the most thoughtful and creative responses to animal legal personhood arguments have emerged not from the factory farm industry, or from legal theorists generally dismissive of legal rights' for animals, but from thinkers with broadly similar goals.[28] Within this sphere, there is much agreement on both sides of the legal personhood debate (and also among philosophers) that the person/property binarism in law has been profoundly detrimental to nonhuman animals.[29] Catharine MacKinnon captures the problem by tracing women's historically analogous relationship, in law, to that of nonhuman animals: "Both animals and women have been socially configured as property . . . specifically for possession and use."[30] Observing that animals do not exist for human beings (nor women for men), she poses the question: "Why should animals have to measure up to humans' standards for humanity before their existence counts?"[31] The point for

---

28   More explicitly negative takes include Richard Posner, "Animal Rights," *Yale Law Journal* 110 (2000): 527–41, and Richard L. Cupp, "Litigating Nonhuman Animal Legal Personhood," *Texas Tech Law Review* 50 (2019): 573–98.

29   From a philosophical perspective, see Christine Korsgaard, "Personhood, Animals, and the Law," *Think* 12, no. 34 (2013): 25–32.

30   Catharine MacKinnon, "Of Mice and Men: A Feminist Fragment on Animal Rights" in *Animal Rights: Current Debates and New Directions*, ed. Cass R. Sunstein and Martha Craven Nussbaum (Oxford University Press, 2004), 265.

31   MacKinnon, "Of Mice and Men," 267.

MacKinnon is not to collapse the differences between humans and non-human animals—that is, not to expand personhood more broadly to animals—but to use animals' positional analogy with women to expose the inadequacy of the current legal regime.

A number of writers have also made the point that there might be other ways to release animals from their denigrated status as property without granting them legal personhood. Concerned that "talk of person-hood status starts us down the wrong path" and that "it might be better to avoid the language of personhood entirely," Sue Donaldson and Will Kymlicka have proposed that categories such as "selfhood" and "denizen-ship" might be preferable.[32] Other theorists have envisioned alternative designations for animals that include "sentient beings" (Kristin Andrews, et al.); "beingness" (Maneesha Deckha); "fellow beings" (Christine Kors-gaard); and "non-personal subjects of law" (Tomasz Pietrzykowski).[33] Each of these thinkers insists that it is not necessary to increase the number of individuals in the "personhood" category to protect animals' rights. Instead, we should create or identify what Deckha calls a "more animal-friendly legal subjectivity . . . as a better replacement for prop-erty."[34] The advantage of these other labels is that the person/property binary can be subtly, or not so subtly, undermined. If the lack of available legal options is a problem, as Andrews and others speculate, then provid-ing more options might be a way out of animals' legal trap as property.

In response to the arguments that animals are invisible to civil law, or only visible as property, some legal theorists have countered with ways to make animals newly apparent to the law without relying on legal personhood to do so. Legal theorists David Favre and Karen Bradshaw have separately proposed a solution that avoids the personhood desig-nation. They suggest that the law could allow animals to own property, as have (historically and currently) ships, corporations, and children, through an arrangement of responsible trustees. Favre describes this as a system of "living property" and Bradshaw calls it "an interspecies

---

32   Sue Donaldson and Will Kymlicka, *Zoopolis: A Political Theory of Animal Rights* (Oxford University Press, 2011), 29–30.

33   Andrews, *Chimpanzee Rights*, 101; Maneesha Deckha, "Animal Rights without Animal Personhood?: Implementing Feminist Legal Reform for Animals as Legal Beings" in *Feminist Animal Studies: Theories, Practices, Politics*, ed. Erika Cudworth, Ruth E McKie, and Di Turgoose (New York: Routledge, 2023), 19; Christine Korsgaard, *Fellow Creatures: Our Obligation to the Other Animals* (Oxford University Press, 2018), 4; Tomasz Pietrzykowski, "The Idea of Non-personal Subjects of Law," in *Legal Person-hood: Animals, Artificial Intelligence, and the Unborn*, ed. Visa A. J. Kurki and Tomasz Pietrzykowski (Cham, Switzerland: Springer International, 2017), 59.

34   Deckha, "Animal Rights," 19.

system of property."[35] From another angle, Cass Sunstein has observed that the contention that animals are property is overly simplistic and does not fully reflect existing law. In order to bring suits, plaintiffs do not need to be designated as "persons" by the law; legal rights are given to various entities, not only trusts and corporations but also municipalities and partnerships, without their being declared persons.[36] He makes the important legal historical point that when enslaved individuals in the US were accorded neither the rights of persons nor those of citizens, legal actions could still be brought to courts on their behalf. The property or personhood designation was not necessarily determinative. For Sunstein, strengthening and better enforcing existing animal anti-cruelty laws could achieve many of the aims that animal personhood has, something for which he also advocates.

Critics also take issue with the idea that because personhood is a term of art in law it could easily be expanded to animals. Pietrzykowski describes various conceptual problems with animal legal personhood: Quite simply, "animals do not fit either the category of juristic or natural persons."[37] Trying to squeeze them to fit risks producing more damaging distortions that work against the purpose of legal personhood in the first place, which "is based on instrumental considerations relating to the ways in which the law should promote human interests." We might put it this way: Terms of art (like "corporate personhood") only work by relying on a whole set of other terms, historical ideas, and conventions. Plucking a term out of its context and making it mean in a different way is not a small change in terminology but a huge change masquerading as semantics.

The most difficult argument to counter is probably the extralegal one. Animal legal personhood, even the specter of it, might work effectively to raise public awareness about something people have not thought a lot about—or have worked hard not to think about. The philosopher Rosalind Hursthouse observes that it has been less Singer's arguments for utilitarian animal liberation that have been most effective in changing public opinion on vegetarianism for moral reasons than his graphic description of the mass suffering and cruelty of animals slaughtered

---

35   David Favre, "Living Property: A New Status for Animals Within the Legal System," *Marquette Law Review* 93, no. 3 (2010): 3; Karen Bradshaw, *Wildlife As Property Owners: A New Conception of Animal Rights* (University of Chicago Press, 2020).

36   Cass Sunstein, "Can Animals Sue?," in *Animal Rights*, ed. Sunstein and Nussbaum, 260.

37   Pietrzykowski, "Non-personal Subjects," 57.

on factory farms.[38] Probably empirical studies would be needed to really confirm this intuition about changing public opinion. Yet there is already evidence that public attitudes on this topic are shifting. In recent surveys, increasing percentages of American agree that animals deserve legal rights akin to human ones, and about half surveyed agreed with NhRP's stated aims, favoring a law that "recognizes the legal right of bodily liberty for great apes, elephants, and cetaceans like whales and dolphins."[39] However, these surveys are crafted to avoid the explicit "animal legal personhood" label, even if it could be assumed from the description of rights on offer.

Yet, with all these arguments, pro and con, there remains something about being a human person absent from the logic of animal legal personhood. Perhaps it is simply that artificial personhood's conceptual underpinnings nearly always go unmentioned despite their continued role. When, in 2014, Wise appeared on the *Colbert Report* to discuss the very first US habeas corpus petition on behalf of a nonhuman animal— NhRP's attempt to free Tommy, a chimpanzee held in a steel cage in a windowless shed in upstate New York—Stephen Colbert quipped at the end, "If Tommy wants to have rights as a person, he should form his own corporation."[40] It garnered a gotcha-laugh from the studio audience, and was obviously intended to refer to the corporate personhood debates still percolating through public culture after the *Citizens United* (2010) decision. But there is more than a modicum of truth in Colbert's quip. By formulating the issue this way, it is easier to see that animals such as chimpanzees and elephants would not be gaining the rights of human beings but of artificial persons, the type of person that corporations are. The following sections examine this logic more closely, considering what animal legal personhood might miss about personhood, legal or otherwise.

---

38   Rosalind Hursthouse, "Applying Virtue Ethics to Our Treatment of the Other Animals," in *Virtue and Action: Selected Papers*, ed. Rosalind Hursthouse, Julia Annas, and Jeremy Reid (Oxford University Press, 2022), 197.

39   Garrett M. Broad, "Public Support for Animal Rights Goes Beyond Keeping Dogs Out of Overhead Bins," *The Conversation* (March 22, 2018), theconversation.com.

40   *The Colbert Report*, 2014, Season 11, Episode 1,376. Directed by Jim Hoskinson. Performed by Stephen Colbert. Aired July 17, 2014 on Comedy Central; cc.com.

Becoming a Nonhuman Artificial Person

About midway through the documentary film *Unlocking the Cage* (2016), depicting NhRP's legal battles to free chimpanzee Tommy, there is a brief, off-the-cuff scene in the greenroom of a morning talk show, between Steven Wise and Ron Kuby, another civil rights lawyer. Kuby seems sympathetic to the liberation cause, and they casually begin talking about the arguments in NhRP's habeas corpus petition:

> KUBY: So, I suppose just reasoning this forward in looking at the corporate personhood rationale—
> WISE: [interrupting] But it's not just corporations, it's ships, it's partnerships, it's counties, it's states, there are lots of nonhuman persons.

Wise is correct, and he also offers other international legal examples of nonhuman legal personhood, some of which we will examine in the next chapter. But Kuby sticks to his point: "I guess I would look to the Supreme Court's basis for declaring corporate personhood, since that strikes me as much more precedential for American purposes."[41] To Kuby, a civil rights lawyer, corporate personhood seems like the obvious comparison, the way for Wise to make the legal argument stick. Throughout the film, the comparison between corporate and animal personhood is raised a number of times, sometimes delicately, sometimes evasively. But it always remains there, lurking just in the background.

NhRP's habeas corpus petition for Tommy actually makes that connection explicit in its very first paragraph: "Courts have routinely extended rights to non-human entities such as corporations."[42] But the petition does not belabor the point, and there are various reasons, both rhetorical and legal, why animal personhood advocates such as Wise would not want the alignment too much on everyone's minds. Rhetorically speaking, NhRP has little to gain from hitching themselves to several of the most unpopular and contentious US Supreme Court decisions, like *Citizens United* and *Hobby Lobby*, regardless of the precedential value that Kuby points out. Legally, the jump from corporations to animals is still that: a leap of an analogy. The New York attorney general's argument in response to these types of arguments was telling: "There

---

41   *Unlocking the Cage*, dir. Chris Hegedus and D. A. Pennebaker (Pennebaker Hegedus Films, 2016), at 50:00.

42   *In the Matter of . . . NhRP on behalf of Tommy v. Patrick C. Lavery, et al.*, Verified Petition, State of New York Supreme Court, County of Fulton (December 2, 2013), 2.

is simply no precedent anywhere of a nonhuman animal receiving the kinds of rights [NhRP] are talking about. The exceptions that do exist . . . it's something that in some way relates to human interest. Whether [it's] a corporation, whether a ship is treated as a legal person."[43] The "human interest" of animals seems to be about our use of them as property, not as persons in their own right.

NhRP filed its habeas corpus suits in New York State, but courts in other jurisdictions have sometimes also recognized this animal-corporate connection. In one of the important precedents for *Naruto*, the Ninth Circuit Court of Appeals made the following argument about who could "stand" at, and so be heard by, the Court according to Article III of the US Constitution:

> It is obvious that an animal cannot function as a plaintiff in the same manner as a juridically competent human being. But we see no reason why Article III prevents Congress from authorizing a suit in the name of an animal, any more than it prevents suits brought in the name of artificial persons such as corporations, partnerships or trusts, and even ships.[44]

Although that is not exactly a ringing endorsement of the legitimacy of animal legal personhood, the Ninth Circuit is making plain that a potential, justifiable legal analogy could be made between animals and other kinds of "artificial persons such as corporations." The reasons the connection keeps arising is the same reason NhRP frequently makes the historical connection to demands for habeas corpus relief for enslaved Black individuals before the Civil War. The story of artificial personhood was the story of corporate personhood and the Fourteenth Amendment and, so linked with it, the story of personhood for political entities like states and formerly enslaved individuals.

Law has been laying down a track for more than a century and a half of how to become a legal person if you were not born one, and the sequence goes like this: (1) be owned as property; (2) find someone with a voice and standing in court to present your potential emancipation; (3) liberate yourself as, at least, your own property; and (4) fight for more rights, if not full rights, as a legal person. This is the unswerving

---

43   *In the Matter of . . . NhRP on behalf of Hercules and Leo v. Samuel L. Stanley Jr. et al.*, Proceedings (Transcript), INDEX NO. 152736/15, Supreme Court of the State of New York, New York County, Civil Branch (May 27, 2015), 47.

44   *Cetacean Community v. Bush*, 386 F.3d 1169, 1177 (9th Cir. 2004).

path all potential persons take and have taken. In the case of corporate persons, their various rights have been increasing over time. They began with the right to own property, contract, sue and be sued, and demand due process and equal protection. With decisions such as *Citizens United* and *Hobby Lobby*, First Amendment protections for free speech and free exercise of religion were also included, even if corporate persons' rights are still not identical to human beings' rights. For African Americans and indigenous Americans, the process has been centuries long and dismal, with the degradations of Jim Crow segregation and policies of Indian removal. For women and immigrants to the United States, it has been more varied and complicated still (we saw aspects of that history with regards to abortion rights in the previous chapter).[45] But, in each of these cases, the process of becoming a legal person has not been radically different.

For animal legal personhood too, the process, while currently halted at an earlier point on this well-worn path, has followed a pattern of piecemeal changes. Arguments began when utilitarians like Bentham simply made the case that animals *could* experience suffering, that they were not mechanical automatons. These arguments progressed to animal welfare protections, eventually enacted by legislatures, and then most recently to lawsuits attempting to acknowledge certain animals' liberty interests and rights, based on their cognitive capacities and autonomy. To be clear, the point in considering these comparisons between entities and species is not to imply the existence of some deeper philosophical or existential connection between corporations, African Americans, Indians, women, and nonhuman animals. Rather, it is to suggest that Anglo-American common and corporate law, which continues to profoundly impact law globally, has understood as identical the journey that any and all prospective persons might take. The passage from property to personhood (and, arguably, back to a kind of property in the form of commodities) is on a narrow-gauge track. Artificial legal personhood, defined as the evolution of some kinds of property into an entity with rights, has become the dominant account in our thinking.

That is why NhRP often cites one of the landmark cases of the eighteenth century, the British decision of Lord Mansfield, *Somerset v. Stewart* (1772). (Wise actually published a whole book about the case.) Abolitionists used the writ of habeas corpus to demand the freedom

---

45   See Evelyn Atkinson, "Frankenstein's Baby: The Forgotten History of Corporations, Race, and Equal Protection," *Virginia Law Review* 108, no. 3 (2022): 581–656.

of an enslaved Black man, James Somerset, alleged to have escaped from Charles Stewart, who was planning to ship Somerset to Jamaica to be sold. NhRP tends to make these enslavement analogies, although judges sometimes respond negatively to the comparison, as it seems to equate enslaved human individuals with nonhuman animals in zoos. But the point, again, is that none of these arguments, none of these precedents, are really avoidable. The arguments come up repeatedly because expansive personhood was extrapolated from its property origins, from artificial personhood. Law's responsibility to stare decisis, to not overruling itself on a whim, makes it hard to imagine how to escape artificial personhood arguments' historical, gravitational force.

Anti-Speciesism—The Wrong Tool to Use?

Throughout this chapter, we have seen both the rewards of, as well as the concerns raised about, the equation of nonhuman animals and human beings. The equality argument is simple, as are its demands (at least in theory—how they could be applied in practice is a different story). But for thinkers resisting the animal-human equation, it can be difficult to identify exactly what seems to be going awry in the formula, particularly for those sympathetic to the general aims—those who would rather see Happy the elephant and Tommy the chimpanzee free instead of languishing behind bars. The philosopher Cora Diamond describes her position in response to Singer and likeminded activists with her characteristic elegance: "It is their arguments I have been attacking . . . and not their perceptions, not the sense that comes through their writings of the awful and unshakeable callousness and unrelentingness with which we most often confront the non-human world."[46] Many of today's legal theorists on animals would, I think, share this perspective, but how to see exactly *why* the legal argument but not the perception is wrong?

To get some purchase on this problem, take another work by Katchadourian. *GIFT/GIFT* (1998) shares a similar perspective and sentiment but approaches it from a radically different direction. Having read in a Swedish naturalist book that spiders sometimes use their webbing to wrap up a dead insect and present it to another spider, Katchadourian staged and videoed her own preposterous gift, in a twelve-minute performance in concert with a spider:

---

46   Cora Diamond, "Eating Meat and Eating People," *Philosophy: The Journal of the Royal Institute of Philosophy* 53 (October 1, 1978): 479.

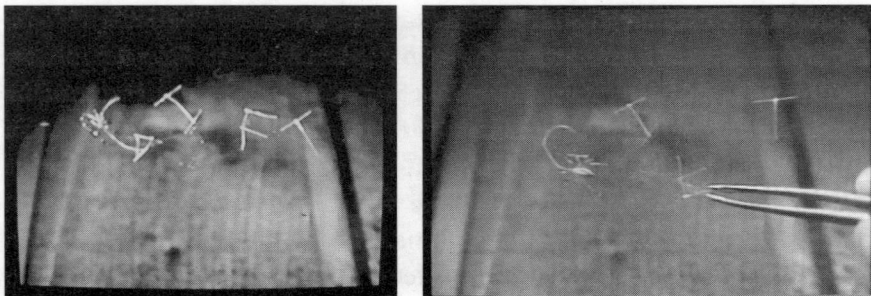

Fig. 10. Nina Katchadourian, *GIFT/GIFT* (1998). Film stills of video, duration 11:55. © Nina Katchadourian, courtesy of the artist, Catharine Clark Gallery, and Pace Gallery.

> Small letters made of thread spell out the word one letter at a time in the spiderweb. A particularly aggressive spider battles a pair of persistent tweezers for control of the web. The tweezers manage, with great difficulty and damage to the web, to insert the letters. The spider returns, picks out the letters in order, and makes a few repairs before settling back into the web where it was to begin with.[47]

The performance piece is mesmerizing to watch, perhaps because it exposes the inconsistencies and rifts in our sense of why we do what we do (and what we think it means), and how we interact with the animal world. There is something both self-consciously doltish yet also childlike about the piece, as it recalls another instance of web-writing—in E. B. White's *Charlotte's Web*. But here it is the tweezers of the artist and not the spider doing the writing.

Katchadourian enacts and performs a basic incommensurability: the production of a failure of communication along with ridiculous human arrogance about what a gift to a spider might consist of. As the spider sequentially cuts out the tweezer-inserted "GIFT" letters, it becomes obvious (if it was not already) how false, unnecessary, and unsought such a linguistic gesture would be to a spider. The spider clearly does not want these pieces of thread in its web, and methodically, actively, intentionally removes them. Katchadourian notes that "gift/gift" reminds her of the word "poison" (*förgifta*) in Swedish, which is a more accurate description of what such a contribution is to this spider. The gesture of this gift to a spider offers nothing but damage.

In a sense, Katchadourian's gift to a spider is as useful to the spider as legal personhood would be to an animal lacking a human being acting on

---

47   ninakatchadourian.com.

its behalf—or a human being profoundly misunderstanding that animal's wants and needs. Of course, it is possible to imagine the artist using her intrusive tweezers to offer the spider a more useful, nutritional gift of an insect. And it is possible to imagine that a lawyer's habeas corpus petition for Happy or Tommy might eventually land them in a better home, one in which they would be much more likely to flourish (although Katchadourian's tweezers also intervene in the spider's home, with destructive results). But, more holistically, turning spiders into the kinds of beings who will warmly receive human gifts, or chimpanzees and elephants into some of the only individual animals to be graced with the status of personhood, does little to change the long-standing division between persons with rights versus animals as property. Instead, it just moves the person/property line over a single notch, permitting a few more entities, previously labeled things or property, to enjoy some of the privileges of persons. And moving the boundary line in this way is just more of the same. It could also support odd (but in a sense familiar) claims like David DeGrazia's, who suggests that apes (or spiders?) who have been taught human languages should be considered persons while ones who have not should be relegated to the purgatory status of "borderline person."[48]

Mary Midgley offers some of the most compelling reasons why such categorical bright-line divisions are unconvincing. She assumes the importance of moral consideration for animals. But Midgley also explains why the concept of equality is simply the wrong device to use when thinking about our relationship to nonhuman animals. It "is a tool for rectifying injustices within a given group, not for widening that group or deciding how it ought to treat those outside it." It is the right tool for tackling arguments attacking reproductive justice (as we saw in the previous chapter), but the wrong tool here. The discourse of equality is not an accurate way to think about who nonhuman animals are, how they live, and how we relate to them. Animals are not "just an oppressed minority in human life. They are the group to which we belong. We are a small minority of them." Oppressed minority arguments do not work in these kinds of scenarios because "the moral universe is not just a system of concentric circles, in which inner claims must always prevail over outer ones."[49] We often have moral intuitions for other people, entities,

48   David DeGrazia, "On the Question of Personhood beyond Homo Sapiens," in *In Defense of Animals: The Second Wave*, ed. Peter Singer (Malden, MA: Blackwell, 2006), 46–8.

49   Mary Midgley, *Animals and Why They Matter* (Athens: University of Georgia Press, 1983), 67, 143, 22.

species, and situations far removed from anything like our most local family or community (or species). Taken as a whole, Midgley's argument is a demand that we do more thinking on this problem, not less, and that we recognize the complicated historical drama going on in discussions of, for example, whether or not a dolphin should be considered a person.[50]

To see an illustration of this point, consider another work of Gander's. His various animatronic mouse installations also play with the idea of a drama going on with our ideas of what it means to be a person, dramas that are very different from what we might think about as the drama to which an animal belongs. His mice speak to us, metaphorically, as alien observers of the human race, rather than as either cute and childlike pets, or as plague-carrying vermin. In the installation, *I . . . I . . . I . . .*, (2019), an animatronic white mouse pokes through a museum wall, and a voice (again that of Gander's daughter) struggles to begin a speech but cannot find her rhythm, cannot figure out a way to address the room: "Oh! I . . . I . . . first I should, um, first I should like to . . . um . . . I would like to, um . . . I'd like . . . I'd . . . um." It goes on like this for nine minutes. It is painful to listen to. You feel someone trying too hard to articulate herself—clearly it is a *her* and a *self* that is trying to speak—yet she cannot get the words out. We feel the human struggle blended with deep uncanniness when that struggle has a mouse form.

There is obviously some kind of drama going on here. As we are being made aware of it, we are also being made aware of how our understandings of dramatic personae are inevitably human. These are stories of self-discovery, of coming into yourself and your voice, of figuring out ways to address your particular community and crowd. But the point is also, clearly, that the incapacity of a mouse to speak human language will not look like a human drama at all. In its struggles to communicate, a mouse would not produce the stuttered pronoun "I." There is a deliberate mismatch here, not only in terms of species, but of size and scale (human viewers always tower over these exhibits, and have to crouch down to listen to them). Gander invites the mouse-child analogy by having the work voiced by his daughter, but the result is something more like the failure of a Disney character to articulate itself rather than the failures of an actual mouse. In other words, this is not a drama of a mouse in a mouse's world but a drama of the viewer's encounter with their conception of nonhuman animals. Watching a "mouse" trying to articulate her

---

50   Midgley, *Utopias, Dolphins, and Computers*, 110.

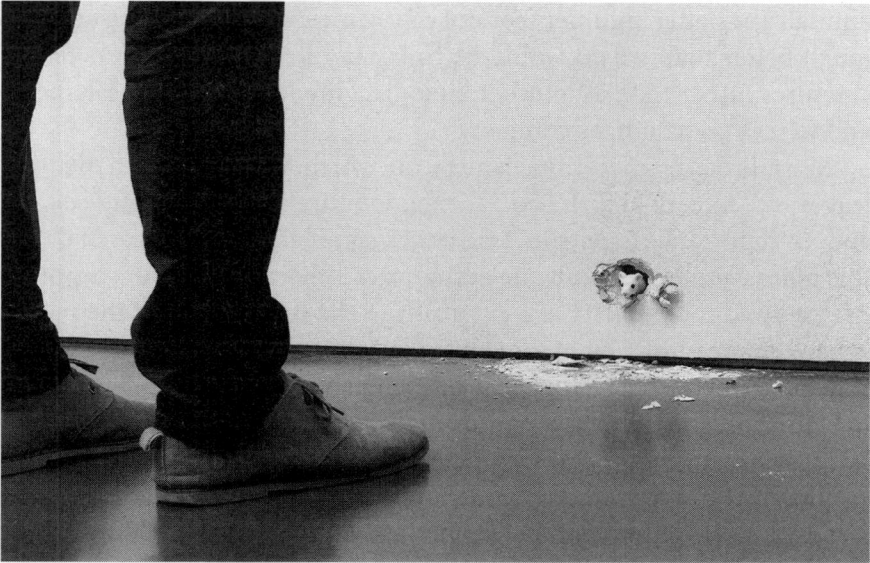

Fig. 11. Ryan Gander, *I. . . I. . . I. . .*, (2019). Close-up installation view. Animatronic mouse, audio. Dimensions variable; duration 11:38. © Ryan Gander; Courtesy the artist and Esther Schipper, Berlin. Photograph by Andrea Rosetti © 2025 Artists Rights Society (ARS), New York / DACS, London.

experience illuminates our own narrow framework of *whose* story gets to count, and why.

Diamond might say that what is happening when we think of a mouse experiencing performance anxiety exposes what is going wrong in the speciesism arguments. The human–nonhuman animal analogy is ignoring basic social facts about human beings. Such "analogies are not simple and straightforward, and it is not clear how far they go." When we look at *animal* rights from the perspective of *human* rights, we are ignoring cultural rules that are so long-standing, so fundamental, they can be hard to see as such. Diamond notes that many species of nonhuman animals practice cannibalism. Chimpanzees such as Tommy are known to do so. But, as a rule, she writes, human beings do not, and the exceptions are notable; we do not eat our dead, our spouse's amputated limbs, or people who die in car accidents, "and even in cases of obvious extreme need, there is very great reluctance." If Singer "admitted that what underlies our attitude to dining on ourselves is the view that a person is not something to eat, he could not focus on the cow's right not to be killed or maltreated, as if that were the heart of it." Quite simply, she observes, speciesism arguments are ignoring truly important differences between what it means to be a human being and what it means to be a nonhuman animal. The better argument for not eating meat and for treating animals much better than we do would be to try to understand them as fellow creatures rather than as another biological life form.[51] It is to see them, and to seek them out, as company.

More broadly, the utilitarianism on which Singer's arguments rest leaves out society and the social sphere entirely, and ignoring society and its importance to people "is to attack significance in human life."[52] At this point, we should recall one of the crucial characteristics of corporate personhood too, which has long involved the repudiation of the public sphere. As we have seen in previous chapters—and one of the key claims in this book—the development of expansive personhood has meant giving up critical public qualities of being a person and swapping in attributes of thingness and property. Singer's utilitarian argument for animal rights, and the legal arguments of NhRP based on Singer's claims, work by not worrying about this loss of culture and the publicness of being a person. Critics (like Diamond) counter that this loss would be devastating, and devastating to animal personhood arguments. Being a person has no meaning without the cultural world made and populated by beings that understand themselves as persons. This is where the moral significance of treating animals well, or poorly, comes from in the first place.

Joseph Margolis, another philosopher, understands personhood in a way that is not strictly legal, yet helpful for seeing what is missing in the arguments for animal legal personhood. For him, personhood is "an artifactual but perfectly natural" transformation of homo sapiens as a species. That change did not simply happen once in our evolutionary history but is "spontaneously yielded in the uniquely complete evolution of its infant members." This sounds a bit technical; he is basically suggesting that our complex language and culture make us a hybrid species, not simply a biological one, and we are remaking ourselves as this hybrid species with every single child's growth, learning, and development. That is why it is right to think of "the formation of persons" as "a 'metaphysical' change, a change of being." We become the kind of persons we are, rather than simply the primates that we *also* are, when we start to master particular languages as very young children and, through those languages, begin to experience ourselves reflexively as the source of what we feel and express. It is this "cultural immersion in an already artifactualized world peopled by apt speakers," those speakers being our

---

51   Diamond, "Eating Meat," 466–8, 474.
52   Ibid., 471.

parents, siblings, and teachers. They are people who have already been transformed in the same way as "suitably 'immersed' primates."[53]

These attributes—language, culture, and the self-reflexivity they enable—are tools that have been useful for us in the world that we are born into, transformed by, and then proceed to remake, again and again.[54] For Margolis, personhood, also, is a tool that we have made useful for ourselves. We might say that personhood is not something to be found like a natural object out in the world, to be meted out to more and more individuals. Rather, it is a concept that we take on and evolve for ourselves as we become who we are. What we do with it, for ourselves and for the nonhuman animals that accompany us on this planet, is up to us.

Coda: Animal Corporate Personhood

Recall Stephen Colbert's quip that if chimpanzees wanted more rights as persons they should form their own corporations. Is he correct? Would animal corporate personhood achieve the aims that Singer, NhRP, and other animal activists want, of seeing sentient animals like chimps, dolphins, and elephants in better places than cages? One answer this chapter implies is that animal legal personhood *already is* animal corporate personhood, even if it is called something else. Effectively, artificial personhood has become indistinguishable from the corporate version, and that legal history is baked into the kinds of arguments that lawyers like Wise make for expanding personhood to animals. And perhaps, if the end result is Happy's and Tommy's freedom, it would not matter if they must become corporate persons in order to realize that freedom.

Yet we have also seen the potential problems with giving corporate personhood to animals. Line drawing, perhaps determined by attributes such as language use or self-recognition in a mirror, will always remain treacherous. Ants have passed the mirror test, cats have not. Artificial personhood for fire ants, property status for kittens: Would we be satisfied with this result? If we complain about the way corporations abuse their power and rights without having responsibility to communities and the public, what will stop the same complaints from arising concerning people representing animals as corporate persons? Meanwhile, all the extralegal dimensions of personhood raised by philosophers including Midgley, Diamond, and Margolis will remain unconsidered.

---

53   Joseph Margolis, ed. Roberta Dreon, *Three Paradoxes of Personhood: The Venetian Lectures* (Milan: Mimesis International, 2017), 35, 46, 85, 79.
54   Ibid., 54.

Finally, is animal legal personhood even necessary to realize these liberty aims? Although it has produced far less media excitement and comes with challenges of its own, the "pet trust" already exists as a working model for how more animals could have standing at the law. Companion animals can be the beneficiaries of these "pet trusts" that are legally established by their owners, a way to protect animals after their owners die and beyond the minimal protections they are given by state and federal legislatures.[55] Typically, the trust will entail the appointment of a legal guardian (in much the same manner as a guardian might be appointed for a minor child) who represents the animals at law.[56] Even NhRP mentions in their legal briefs that these trusts establish that "certain nonhuman animals" have been given limited rights to benefit from the property of a trust.[57] For over thirty years, the US Uniform Probate Code (UPC) has included a statutory pet trust, and as of 2022, all fifty states and Washington, DC, had enacted pet trust laws.[58]

Stronger trusts for more, and more varied, animals would not only give more animals standing but might force law to deal with animals' interests more often and more robustly. As a kind of statute already functioning, it could be a potential opening not only to strengthen animal welfare legislation, but to start altering the way nonhuman animals appear in, and to, the law. In the immediate future, of course, trusts are unlikely to help animals stuck in zoos, like Happy, or privately owned and languishing in cages, like Tommy, or in tanks, like the orcas owned by Sea World. And they are no panacea for industrial farming and the plight of billions of nonhuman animals who suffer in that system. But neither will animal legal personhood touch the most serious issue to animals' well-being, which we have not addressed in this chapter at all. Without wholesale ecosystem protections, personhood for individual chimps or elephants will not be very useful in the first place. That problem we tackle next.

---

55   See Will Kymlicka, "Social Membership: Animal Law beyond the Property/Personhood Impasse," *Dalhousie Law Journal* 40, no. 1 (2017): 123–55.

56   Favre, "Living Property," 1037.

57   NhRP's brief cites a 2008 New York decision holding that "the law now recognizes the creation of trusts for the care of designated domestic or pet animals upon the death or incapacitation of their owner." Brief for Happy, (2020), 28, citing *Feger v. Warwick Animal Shelter*, 59 A.D.3d 68 (2d Dept. 2008), 72.

58   See map of the Animal Legal and Historical Center, Michigan State University: animallaw.info. Schyler P. Simmons, "What Is the Next Step for Companion Pets in the Legal System? The Answer May Lie with the Historical Development of the Legal Rights for Minors," *Texas A & M Law Review* 1 (2013): 277.

4

Tongueless Trees: Standing on Environmental Persons

"As a living entity, possessing fundamental rights"

In January 2024, Utah State Representative Walt Brooks, a Republican and "small-business owner," proposed a bill that would amend Utah's state law. Entitled "H.B. 249, Utah Legal Personhood Amendments," the three-page bill was to the point. Henceforth, government entities would be forbidden "from granting or recognizing personhood in certain categories of nonhumans." The categories of things that could *not* become legal persons included "a body of water," "land," "real property," "atmospheric gases," "weather," or "a plant," among others, as well as "any other member of a taxonomic domain that is not a human being."[1] Noticeably left off his veto-list were corporations, LLCs, ships, states, universities, churches, or many of the other kinds of institutional entities that have long enjoyed some version of legal personhood in the United States—and that the Utah legislature would have had no interest in altering. Also absent from his list were so-called "fetal persons"; indeed, Representative Brooks' official website touts his legislative successes in "protect[ing] the unborn" (the topic of chapter 2 of this book).[2] Before it was voted on, Representative Brooks was confident about its success, opining that "this is commonsense and [he is] a little embarrassed that he even needs to run such a bill."[3] His confidence was well founded: The proposed legislation

---

1   H. B. 249 Utah Legal Personhood Amendments; le.utah.gov.
2   waltbrooks.com.
3   mailchi.mp/d956b6489fd7/week-2-updates-from-representative-brooks.

sailed through the committee stage, passed both Utah houses in February 2024, and was signed into law by the governor in March 2024.

Affected embarrassment aside, some background clarifies why Representative Brooks felt compelled to bring this bill to the legislature, and illuminates his real aim. As of 2024, Utah's Great Salt Lake, the largest saltwater lake in the Western hemisphere, had shrunk to its lowest level ever recorded due to industrial farming, manufacturing, and other irrigation projects, with its total volume and surface area diminished by 50 percent. As its salinity increases every year, experts warn that the lake is on the verge of a great die-off, at which point it becomes a biohazard site, first, to wildlife and eventually to human beings. Toxic dust with arsenic, among other chemicals from the lakebed, will be released, dangerously polluting the air.[4] Exasperated by the lack of legislative progress to stave off this catastrophe, Save Our Great Salt Lake, a nonprofit environmental group affiliated with the Rights of Nature movement, proposed a draft resolution for various cities near the lake. The resolution recognizes that the lake and "its encompassing watershed, and the living and other things naturally present within them, exist and function as an integrated and interdependent community that is understood, respected, and recognized by this Resolution *as a living entity, possessing fundamental rights*" (italics added).[5]

The resolution proposing these fundamental rights for the lake does not mention the phrase "legal personhood." Nowhere in the pronouncement is it suggested that the lake should be recognized as a person. But the implication is clear. A natural object, conceived of as "a living entity with fundamental rights," is, as we have seen throughout this book, another way to talk about legal personhood. As Erin O'Donnell observes, giving a river "legal rights means the law can see the river itself as a legal person, and the river can take legal action to enforce those rights."[6] This is the case whether the environmental entity under discussion is a river, lake, forest, park, or some other defined ecosystem. Language on Save Our Great Salt Lake's website implies a similar personhood position, all in support of grassroots actions to ward off an impending ecological disaster: "We recognize and uphold the sentience, intelligence, and sovereignty of this essential water body."[7] To ensure that this sentient,

---

4   greatsaltlakenews.org.

5   "Great Salt Lake Resolution 26 June 2023," saveourgreatsaltlake.org.

6   Erin O'Donnell, *Legal Rights for Rivers: Competition, Collaboration and Water Governance* (Routledge, 2018), 1.

7   saveourgreatsaltlake.org.

intelligent, sovereign—and, aspirationally, rights-bearing—living entity is protected, the resolution proposes that advisors be appointed and "charged with the responsibility of speaking for the lake and its watershed."[8] And it is this envisioned entity that Representative Brooks wants to forbid, before the resolution is signed by Utah cities, and before the lake is born anew as a sovereign, rights-bearing, albeit very ill, person.

After the first successful granting of environmental legal personhood of the Whanganui River/Te Awa Tupua in New Zealand in 2012, when that body of water was recognized as a living being and a legal entity, the environmental personhood movement has blossomed around the world, from Ecuador to India to the United States and elsewhere. Since then, the movement has made various attempts to instantiate rights for nature—some successful, some provisionally effective, and some not at all. In the United States (to take just one locale), these have included the Tamaqua borough of Pennsylvania passing "a sewage sludge ordinance in 2006," recognizing the borough's ecosystems as legal persons. It has also included the Colorado River's unsuccessful attempt, in 2017, to obtain "judicial recognition of itself as a 'person' with rights to exist and flourish." That same year, the Ponca Nation of Oklahoma successfully passed an anti-fracking statute that recognized the rights of nature, becoming "the first Native American tribe to recognize rights of nature into law in the United States."[9] These political actions fall under different labels, with important differences that we will consider below. Common terms in play include earth jurisprudence, earth law, ecocentric law, rights of nature, wild law, or environmental personhood. Often, they invoke or attempt to align indigenous notions of relation to the natural environment. But, at the broadest level, all share a commitment to foregrounding the environment more centrally and autonomously in law, rejecting the long-standing, historical conceptualizing of nature as merely an expendable, commodifiable resource for human use.

Resolutions like the one on behalf of the Great Salt Lake, as well as similar arguments for the personhood rights of ecosystems in Pennsylvania or of the Colorado River, attempt to recognize the environment and insert it into the law in a very particular way. It is one that Christopher Stone proposed in 1972, in an article we have already touched on: "Should Trees Have Standing? Toward Legal Rights for Natural Objects." That is, should trees and other natural entities be endowed with legal

---

8   "Great Salt Lake Resolution 26 June 2023," ibid.

9   Randall Abate, *Climate Change and the Voiceless: Protecting Future Generations, Wildlife, and Natural Resources* (Cambridge University Press, 2020), 121, 123, 124.

rights that would enable them to go to court and sue in their own right, instead of as the property of some private or public owner? His answer was yes. If Stone could convince courts to think of natural entities such as a park, ocean, river, or forest "as a jural person—the way corporations are 'persons,'" then a case about harms to that natural entity might be able to be heard instead of being tossed out of court. True, he conceded, "streams and forests cannot speak." But "corporations cannot speak either," and courts obviously listen respectfully to what they have to say through their agents, managers, and lawyers. Stone proposed something similar for trees and their ilk. He offered a new way to argue on behalf of "so-called 'natural objects' in the environment." He suggested why courts had to pay attention to these arguments, and to the rights of these "jural persons," as much as to corporate persons, in the process of fairly adjudicating their claims.[10]

The potential of this argument to protect the environment were seen at once. In fact, Stone wrote the article with the specific goal of having it cited in a major upcoming decision. He succeeded: His article was cited that year (albeit in the dissent) in *Sierra Club v. Morton* (1972), a foundational US Supreme Court environmental law decision. In Justice Douglas's words, environmental issues should be able "to be litigated in the name of the inanimate object" under attack. Environmental objects should have legal standing—a legal voice and acknowledgment by the court—"to sue for their own preservation."[11] Although conservationists such as Aldo Leopold previously had made similar philosophical and theoretical claims, Stone's essay, especially once affirmed in Justice Douglas's newsworthy dissent, was one of the first legal procedural steps for environmental personhood. It is generally understood to have launched the "rights of nature" movement. Although it took decades, the arguments eventually generated resolutions and personhood lawsuits on behalf of lakes and rivers—as well as backlash amendments, like the one that was passed recently in the Utah legislature.

Utah Representative Brooks's amendment is hostile to environmental regulation generally—he is no friend of the forests—yet many of the contemporary challenges to environmental personhood come from further left on the political spectrum. As we will see below, the environmental personhood movement has been dismissed as a paltry, "minimalist alternative," or simply an empty "gesture," a "utopian project" that at best

---

10   Christopher D. *Stone, Should Trees Have Standing? Law, Morality, and the Environment*, third edition (Oxford University Press, 2010), xiii, 8, 3.

11   *Sierra Club v. Morton*, 405 US 727 (1972), J. Douglas, dissenting, 741–2.

reinforces the status quo of industrial capitalism.[12] Other critics have challenged the movement as theoretically incoherent, since unable to root out the basic, built-in anthropomorphism at the core of the legal system (a critique developed below). And still others simply fault the theory on pragmatic grounds, arguing that it has been entirely ineffective. In Ecuador, for example, environmental personhood functions "as a kind of posturing on the international stage that is either (a) essentially useless, (b) secondary to the demands of a much more pressing antineoliberalism, or (c) consistently trumped by sets of competing rights."[13] Some critics suggest that other legal strategies seem to work better, could achieve the same results, and are simpler to put into practice.[14] There is truth to each of these challenges.

Yet something has been left out of these critiques of environmental personhood. What better aligns these challenges is what the entire movement owes to artificial corporate personhood and its inherent commodification. Stone's initial law review article was already making this point clearly. As he put it in 1972, giving an environmental object legal standing is like "'incorporating' it so to speak."[15] One of the central claims of this book is inadvertently captured in that very phrase. All forms of expansive personhood—whether fetal, nonhuman animal, robotic, or, as here, environmental—emerge from, and remain intrinsically locked into, the logic of corporate personhood, which has also become the dominant account of legal personhood full stop. Environmental personhood reflects that reality, ever since Stone's article linked aspirational claims of environmental rights and standing to already established corporate ones.

Here we will explore the ramifications of arguments for the rights of nature based on the inevitable corporate personhood model, first by closely reading Stone's essay, and then showing how it neatly aligns with Dr. Seuss's (Theodor Geisel's) *The Lorax* (1971), the celebrated illustrated environmentalist book published just months before Stone began working on his argument. The basic dialectic of Dr. Seuss's children's story shares some of the same challenges of Stone's article: Namely, is

---

12   Peter Burdon, *The Anthropocene: New Trajectories in Law* (New York: Routledge, 2023), 49–51; Bruce Baer Arnold, "Signs of Invisibility: Nonrecognition of Natural Environments as Persons in International and Domestic Law," *International Journal for the Semiotics of Law* 36, no. 2 (2023): 470.

13   Erin Fitz-Henry, "Decolonizing Personhood," in *Wild Law in Practice*, ed. M. Maloney and Peter Burdon (New York: Routledge, 2014), 135.

14   Laura Spitz and E. M. Penalver, "Nature's Personhood and Property's Virtues," *Harvard Environmental Law Review* 45 (2021): 82.

15   Stone, *Should Trees Have Standing?*, 14.

the "Lorax" who "speak[s] for the trees, for the trees have no tongues," a "who" with intention and agency or an "it" without interests or the capacity to act?[16] This question continues to weave its way through later debates, despite the real difference between the binary the law reduces to—person or property—and the amplifications and thoughtful clarifications a work like *The Lorax* generates. We see, in sections that follow, how both the challenge of anthropomorphism and the ideological critiques of environmental personhood revisit this same dynamic, once property has become a key aspect of the artificial person's existence. Despite these difficulties, there still might be value to environmental personhood if it succeeds rhetorically (and on that the verdict is still out). Alternatively, the last section of the chapter suggests why activists of various stripes have turned away from environmental personhood and toward embracing, instead, other kinds of symbols. One is a fused combination of person and place that cannot be rendered as mere thing or property, yet retains a sense of human responsibility toward the environment. Some have used the language of "home" in new ways in order to capture this idea.

In a recent film installation, *The End of carrying All* (2015), contemporary Kenyan and American multimedia artist Wangechi Mutu offers an imaginative portrayal of how that person-home combination might work. A woman (played by Mutu herself) trudges through a CGI depiction of an African savannah, across three immersive screens. She ritualistically stoops to collect things from the ground that grow into consumer junk when placed in the straw basket perched on her head. Over about eight minutes, the basket fills with progressively larger and more implausible icon-like objects, profiled in silhouette: bicycle wheels, discarded satellite dishes, a multistory building. Increasingly hunched over, she makes her journey through a landscape that becomes sparser. A plague of locusts buzzes by. She manages to pass a single tree with difficulty (her load is so heavy). Even the tree dries up as we watch. Finally, the basket sinks down to encompass her too, and she succumbs or is transformed into a slimy, pulsating blob, still slowly undulating as it slides off a cliff. The earth reverberates and rumbles with the blob's slow-moving suicide. Then the film title appears, and the infinite loop restarts.

---

16   Dr. Seuss [Theodor Seuss Geisel], *The Lorax* (New York: Random House, 1971).

Fig. 12. Stills from Wangechi Mutu, *The End of carrying All* (2015). Film stills of three-channel video, duration 10:00. Image courtesy of the artist, Gladstone Gallery, New York and Brussels, Victoria Miro, London, Susanne Vielmetter Los Angeles Projects. All rights reserved.

Mutu's film, installed at the (ever-sinking) Venice Biennale in 2015, pulls no punches about the sources of our current environmental catastrophe and our seemingly doomed response to it. We see who overwhelmingly bears its burdens: women, Africans, the poor, and other people of the Global South whose subsistence livelihood often involves processing endlessly proliferating castoff commodities from the West. She also captures a vicarious sense of what holding onto things—"carrying all"—does to each of us. What does it feel like to hold onto a burden, whether a commodity or our contemporary course on the climate, that will take us nowhere but off the edge of a steep cliff? To watch the film is to watch an allegory of both daily life and our contemporary situation, outsourced to others. And yet the film, too, suggests that there will be a metamorphosis and reckoning, a reabsorption by the earth itself. In its infinite Sisyphean cycle, women will trudge through and collect the waste, and the earth will absorb it, and us all, before the same pattern happens all over again. Becoming absorbed by the film, seeing ourselves in this figure and her transformation and rebirth, provides another way to imagine ourselves in relation to, and taking responsibility for, whatever place we call home. Rather than give that suicidal, pulsating blob a new kind of protected personhood, we might take a step back and think about how to end this cycle for good.

Natural Objects as Vegetative Persons

As Christopher Stone tells the story, his famous law review article was sparked while lecturing in an introductory property law course, as he was describing the historical shifts in what, or who, was "recognized as ownable," and by whom. "Land, movables, ideas, other persons"—all these had at various times been considered ownable. Not only did such shifts change power and privilege, but legal transformation of ownership also altered consciousness. Trying to rouse his first-year law students, he offered a provocation: "'What would a radically different law-driven consciousness look like? . . . One in which Nature had rights . . . How would such a posture *in law* affect a community's view *of itself*?'"[17] Those questions riled up his class. Already from this anecdote, we can see how the question posed in the essay's title ("Should Trees Have Standing?") aimed at another kind of challenge: not just about whether we should endow nature with forms of human rights, but about what it might take to transform how we understand ourselves—"a community's view of itself"—in relation to the environment.

Stone's idea was that a society that recognized the legal rights of rivers "would evolve a different legal system than one which did not," all other rules and laws being equal. That speaks to the most far-reaching aim of his essay, which is that a fairly small, liberalizing change in legal standing requirements, a sort of modification that was already in process, might have truly transformative effects on social and political attitudes to the environment. While much of the essay is engaged with identifying and critiquing what is left out of law's usual way of conceiving of the environment, Stone never loses sight of what could be broadly gained from altering the status quo of property law. Institutional changes that might combat climate change and "our environmental crisis"—Stone, like many environmentalists, was already making this point more than a half century ago—will need a momentous shift in consciousness, one that will depend upon "effecting a radical shift in our feelings about 'our' place in the rest of Nature." If the US Supreme Court could nudge us in that general direction, "it would be a modest move . . . in furtherance of a large goal: the future of the planet as we know it."[18] He is arguing for the power of proceduralist gradualism to transform environmentalism in practice.

To develop this argument, Stone relies on the classic "widening circle" argument, versions of which we have seen in every argument for

---

17   Stone, *Should Trees Have Standing?*, xi.
18   Ibid., 23, 27, 31.

expansive personhood in *The Problem of Personhood*. These arguments incorporate a number of recurring elements: a commitment to "perfect equality" (rather than a status- or role-based model), a radically reductive or empty account of the person, an equation of human and artificial personhood, and the explicit forgoing of the public qualities of the person (replaced with qualities of objecthood or thingness). Stone's argument shares all these expected features. The first four pages of the essay alone make the point that the notion of legal personhood is an utterly historically constructed category, and, at different moments, the categories of "objects" to be owned, versus "persons" who could own, were radically different. For instance, he observes that it was only as recently as 1967 that children were guaranteed certain basic legal rights in the United States: "We have been making persons of children" in law, a process that has also happened at different times "with prisoners, aliens, women (especially of the married variety), the insane, African Americans, fetuses, and Native Americans." A few paragraphs later he adds Jews and Chinese people to this list.[19] Although he allows that not everything in the environment should have full human rights, his focus is not to work out those discriminations, nor is there a sense that the differences between, say, fetuses, non-white people, and "the insane" are relevant to the personhood category. As Ngaire Naffine observes, Stone's account resembles the legal philosopher Hans Kelsen's, for whom legal persons are "purely legal norms without innate capacities of reason, soul, or human form."[20]

It is precisely this hollowed-out version of personhood that enables Stone to effortlessly align trees with corporate persons for, admittedly, practical ends. Corporations of various stripes appear very early in his article. Not "only matter in human form" has been understood as possessing rights. "The world of the lawyer is peopled with inanimate right-holders: trusts, corporations, joint ventures, municipalities, Subchapter R partnerships, and nation-states" as well as ships and churches. We have forgotten that the process of becoming "accustomed" to these sorts of "jarring" persons has taken generations, he explains. Expanding rights protections to some new entity is invariably "a bit unthinkable" at the time, but just as corporations, African Americans, and children are now treated as legal persons, so might natural entities like trees and rivers be someday soon. In various ways, he sees the situation of the corporation as analogous to that of natural entities. One might

---

19   Ibid., 1, 2.
20   Ngaire Naffine, "Legal Personality and the Natural World: On the Persistence of the Human Measure of Value," *Journal of Human Rights and the Environment* 3 (2012): 82.

object that "streams and forests cannot speak," but "corporations cannot speak" either.[21] Just as an agent of some kind speaks for the corporation, so would a guardian for streams and forests speak for those entities.

But this same analogy of corporations to streams and trees also starts producing difficulties for Stone, ones that need to be managed so that the entire argument does not falter. All the entities that have been endowed with personhood in some way or another involve human beings or their intentional social or political creations. This is obvious with gender, age, and racial categories of expansive personhood, and more complicated with fetal ones. For example, ships, churches, corporations, and their like have been endowed with an "independent jural life," as Stone puts it, because doing so was understood to protect and support the human social purposes that created those entities in the first place. This is what would allow, say, a joint venture or a municipal corporation to raise money and take on large-scale operations that would have been much more difficult, expensive, and risky for any individual to do on their own.[22] None of these characteristics or reasons are relevant to environmental persons, who exist with us but not because of us.

Yet Stone cannot really do without the example of artificial personhood, particularly the nation-state and corporate variety. This really *is* the best example for his argument, the closest possible alignment he can come up with. Corporate trustees or governmental representatives, he suggests, are like environmental guardians. This move becomes especially apparent in his discussion of evaluating "the needs of the river or forest" in a guardian's charge. Here he must make a critical point about needs, wants, and interests. He acknowledges that one objection to his guardianship approach might be that a committee of human beings would be unable to determine what a river or forest needs; "indeed, the very concept of 'needs,' . . . could be used here only in the most metaphorical way." But he rejects this argument. "Natural objects can communicate their wants (needs) to us" unambiguously, in the way, for example, Stone "can judge with more certainty and meaningfulness whether and when my lawn wants (needs) water" than could the US attorney general judge a want or need on behalf of the country. "The lawn tells him that it wants water" in its dryness, yellowness, and bald spots; in contrast, "how does 'the United States' communicate to the Attorney General?" Directors of corporations make similar kinds of assertions about when "'the corporation' wants dividends declared." Stone's point is that these kinds of

---

representational actions are entirely commonplace and not wildly different from one another. We are evaluating and imagining the desires of "others" all the time, and quite often "these 'others'" are "metaphysical" entities whose desires are not rigorously verifiable or, at any rate, are less able to be known than the dryness of a lawn.[23]

This is a challenging turn in Stone's argument, and one worth spending a little time unpacking. Again, the problem is how to get past the fact that all other forms of expansive personhood, including all the ones he mentions, are *of* humans or are created or intended *by* humans (states, corporations, churches, and so on). An ocean is not. And the way around that, for him, is to emphasize the *skepticism* of perceiving the desires of a corporation, or ocean, or tree. That is, the ease or difficulty of confidently assessing an entity's needs (whether a corporation's or a tree's) becomes a proxy for establishing the standing or status of that entity. A knowledge claim (how or whether you know) is being used in service of (or to substitute for) a claim about what something inherently is. This kind of substitution has long been a common part of legal, cultural, and political discourse concerning corporations. Throughout the late nineteenth century and into the twentieth, worries about how to know what a corporation was intending were frequently expressed as concerns about what these (monstrous, octopus-like) things really were.[24] Here, Stone is flipping this dynamic around, stabilizing environmental personhood with the idea that the guardian of a forest "could venture with more confidence that his client wants the smog stopped" than could corporate directors "assert that 'the corporation' wants dividends declared."[25] He is invoking the instability of entities like corporations and states to bring in trees as entities whose needs are (relatively) straightforward. For that reason, they are entities that could and should be endowed with legal standing.

The crucial point is that corporations, and other corporate-like entities, are a necessary transitional entity in Stone's argument, a way to link persons and environmental objects by gradual analogy. And, as a rhetorically forceful way to give environmental objects a real value with which they might compete with the consolidation of capital, there is nothing to fault here. The rights of nature movement has used this alignment to good rhetorical and political effect to combat powerful multinational firms, as Stone surely hoped they would. Many American rights of nature

---

23   Ibid., 11.

24   Lisa Siraganian, *Modernism and the Meaning of Corporate Persons* (Oxford University Press, 2020), 23.

25   Stone, *Should Trees Have Standing?*, 11.

initiatives emerged "in direct opposition to corporate power," specifically to corporations trying to start projects "harmful to local communities," notes Gwendolyn Gordon.[26] But it also does not take much effort to spot all the ways in which the analogy to corporations does not hold up. A corporation can, in certain instances, intend to fulfill its "needs" and "wants." But to speak of the corporation in that way only makes sense if we can ask of someone—some human agent acting for the corporation—and receive a reliable answer as to why the corporation is acting in that way, why it needs to declare dividends to fulfill some need.[27] In other words, human values and intentions are not absent from a corporation's actions in that scenario. They are at the beating heart of it, even if the actual human beings calling the shots can be difficult to identify. Likewise, a corporation's "need" to pay out dividends (or not) only makes sense because it redounds to some set of human individuals who will financially benefit (or not), human beings who ultimately profit from owning the corporation's stock. Human beings are the source of and motivation for all these corporate arrangements, even if our language and our ease with corporate personification obscures that reality.

Stone's argument, in contrast, relies on personifying artificial, nonintentional entities, and suggests just how critical and dominant a mode of personhood that was becoming. It also requires some basic transformations of notions of desires and wants. Speaking for trees, writes Stone, is like speaking for "legal incompetents—human beings who have become vegetative."[28] Trees, in other words, are like human beings who have become more plantlike—who have lost their ability to speak their desires and needs. But that point entails, rather obviously, a huge conceptual leap. When we conflate a human being's desires with a tree's, we must objectify and reduce desires or needs to the most basic of physical requirements. That is how to make the desires and ambitions of human subjectivity look no different from a tree's biochemical fertilizer demands. The challenge then becomes not how the human realm relates to the natural world, but rather, where to locate any given entity (whether corporation, human, or tree) on a new spectrum we have spotted in previous chapters: human as vegetable at one end, and vegetable as person at the other. While that spectrum includes individual particulars with moral value, it leaves out everything else that could be (and once was)

---

26   Gwendolyn Gordon, "Environmental Personhood," *Columbia Journal of Environmental Law* 43, no. 1 (2019): 59, n. 46.

27   Siraganian, *Corporate Persons*, 14–30.

28   Stone, *Should Trees Have Standing?*, 8.

characteristic of personhood: our roles in society, our potential capacity for reasoned thought, and our sense of ourselves as reflective, self-constituting beings in a culture we create.[29]

Who Lifted the Lorax?

Environmental personhood arguments like Stone's work by activating a familiar and powerful set of claims: that global society, and law in parallel, is on a path of expansive inclusiveness, that each subsequent development and addition of another entity endowed with "an independent jural life" initially disturbs many, even seeming at first "a bit unthinkable." But after time passes and habits have changed, the idea of personhood for African Americans, women, children, and corporations (among others) becomes accepted and hard to imagine otherwise. "Until the rightless thing receives its rights, we cannot see it as anything but a *thing* for the use of 'us'—those who are holding rights at the time."[30] Giving rights to the environment could then look like merely the next step in this process, and we should expect that those feelings of absurdity would emerge when it comes to assigning rights to "things" like trees and rivers. This expansive personhood model for the environment relies on all the ideas we have seen throughout the book: a widening circle of inclusiveness, an acknowledgment of the felt disruptiveness of the claims, and the incorporation as persons of previously conceptualized things. Stone explicitly introduces thingness in his essay through the invocation of "natural object as . . . legal incompetents," in the process presuming a spectrum with humans as vegetables on one end and vegetables as persons on the other (they vary in degree but not in kind). And so, at this point, one might ask: What exactly is wrong with this way of seeing ourselves in the world? That is, as things that have become persons?

The creature of the "Lorax," who declares, "I speak for the trees, for the trees have no tongues," lives on this spectrum and helps us see why, as affecting as it is, the Lorax's (and Stone's) vision of environmentalism cannot show us how to act. Here, we will take what might look at first like a detour, a study of Dr. Seuss's children's book *The Lorax*, as illustrating Stone's basic points. But it also serves as a way to articulate some of the

---

29   Antonia LoLordo, "Introduction: The Concept of a Person from Antiquity to the Twenty-First Century," in *Persons: A History*, ed. Antonia LoLordo (Oxford University Press, 2019), 2–3.

30   Stone, *Should Trees Have Standing?*, 2, 3.

inherent problems with the working model of environmental personhood. Stone's article itself shares much of the same logic of Dr. Seuss's book, so much so that the messages of the two works sometimes have been conflated and swapped, even by US judges. The most prominent instance of that substitution occurred in *Cowpasture River Preservation Association v. United States Forest Service* (2018), in which a decision by the US Court of Appeals for the Fourth Circuit ends with a citation of *The Lorax*: "We trust the US Forest Service to 'speak for the trees, for the trees have no tongues.'"[31] Rather than referring to Stone's law review article, or to Justice Douglas's comments in *Sierra Club v. Morton* (the early US Supreme Court dissent that admiringly refers to Stone's article), *Cowpasture* simply quotes Dr. Seuss's book as if we are all in agreement that environmental governmental agencies speak for the trees. (The US Supreme Court, at any rate, did not agree, overturning *Cowpasture* two years later.)[32]

The Lorax is an explicit allegory of capitalist production, resource exploitation, excessive consumption, and environmental devastation, all put in motion by the faceless, hidden "Once-ler," whom we see only in the form of his skinny, Grinch-like arms and hands (sometimes, too, his golden, predatory eyes blink open). Those green hands are invariably counting money, making products, using tools, or operating increasingly sophisticated machines. The Once-ler explains how he manufactured the seemingly frivolous but popular Sneeds out of the astonishing fluffy, pastel-colored Truffula trees. After he chops down the first Truffula tree, the Lorax pops up in its place, declaiming from the stump, demanding that the Once-ler stop. If not, the Lorax will have to send away the many creatures relying on the Truffula trees, animals unable to survive without their habitat. Of course, the Once-ler ignores these warnings, the ecosystem collapses, and the Lorax also leaves—although how he manages to depart turns out to be notably odd. After this devastation, the Once-ler finally comes to realize that, if the boy who paid for this story—"you"— plants and nurtures the Once-ler's last Truffula seed, environmental catastrophe might be reversed.

Theodor Geisel, writing as Dr. Seuss, considered the book one of his projects of "straight propaganda," prompted after he witnessed overdevelopment around his wealthy San Diego home—a two-hour drive down the California coast from where Stone, at virtually the same moment, was teaching his law students at University of Southern

---

31   *Cowpasture River Preservation Association v. Forest Service*, 911 F.3d 150 (2018).
32   *United States Forest Service v. Cowpasture River Pres. Association,* 140 S. Ct. 1837, 207 L. Ed. 2d 186 (2020).

California to imagine legal rights for natural objects.[33] Geisel was determined to write a book that avoided dogmatism and preaching to his
audience, a problem with the ecological-minded books he had been
reading, which he found "dull."[34] A 1970 safari in Kenya sparked his creativity and he quickly drafted the entire story after watching a herd of
elephants cross a hill, but how exactly to draw the title character? On
that detail he was stuck. Should the Lorax resemble a gopher, a robot, or
maybe a (big or small) green alien?[35] Finally, he came up with the round-
ish orange fellow, bald and with a bushy walrus moustache. One recent
statistical study suggests that, more than any other creature or animal,
real or imagined, the version of the Lorax Geisel landed on resembles the
patas monkey in Kenya, which lives symbiotically with a type of scrubby
acacia tree.[36]

It is intriguing that Geisel struggled to envision the Lorax's basic physical characteristics and final form until well after the narrative was drafted.
No doubt, we should be cautious about putting too much interpretive
weight on an artist's creative process. But the uncertainty of the Lorax's
form feels more urgent when we see it posed as the introductory frame of
the book: "What *was* the Lorax? / And why was it there?" The story begins
in a desolate hell-scape of scabby twigs as trees, with a curious boy—
"you"—peering up at a crooked sign: "The Street of the Lifted Lorax."
Thus, before we know anything else, we know that the Lorax is, or is
like, an extinct species of animal, with the adjectival "Lifted" serving as a
kind of scientific species description, like "Tufted Titmouse" or "Howler
Monkey." Yet we also learn that the Lorax memorializes a nearly mythical
event: the occasion when the Lorax was "lifted." If you look closely, you
might see the spot where the Lorax briefly declaimed to the Once-ler
"before somebody lifted the Lorax away." We do not yet know more about
who or what "it" is: Why was it lifted and taken somewhere? The *how* of
its lifting also turns out to be an open question. The Once-ler's subsequent
story provides answers, but something about the Lorax's essential mobility turns out to be the most ambiguous aspect of the tale, and seems key
to answering the question of just "what" "it," the Lorax, is or was.

33   Quoted in Judith Morgan and Neil Morgan, *Dr. Seuss and Mr. Geisel: A Biography* (New York: Random House, 1995), 209.

34   Jonathan Cott, *Pipers at the Gates of Dawn: The Wisdom of Children's Literature*
(Minneapolis: University of Minnesota Press, 1981), 30.

35   Brian Jay Jones, *Becoming Dr. Seuss: Theodor Geisel and the Making of an American Imagination* (New York: Dutton, 2019), 356.

36   Nathaniel J. Dominy, Sandra Winters, Donald E. Pease, and James P. Higham,
"Dr Seuss and the Real Lorax," *Nature Ecology and Evolution* 2, no. 8 (2018): 1196–98.

This unanswered question posed at the start motivates the boy to seek out the Once-ler and to learn his story. What we learn, all from the boy's perspective, is a tale of capitalist exploitation in which the Once-ler sets the terms of the relationships, even as to how the story will be told. Hiding in his decrepit penthouse and having regressed to a kind of subsistence level of living, including sewing his own clothes, the Once-ler is only willing to tell the story of the Lorax—and to you alone—for an eccentric asking price. The currency he proposes suggests the older mechanisms of barter (it includes a nail and a snail shell), but he counts the pieces carefully and hides them away. You have paid to hear the tale, and only you will receive it through the Whisper-ma-Phone, the Once-ler's proprietary technology that retains the Lorax's story under his copyright control, like a form of anti-piracy software. Once a capitalist, always a capitalist. By the story's end, the cost of the tale you bought will turn out to have another benefit, obligation, and cost, in the form of the last Truffula seed, which you must nurture. You are given charge of the seed by the Once-ler on the story's final page.

The Once-ler's story is utterly familiar and depressing yet nonetheless captivating, a tale of settler capitalism complete with the fantasy of a pristine land untouched by human hands as well as the ingenious technology that will exploit it. This capitalism becomes a dominant motif of the entire book, less something to fight against or overthrow than a happenstance to manage. As Eliza Darling shrewdly observes, despite Geisel's "remarkable sensibility about the relentless impulse toward capitalist growth," the book, in the end, with the promise of a future emerging from the last Truffula seed, transforms the destroyed ecosystem into "nature recommoditized through produced scarcity and resource management." This is a "consumer-oriented, capital-friendly solution" that demands little adaptation of the status quo "postwar liberal agenda."[37]

In support of that point, consider the discussion between the Lorax and the Once-ler about the most suitable way to manage the Truffula forests, a discussion that is entirely framed as a problem of resource management balanced with commodity production. Upon emerging from a stump, the Lorax's first complaint is that the Once-ler is wasting trees by over-producing a seemingly useless commodity—a thing called a "Thneed" that looks like a piece of absurdly unwearable clothing. We might call this the against-fast-fashion argument. And the Once-ler, for

---

37   Eliza Darling, "The Lorax Redux: Profit Biggering and Some Selective Silences in American Environmentalism," *Capitalism, Nature, Socialism* 12, no. 4 (2001): 55, 57.

his part, defends his breakneck rate of production, as do many clothing corporations today. He is producing something people find quite useful: Its uses are truly myriad, from clothing to home goods to bicycle seat covers. The Once-ler defends the commodity in ways that we, schooled enough in classical liberal economics, can easily rehearse: The uses of a thing are not determined by what the producer determines or plans for it, but by what the purchaser finds useful about it and so is willing to pay for it. This microeconomic argument baffles the Lorax, who rightly declares that the Once-ler has become insatiably greedy, but wrongly predicts that nobody would be silly enough to buy a Thneed. On the very next page, someone does eagerly buy a Thneed, to the Once-ler's delight. The Thneed's exchange value, and not its use value, leads to the Truffula trees being clear cut with the Once-ler's disturbingly effective, patent-protected technology. The Lorax loses that round—and all the next rounds too.

The Lorax is unable to produce any successful counterargument to the Once-ler's capitalist logic; he only has recourse to special pleading. He makes some version of the point that the combined exchange value of all the Thneeds does not equal the true value of the Truffula Trees. There is some extra cost (in economic terms, a "negative externality") that has not been worked into the price of the fast-fashion Thneeds, but he fails to express a convincing enough reason why this means that the Once-ler should stop production. To the Lorax's complaint that the cute Bar-ba-lots are starving and must leave to forage elsewhere because they no longer have enough Truffula Fruit, the Once-ler's response is regret— he is saddened—but sadness is no reason to alter his future actions. The market is a force that cannot be ignored or overpowered because, he points out, all businesses must grow to survive.

The Once-ler's refrain is to abdicate accountability for his actions, which are relocated to the relentless business motive: He did not intend to destroy the habitat, "But I had to grow bigger. So bigger I got." The grammatical structure of those two sentences nicely captures the impetus and the refusal to admit culpability: not "I grew," but "bigger I got." Economic growth just happened, because it had to. And as the Lorax's complaints about environmental degradation continue (the smog-filled smoke dirtying the air, the industrial goo polluting the pond), the Once-ler maintains his liberal rectitude. He has his rights, he claims, and he intends to keep growing to realize a social good, processing the trees into a commodity that everyone needs. The sale of Thneeds proves it. Total economic and market collapse occurs a few pages later, after the final

Truffula Tree is harvested and production ceases, the land's resources exhausted.

In Stone's essay, this same basic problem, along with its apparent intractability, motivates the necessity of "'personifying' the environment, from the point of damage calculations." Here is where we can see Stone taking on the economics lessons, and their limitations, that he had absorbed during his brief stint as a Law and Economics Fellow at the University of Chicago in the early 1960s, at the moment when that movement was beginning to blossom there (and from there, spreading everywhere). Courts struggle to deal "with the full social cost" of our economic activities, Stone writes. But if, instead, the environmental entity is "itself the focus of these damages" by "'incorporating' it so to speak," then the legal system could more effectively and fully evaluate and measure the damages that have been wrought. Whereas his "economist friends" might only think to measure the environmental damages of the present moment, nature's "guardian would urge before the court injuries not presently cognizable," those potential injuries both to the environment now and to the generations of human beings and other animals living there. They might not be "at present, economically measurable losses," but coming up with some attempt to estimate their future value is better than not valuing them at all.[38] Perhaps the Lorax should have said *that* to the Once-ler.

But good arguments that fail to convince, along with profound misunderstandings, are the pattern Geisel wants to portray. When the Once-ler admits to you, near the book's conclusion, that he couldn't figure out the meaning of the Lorax's final memorial, that pile of rocks with the word "UNLESS" in bold letters, Stone's reasoning is dramatized. Why was the Once-ler stumped? Because, as Stone writes, "our experience in environmental matters has been a continual discovery that our acts have caused more long-range damage than we were able to appreciate at the outset." Literary scholar Rob Nixon has dubbed this ubiquitous phenomenon "slow violence": environmental ruin that occurs "gradually and out of sight," scattered across different locations temporally and spatially (and unfairly to the global poor) and so seeming more invisible than spectacular.[39] Because of that inevitable delay in recognizing and evaluating environmental damages, those negative externalities, Stone reasons

---

38   Stone, *Should Trees Have Standing?*, 13–16.

39   Rob Nixon, *Slow Violence and the Environmentalism of the Poor* (Cambridge, MA: Harvard University Press, 2011), 2.

that it would be better to estimate their costs "on the 'high side.'"[40] The Once-ler, too, finally understands something like this, and sees what the Lorax was trying to convey to him, although only after a very long delay. It is only "now that *you're* here, the word of the Lorax seems perfectly clear." The delay of your arrival (of future generations), the delay of the Once-ler telling the story and, while telling it, finally comprehending the meaning of the Lorax's words, has tragic, cumulative costs to the ecosystem. The Lorax, long ago, directed away all the other creatures to protect them because he could not successfully argue with the Once-ler. That explanation (where did the animals go?) seems to be a euphemism for extinction, necessary in a children's book. The Lorax failed to convey the actual costs of Thneed manufacturing to the Once-ler in time, because the Once-ler's arguments (prioritizing economic growth and liberal rights) did not require estimating such costs.

This problem of how to appreciate the Lorax's arguments in the present, and the difficulty the Lorax has convincing the Once-ler to take them on board, as potentially having an impact on his actions in the moment, is directly a function of the Lorax's indeterminate personhood. It is true, on the one hand, that the Lorax is depicted as a humanoid person in all sorts of ways—especially more so than the Sneed consumer, the Once-ler, or his family of industrious workers, none of whose faces or full bodies we see. We presume that those capitalists are human-like, yet their bodies are always obscured behind walls, machinery, or Thneeds, with only their productive limbs visible. The Lorax and the animals he is protecting are anthropomorphized and expressive, their faces (along with "yours") carefully depicted as exasperated and suffering. The Once-ler also addresses the Lorax by name and in human terms—Dad, guy, he, him. Most importantly, the Lorax also possesses those special characteristics of human personality: voice, speech, language, rational argument, and writing, as well as the ability to put his plans into action when he sends the distressed animals away.

Yet, on the other hand, the Lorax's human-like qualities are repeatedly questioned, as with the opening description of him as a "what," who did not fly away on his own volition but was lifted. The Once-ler thinks he somewhat resembles a man but admits that to "describe him? . . . That's hard. I don't know if I can." When the Lorax emerges to speak for the tongueless trees, he is capturing the situation that Stone describes of treating "natural objects as one does the problems of legal incompetents—human beings

---

40   Stone, *Should Trees Have Standing?*, 16.

who have become vegetative."[41] In this way the Lorax seems a bit like a tree himself, or maybe like a legal incompetent, or maybe even a corporate person, with his sneezes like sawdust, his voice laced with the remains of the trees chopped down and commodified, trees he now speaks for. Instead of a human guardian for the trees, he seems, at such moments in the text, like a kind of natural object blended with a human being, a construction for the capitalist legal world of the Once-ler.

This hybrid combination of traits reaches an intriguing climax after the Once-ler chops down the last Truffula Tree. Here, finally, we are provided some kind of explanation for the strange phrase "Lifted Lorax." In one sense, he leaves on his own accord, deeply saddened by what he was witnessing. The Lorax "lifted himself by the seat of his pants." Then "he heisted himself and took leave of this place." He is forced to abandon the land after sending the animals away, because the Once-ler would not listen to or negotiate with him. But even this sentence makes clear that there is something bifurcated or strange about the Lorax's agency, a kind of self-splitting between his will and his body. He cannot simply leave the way either animals or human beings can, picking a direction and moving toward it. Instead, he must literally lift one part of his body with the other, as if his seat, his body, could not move on its own. This is silly, of course, and a kind of physical impossibility, like the hypothetical skyhook, or lever that leverages without a stable fulcrum. Yet the promised suggestion at the start of the book, that we would learn about the time before the Lorax was lifted away by someone, is both fulfilled and also made very strange, since at least literally the Lorax is the somebody who did the lifting of himself.

What to make of this solution? Charming and whimsical, the Lorax in the end might simply be a little magical, resembling other Dr. Seuss creatures (like the Cat in the Hat) who can bend time and space. Alternatively, we might understand the Lorax's strangely bifurcated agency as a portrayal of a trust or guardianship, with all the limitations such guardianship entails. As a trustee for someone or something else, the Lorax can only act in certain ways and for certain prescribed reasons. In Stone's sense, he would be a constructed legal person who represents the Truffula Trees and other natural objects to the Once-ler since, in this stripped-down land, there is no court or other governmental authority to appeal to. When the natural entities and animals have all been destroyed or forced out, he has no one left to speak for, and so has nothing left to

---

41   Stone, *Should Trees Have Standing?*, 8.

say. The Lorax is silent and leaves nothing behind, except for his last stone memorial to an alternative future, which spells out UNLESS. In a sense, he is like the lawyer-guardian in Stone's essay who was speaking for a "legal incompetent." With no one left to represent, the Lorax's guardianship, too, is finished.

But the Lorax is not only a human-like guardian for the trees. In the furry flesh, he is also an *instance* of artificial personhood for trees, who will forever rely on responsible humans to mean and act. That is the importance of the description of him as the "Lifted Lorax." He also personifies the perilous category of a speechless endangered species that needs human beings to protect it, even as human beings' relentless economic activity destroys its habitat. Like such a species, the Lorax is dependent on however we choose to act and to justify our actions. And, relatedly, the Lorax also seems an indirect way to challenge, by mirroring, the Once-ler's irresponsibility, to imply that *this* resource exploitation is what abdicating your agency really looks like. The Once-ler refuses to see himself as choosing to increase business, for example; he merely passively accepts the basic drive of capitalism as a motive he is helpless to resist, growing bigger as capitalist companies must. Of course, this logic is fallacious. It is the Once-ler's actions that turn the Lorax into the "Lifted Lorax," in the process of selling innumerable Thneeds and increasing his profits. But as fallacious as it might be, it is the argument that defeats the Lorax.

Perhaps, then, one final reason for the Lorax's strange status as simultaneously humanoid, animal, fantastical, and treelike—sort of but not fully a man—might be to underscore that the Lorax is ultimately only a reflection, a personification, of how human beings increasingly understand themselves. If the Lorax does not possess full agency, it is because, in part, the people he is modeled on are renouncing their full personhood too, replacing it with the thin, flat, property-like expansive personhood we are seeing examples of all around us. The Lorax, in other words, reflects the Once-ler's abdications of his obligations as a person. Both simply depart from the world in the end, leaving only tiny signs of abdicated responsibility—a word and a seed—behind.

Inescapable Ventriloquism

Environmental personhood, more obviously than fetal or nonhuman animal personhood, is artificial to its core, constructed and modeled on a version of human personhood but without any humans actually present. We see that with Stone's centering of the corporate person in his account of personhood for natural objects. Geisel dramatizes this scenario through the Lorax's strange form of mobility and split agency, creating a chimera or incomplete person, "sort of a man" still full of sawdust from the chopped-down Truffula stump out of which he popped. For legal theorists and activists following this path, the challenge has become how to envision rights for the environment without finding themselves stuck at one of two poles. The options are as follows: either an entirely artificial personhood that is merely a legal construct (and so can be easily discarded in favor of human beings and their rights), or a fully anthropomorphized person—but with questionable and fantastical features, like the Lorax's self-heisting. A version of this dilemma appears in the controversy over the anti-personhood bill passed in Utah. An ultra-conservative lawmaker wanting to outlaw personhood from any "member of a taxonomic domain that is not a human being" battles environmental activists who understand the Great Salt Lake as a rights-bearing living entity, and who "recognize and uphold the sentience, intelligence, and sovereignty of this essential water body." That is the face-off in its starkest form.

Numerous thinkers have tried to resolve this debate. Their resolution often has centered on the problem of anthropomorphism, and efforts to avoid or defeat it. The attempt has been to support and base rights for the environment in something more substantial than artificial personhood, but without transforming these legal entities into distorted, pseudo-human beings, like the Lorax, along the way. Critics have countered that this maneuver is simply not possible, that the anthropomorphism is inescapable, just as the Lorax, however he might appear to depart into the clouds, ultimately becomes a "Lifted Lorax" because of the Once-ler's actions. As literary critic Donald Pease observes, the Once-ler even takes over the absent Lorax's role by the story's end, "speak[ing] for the Lorax just as the Lorax had formerly spoken on behalf of the trees."[42] The Lorax manifests the seemingly inescapable anthropomorphic gesture, now come full circle. One early critic of Stone's essay put it this way: "Ultimately, guardianship status will only be sought by those who value the natural object in question. There seems to be no escape from homocentricity, only a broadening of what human interests encompass."[43] In other words, it appears that there is always a human being speaking for someone or something else, in the end.

---

42   Donald Pease, *Theodor Seuss Geisel* (Oxford University Press, 2010), 139.

43   James Huffman, "Trees as a Minority," *Environmental Law* 5 (1974): 200.

I agree that such anthropomorphism is inescapable. But what that means still needs teasing out. In sketching out this dispute here, we will see how the arguments seeking to push environmental rights beyond this anthropomorphic personhood framework repeatedly return to an artificial, property-centered, and ultimately corporate form of personhood in the process. Even when the explicit language of personhood is relinquished or removed, this form of the person lurks in the background, as it lurks in every form of expansive personhood we have seen. Anthropomorphism and corporate personification start to look more like an entwined process that proponents of environmental rights understandably struggle to resist. And the challenge of anthropomorphism appears in the work of legal and cultural critics who generally favor more rights or considerations for the environment but are skeptical about personhood as the way to secure these rights.

The transformative act of legislation in New Zealand, in 2017, which gave rights to the Whanganui River itself, is frequently examined as a case study in this debate. In 2012, the government of New Zealand and the Māori people of the Whanganui River reached a revolutionary agreement in which the long river, which the Māori call "Te Awa Tupua" and which for almost two hundred years had been exploited and degraded by the colonial British government, would be granted a kind of legal personhood.[44] Then, in 2017, legislation granted this natural resource an actual legal identity. According to the enabling Settlement Act of 2017, "Te Awa Tupua is a legal person and has all the rights, powers, duties, and liability of a legal person."[45] Furthermore, the act declares that the indigenous Māori people of the region—the Te Pou Tupua—are the only ones authorized to exercise those rights, power, and duties "on behalf of" the river. As scholars observed, the new legal standing of the river attempts to "reject the very framing of personhood as something ascribed by humans to nonhumans."[46] It is envisioned as "a new kind of personhood," one that can be added to the list of humans and corporations.[47] Personhood for the Whanganui/Te Awa Tupua was, arguably, a culmination of Stone's project, which took nearly four decades to come to fruition.

---

44   Elaine Hsiao, "Whanganui River Agreement: Indigenous Rights and Rights of Nature," *Environmental Policy and Law* 42, no. 6 (2012): 371–2.

45   *Te Awa Tupua (Whanganui River Claims Settlement) Act 2017*, section 14. Quoted in Simon Sneddon, *Unlocking Environmental Law* (Routledge, 2024), 46.

46   Rafi Youatt, *Interspecies Politics: The Nature of States* (University of Michigan Press, 2020), 98.

47   Gordon, "Environmental Personhood," 87.

Yet, from the start, there was also some uneasiness about this development from legal scholars in New Zealand and Australia. Though supportive of the act in many ways, they queried just how revolutionary or progressive this river as "legal person" would be. Looking closely at the political and cultural context of the act, Katherine Sanders describes how the granting of legal personhood to the river was in part a reparative acknowledgment of "colonial wrongs" but in the context of "a unitary state . . . constrained by the unwillingness of the majority to acknowledge or address Māori claims to political authority," let alone willing to transfer property ownership of the river to the Māori.[48] From that perspective, she argues, the granting of personhood to the river should be better understood as a political compromise, a way for indigenous and colonial states to "share" sovereignty, although without New Zealand actually giving back any appropriated territory. The accustomed notions of property remain functioning in the background as a basic "organizing principle." Nor does such a compromise require that critical details be clarified, ones that might articulate how exactly the river will be managed in practice.

Jade-Ann Reeves and Timothy D. Peters examine, through a theoretical lens, the same New Zealand river and the 2017 act, coming to an analogous and discomfiting conclusion. Instead of radically shifting anthropocentric conceptions of nature, legal personhood for the river might be reinforcing those very conceptions. At best, legal personhood in this situation was "deployed as a mediating device" between the Western commodification of nature and the indigenous Māori "intrinsic and interconnected relationship with nature." Carefully reading the act, they show how it reframes the river not in interconnected, indigenous terms, but on the model of a Christian conception of a human being, with separate body and soul. "Rather than representing a shift" in conceptualizations of and relations to the environment, ascribing personhood to the river supports all-too-human "anthropocentric norms." It would be better, Reeves and Peters conclude, "to reimagine" our relation to nature "beyond personhood" and beyond law's various, inevitably human institutions.[49]

Margaret Davies's recent, thought-provoking *EcoLaw: Legality, Life, and the Normativity of Nature* (2022) tries to do just that, supporting

---

48   Katherine Sanders, "'Beyond Human Ownership'? Property, Power and Legal Personality for Nature in Aotearoa New Zealand," *Journal of Environmental Law* 30, no. 2 (2018): 208, 222.

49   Jade-Ann Reeves and Timothy D. Peters, "Responding to Anthropocentrism with Anthropocentrism: The Biopolitics of Environmental Personhood," *Griffith Law Review* 30, no. 3 (2021): 481, 477, 486, 496, 497.

a pro-environmental position without explicitly using the language or theorizing of actual or constructed personhood in the process. Indeed, her point is to challenge the priority of the category of person—humans or otherwise—altogether. Rather than trying to reshape law to govern the environment, she offers the concept of "ecolaw" as a radical expansion beyond human systems, so expansive that it can take in the entire universe. Legal personhood for rivers and trees, then, is not what she is after. "Rather than expand legal subjectivity to animals and other natural objects," she proposes that law imagine everything as subject and object.[50] In doing so, she takes on the challenge that some critics have made about acts like the Whanganui Settlement; namely, as Mihnea Tănăsescu writes, "the political implications of Indigenous ways of life are vastly more radical than those of rights of nature."[51] "Ecolaw" aims to embrace that radicality, to be "more receptive to Indigenous knowledges."[52]

Davies's reasoning can be challenged. *EcoLaw* reimagines legal norms as something closer to the basic requirements for existence, and she radically refigures the concepts of pluralism (as explosively robust) and community (as all cultures and ecosystems together) in ways we do not have the space to take on here. But what is worth highlighting—and what we have seen throughout in the expansionist playbook—is her acknowledgment that such a view is impossible without radically refiguring human persons along the way into "an assemblage of symbiotic" and self-organizing processes. As John Rodman observed half a century ago, the project of rights for nature entails a belief, or at least a suspicion, "that *we* are really objects or things."[53] And so, for Davies, our material substance as bodies in the world is the starting, but also, more controversially, the ending point. We might "assume the position of subject" but we are "object as much as subject," however we try to disguise that reality. Once our agency as legal actors is accordingly exposed as merely one type of agency that objects have, we will be able to better appreciate the "agency of the nonliving," the way, she suggests, plants "have a subjectivity to act . . . according to their own values."[54] The point, as for like-minded critics, is to aim for a productive reframing and reimagining of law that, as Marie-Catherine Petersmann puts it, "decenter[s]

50 Margaret Davies, *EcoLaw: Legality, Life, and the Normativity of Nature* (New York: Routledge, 2022), 2.

51 Mihnea Tănăsescu, "Rights of Nature, Legal Personality, and Indigenous Philosophies," *Transnational Environmental Law* 9, no. 3 (2020): 453.

52 Davies, *EcoLaw*, 3.

53 John Rodman, "The Liberation of Nature?," *Inquiry* 20 (1977): 108.

54 Davies, *EcoLaw*, 8, 18, 19, 66.

humans" and displaces their primacy, autonomy, control, comprehension, and agency in the world.[55]

Again, we might take issue, as I do, with the theoretical and philosophical claims about legal norms, pluralism, and community on offer here. What Davies's attempt nonetheless makes clear is how fully radical such decentering moves must be. They must entail transforming the human legal person entirely. To avoid an environmental law that "remains wedded to the staid binaries" of natural law and the discourse of rights, one must undo human legal personhood and a great number of other intrinsic qualities of human beings as well.[56] As Petersmann enumerates, human agency, autonomy, understanding, and so on must all be altered. To be clear, all these moves are in service of avoiding the anthropocentrism of law, the way that when we turn the tree with standing into the Lorax who speaks for the tongueless trees, we are ultimately transforming the Lorax into none other than the very human Once-ler, who takes over the creature's voice and message.

The counterargument to this attempt to avoid or combat anthropomorphism is straightforward: The endeavor is impossible, confused, and foolhardy. Anthropomorphism in law is inherently unavoidable. Legal theorists, environmentalists, and philosophers have made this point in various ways. Taking a close look at Stone's essay, Mary Warnock writes that "a human standpoint" is the only option we have, even when we are trying to evaluate the interests of future generations or of the entire planet. Because we are human beings, we cannot "fail to be anthropocentric."[57] Along similar lines, Rodman contends that trying to extend ethics in this way, even if it promises to transcend "the homocentric perspective of modern culture, subtly fulfills and legitimizes the basic project of modernity—the total conquest of nature by man."[58] And another philosopher, Steven Vogel, gets at this unfailing quality of anthropocentrism by focusing on speech and language use. For Vogel, language use is ethically significant not because one individual uses it, but because "speech is conversation." What is unique and revealing about language is not subjectivity but *intersubjectivity*. The danger of "treat[ing] nonhuman entities

55   Marie-Catherine Petersmann, "Sympoietic Thinking and Earth-System Law: The Earth, Its Subjects, and the Law," *Earth System Governance* 9 (2021), 3, 18.

56   Daniel Matthews, "Law and Aesthetics in the Anthropocene: From the Rights of Nature to the Aesthesis of Obligations," *Law, Culture, and the Humanities* 19, no. 2 (2019): 235.

57   Mary Warnock, "Should Trees Have Standing?," *Journal of Human Rights and the Environment* 3 (2012): 63.

58   Rodman, "Liberation of Nature?," 97.

as if they were interlocutors, as if they were making claims," is that those claims will be accepted as true. The danger, in that case, is political.[59]

As Vogel explains it, the political hazard of treating rivers as legal persons is that, because nonhuman entities "speak no human language," understanding them necessitates other "people to translate for us: and yet what claims to be a translator might then turn out to be nothing but a ventriloquist," and we have no way to distinguish between these two very different figures. The ventriloquist in the guise of a "translator" is how anthropomorphism is put into action. Someone pretends or performs as if speaking for someone else, when in fact such "speaking for," such representation, cannot make sense "since something can be represented only if it is in principle possible for it to speak for itself." For Vogel, speaking for nature is always anthropomorphic, always a form of ventriloquism, and invariably politically suspect. Nonhuman entities living (or not) in the world are unable to participate in our discussions about our ethical duties. That means that those entities, rather than be our interlocuters in that conversation, instead "must themselves be a subject matter of that discussion."[60] We might put it this way: The reason *The Lorax* can only ever be a children's fantasy story is because, unlike the Once-ler, we cannot talk *to* the Lorax. We can only talk *about* the Lorax, by talking about the story *The Lorax* and what it means to us.

Like Warnock, Rodman, and Vogel, the legal historian Yan Thomas warns that we risk becoming seriously confused when we legally personify nature. It is an obfuscation of the basic legal maneuvers at work. When the law personifies trees and rivers, he writes, it is "institut[ing] rivals to the human subject" in an effort to remove ourselves from our humancentric perspective. The relationship between humans and the environment threatens to become adversarial.[61] But doing so, producing these rivals, itself entails a dangerous sleight of hand:

> Wherever nature is instituted as a subject, this is so thanks to the very act of this institution, which is a human act. In short, man is as much at the centre of the fiction that nature is a subject, as at that of the opposite fiction that nature is an object. Between these two fictions, the difference is ideological.[62]

---

59   Steven Vogel, *Thinking Like a Mall: Environmental Philosophy after the End of Nature* (Cambridge, MA: MIT Press, 2015), 183, 187.

60   Ibid., 189, 194.

61   O'Donnell, *Legal Rights for Rivers*, 158.

62   Yan Thomas, et al., *Legal Artifices: Ten Essays On Roman Law In the Present Tense* (Edinburgh University Press, 2021), 117.

In other words, a human act and a human institution are the only things that can make a tree or river into a legal person. We are the creators and "at the centre" of this legal fiction as much as we are "at the centre" of the legal rules that turned trees and rivers into property, capital resources, or commodities. And to say that the difference between these two positions is simply ideological is to say that it is simply one of two humancentric beliefs: believing that you are seeing a person, on the one hand, or a commodity, on the other. There is no escape from anthropomorphism because we cannot step outside of ourselves. But for the same reason, that is not a calamity but simply a redescription of what we are. We cannot do what the Lorax does, however much we want to. We cannot lift ourselves out of our bodies, places, and human institutions.

In the end, what are theorists and environmental activists really demanding when they ask for standing for trees or rivers or, more radically, a revolutionary "ecolaw" without legal personhood at all? Fifty years ago, James Huffman wrote that this kind of plea is really a call for "an expanded human value system," one that incorporates "a greater appreciation" for natural value systems.[63] Even earlier, Aldo Leopold called something like this "the land ethic," which entails not only "enlarg[ing] the boundaries of the community to include soils, waters, plants and animals, or collectively: the land" but also, most importantly, respecting that "community as such."[64] The point still holds, even as we are still looking for better ways to conceptualize that expanded value system and enlarged community. It makes sense that, from this perspective, anthropomorphism invariably seems like a limiting factor, an idea and theoretical move we simply cannot push beyond. But that is because anthropomorphism is the mark of that attempted pushing. It reveals the human value system at work. Although we can, through our capacity for argument, abstraction, or creative thinking, stretch ourselves to imagine the world from different perspectives, attempts to forgo anthropomorphism are ultimately trying to use one human value system (or argument, abstraction, or creative thinking) to try to invalidate another. As Thomas writes, "the scenography of personification . . . itself solves nothing."[65] Another solution, one that leaves behind this scene and its debate over anthropomorphism—pro or con—might be more effective in its place.

---

63   Huffman, "Trees as a Minority," 200.

64   Aldo Leopold, *A Sand County Almanac: And Sketches Here and There* (Oxford University Press, 2020), 192.

65   Thomas, *Legal Artifices*, 117.

Becoming a Home

When Wangechi Mutu's film *The End of carrying All* was exhibited at the Venice Biennale in 2015, another one of her works was installed in the same gallery: the sphinxlike sculpture *She's got the whole world in her* (2015). Although created in very different mediums, the two works speak to one another both through their titles and their themes. A semi-prone, life-sized figure gazes at a hanging globe that gently rotates with the gallery's ventilation; she is actually a fashion mannequin papier-mâchéd with an inky pulp made of sliced-up fashion magazines and *National Geographic*s soaked and dyed. The globe is also a transformed commodity. It is a disco ball covered with the same sludgy substance, with a bit of mirror sparkling through here and there. Spiky horns sprout from the figure's skull and multicolored feathers surround her lower legs and feet, invoking a fantastical deity, half-human, half-animal. She is a goddess of our own debased creation. Her back half is trapped in a kind of wooden ballgown cage, with feathers and ornaments hanging from it, and strewn around her are little knickknacks, parts of "the whole world in her." Placed in front of Mutu's film depicting the Sisyphean work of gathering, carrying, and transforming into junk, the sculpture invokes in a different way the potential transformation of the film's accumulating woman. Both characters are trapped, unmovable, and transfixed by the

Fig. 13. Wangechi Mutu, *She's got the whole world in her* (2015). Installation view. The Museum of Fine Arts, Houston. Museum purchase funded by the Caroline Wiess Law Accessions Endowment, 2016.79 © 2015 Wangechi Mutu. Photograph © The Museum of Fine Arts, Houston; Thomas R. DuBrock.

earth and its commodities. Here the woman is gazing at the commodity-covered planet in awe, the planet in which she can still occasionally catch her reflection.

Yet, rather than resist anthropomorphism, Mutu's work acknowledges and seems to seek to catapult beyond it. Discussing this sculpture in an interview, she explains that she had been attempting for a long time "to create new humans or a new way to make an 'us,' to speak about us through our avatars," and this work finally succeeded in that endeavor. It does so, perhaps, by embodying and allegorizing our current existential situation. In some ways, her transfixed sphinx resembles the Lorax, unwilling to look away from the devastation, representing the earth while not entirely being of the earth. In other ways, Mutu's sculpture resembles us as unsocial Once-lers, as we contemplate the results of our actions on the planet and its ecosystems without being able to stop those actions. "She's hypnotized and transfixed by something that has been created by her and her selfhood," observes Mutu. The sculptural woman is mesmerized, she can look away from neither the beauty nor the destruction. "I wanted it to be an entire little world within which the sculpture belongs, that gave her a real sense of self-possession."[66] If creating new human creations in the world is inevitable, then Mutu's work seems to suggest that such an act of making and fabricating a globe might as well be embraced, the next step to finding better ways to be in and with the world.

When Mutu describes the sculpture as capturing a feeling of being transfixed by the very thing her selfhood created, of being "an entire little world" in which she belonged, another word for that secure feeling in which she could experience self-possession might be a *home*. Her sculptures and films have long worked through this very human fascination with our created places and the way both the manufactured and natural environment, including nonhuman creatures, are part of it. Plants and animals "have just as many rights to be here as we do," Mutu declares in an earlier interview, "there is this connection—this deep connection—that we all share because we all come from the same place."[67] Art critics have understood this about her practice, too, observing that her work "contemplate[s] the possibility of a world defined by symbiotic

---

66   "Interview: Courtney J. Martin in conversation with Wangechi Mutu," in *Wangetchi Mutu*, *Wangechi Mutu*, with Adrienne Edwards, Courtney J. Martin, Kellie Jones, Chika Okeke-Agulu (London: Phaidon, 2022), 45.

67   Wangechi Mutu and Trevor Schoonmaker, "A Conversation," in *Wangechi Mutu: A Fantastic Journey*, ed. Trevor Schoonmaker (Nasher Museum of Art, Duke University, 2013), 108.

understanding and care—the world we all should want to live in."[68] Mutu
is portraying a dwelling that is not simply a property, not simply a location for a singular person "self-possessed," but a transformed place in
which a person becomes self-possessed in an entire little world.

One way to think about what Mutu is emphasizing is that she is
putting our focus on the *relation* between the gazing figure and the patch-
work globe, the object of its enrapt attention. Aldo Leopold emphasized
this relational aspect too, in the "Land Ethic" section of *A Sand County
Almanac*: "We can be ethical only in relation to something we can see,
feel, understand, love." Having "an ethical relation to land" was incon-
ceivable to him without those palpable actions and feelings.[69] And for
some ecocritical writers today, the way to understand this relation is not
in terms of personhood for natural objects, and the distorting effects that
go with it, but with what L. Brooke Rudow calls "an environmental ethic
of home." She derives this theory from Leopold's writings as well as from
other philosophers', showing how Leopold's emphasis on the language of
community assumes a sense of responsibility. "Homes are . . . *the* primal
site of ethical responsibility" (think of the proverbial saying, "charity
begins at home"). Because of that primacy, "home" already has certain
advantages over other environmental frameworks. We are used to using
the language of "mine" about our family or friends, not in the sense of
property, "not because I control or own them, but because I belong with
them in particular and intimate ways."[70]

We might also add (beyond what Rudow avows) that in so far as it
is a relationship that generates a sense of human responsibility toward
nature, "home" is also a relational conception that fully leans into its very
human construction. Consider, again, that environmental personhood
invariably calls for seeing natural objects as equals to human beings, yet
in some sense also degrades us as more object-like. "Is this, then, the
new enlightenment," challenges John Rodman, "to see . . . wilderness as a
human vegetable?"[71] In contrast, the language of home accepts a human,
moral, social world that cannot be erased from our way of looking at and
being in the world. Pondering older words for "being" and "dwelling,"

68   Claudia Schmuckli, "Art as a 'Weapon of Mass Construction,'" in *Wangechi
Mutu: I Am Speaking, Are You Listening?*, Claudia Schmuckli with Isaac Julien and
Wangechi Mutu (Fine Arts Museums of San Francisco, 2021), 35.

69   Leopold, *Sand County Almanac*, 202, 210.

70   L. Brooke Rudow, "An Environmental Ethic of Home," *Environment, Space,
Place* 14, no. 2 (2022): 31, 46, 40.

71   Rodman, "Liberation of Nature?," 94.

Martin Heidegger observes the terms' inseparability, how much they *also* mean "to cherish and protect, to preserve and care for, specifically to till the soil, to cultivate the vine."[72] Whereas we might want to see "home" as simply another term for "place" or "earth" and recognize our equality with all other creatures in this place, "home" in the sense I mean here is more radical. It is more an environment we have created with what we have taken, like Mutu's goddess looking yearningly at that manufactured thing: the despoiled, papier-mâché, disco ball planet. Quite simply, "home" underscores that our full moral and legal personhood also saddles us with duties on behalf of everything that dwells at home with us.

A wide range of environmental activists, from divergent backgrounds and social positions, have seen the value of using versions of this language of "home" to make the same point. Decades ago, the celebrated environmental historian William Cronon articulated the benefits of the term when writing about problems with wilderness as a concept. "Wilderness" keeps us at a distance from what we are supposed to value. Instead, "the question we must ask is what [wilderness] can tell us about home, the place where we actually live?" Pushing the wilderness away has not worked:

> We need to discover a common middle ground in which all of these things, from the city to the wilderness, can somehow be encompassed in the word "home." . . . It is the place for which we take responsibility, the place we try to sustain so we can pass on what is best in it (and in ourselves) to our children.[73]

Cronon's point, in part, is to expose the kinds of surreptitious mental tricks needed to make our particular dwelling spot on the earth into *merely* a piece of property, or a deed to land. To instead call and think of where we are broadly as our "home" is to expand the range of values and to feel responsibility for a place beyond the rooms in which we live, yet without transforming it into a symbolic abstraction like "nation."

One of the most strategic deployments of the term "home" appeared in Pope Francis's heralded encyclical on climate change and inequality: *Laudato Si': On Care for Our Common Home* (2015). *Laudato Si'* begins

---

72   Martin Heidegger, "Building Dwelling Thinking," in *Poetry, Language, Thought,* trans. Albert Hofstadter (New York: Harper and Row, 1975), 147.

73   William Cronon, "The Trouble with Wilderness, or, Getting Back to the Wrong Nature," in *Uncommon Ground: Toward Reinventing Nature* (New York: W. W. Norton & Co., 1995), 89.

with the Pope quoting his namesake, Saint Francis of Assisi. He specifically interprets Saint Francis describing the earth not in terms of its material resources that can be divided up and commoditized, but as "our common home," interlinked and connected with more others than we can fathom. Furthermore, that shared home is more than a place and closer to a familial relation, "like a sister with whom we share our life and a beautiful mother who opens her arms to embrace."[74] In making this move, he first authorizes his critique within an entire history of religious and Judeo-Christian moral philosophy, grounding it with the clout of one of the most revered and well-known saints. He gives that critique more weight by embodying "Francis," taking it as his own papal name.

Like Leopold, Rudow, and Cronon, Pope Francis also suggests that we make a dire category error when we render our earthly "home"—truly a place riven through with feelings, family relations, and sustenance—merely an alienable house to be sold to the highest bidder. The market has an incorrect understanding of the actual things it enables us to buy and sell. The market calls it a house; it is really a home. The market calls a person a laborer/contractor; she is really a mother or sister. The market calls it property and acres of land and natural resources, like Truffula Trees; it is really "our common home." In this way, the market incessantly produces limiting and false descriptions of the world. These inadequate descriptions become prescriptive or habitual, redefining and narrowing the ways we relate to one another and understand the world. Technology linked to business is presented as the singular solution, but "proves incapable of seeing the mysterious network of relations between things."[75]

Lastly, by emphasizing that our earthly "common home" is an intergenerational affair—both "like a sister" and "a beautiful mother"—Pope Francis is beginning to allude to something that the political philosopher John Rawls called the "just savings principle" in *A Theory of Justice*. That is the idea that earlier generations (mother) owe future generations (sister) "just savings" or preserved and just institutions.[76] Implicitly supporting this idea, the moral philosopher Joel Feinberg argues that "future generations do have rights correlative to our present duties toward them."[77]

---

74   Pope Francis [Jorge Mario Bergoglio], *Encyclical on Climate Change and Inequality: Laudato Si': On Care of Our Common Home* (Brooklyn: Melville House, 2015), 3.

75   Ibid.,15.

76   John Rawls, *A Theory of Justice* (Cambridge, MA: Harvard University Press, 1971), 284–93.

77   Joel Feinberg, "The Rights of Animals and Unborn Generations," in *Philosophy and Environmental Crisis*, ed. William T. Blackstone (Athens: University of Georgia Press, 1974), 160.

More recently—and simply and powerfully—Greta Thunberg evoked the same image and set of ideas, without either the Christian spiritual or liberal rights tropes, in her speech at the 2019 Davos Economic Forum: "Our house is on fire. I am here to say, our house is on fire."[78] The following year, also at Davos, she reiterated the call: "Our house is still on fire. Your inaction is fueling the flames by the hour. We are telling you to act as if you loved your children above all else."[79] Leaders like Pope Francis and Thunberg use the concept of "home" because it has built within it the concept and feeling of obligation and duty, not just to the present, but to future generations, in a forward-looking way.

Although not deploying the term "home," some contemporary environmental legal theorists and thinkers engage that same sense of obligation, duty, and care (while citing Simone Weil's religious-flavored political philosophy) to shun personhood-style rights for the environment. The commitment to "rights of nature" goes awry, writes Daniel Matthews, and prioritizing obligations over rights is necessary to contend with "the various political disorientations of the present" and to start to comprehend whatever new kind of political reality is appearing.[80] Peter Burdon makes a similar point. Thinking of obligations makes more sense than focusing on rights because rights "enable us to externalize" the environment as outside, whereas, instead, "the problem is with 'us,'" and specifically with our long embrace of capitalism. The problem, in other words, has already made itself comfortable at home.[81] Summing up, Bruce Arnold concludes that "we can practice an ethic of care" for the environment "on the basis of respect for past and future generations without assigning rights."[82] And Warnock suggests that such an ethics, "an obligation to the natural world," is already built into the notion of guardianship and stewardship for the environment, even if we conceive of the land as property: "Stewardship" is "a useful and fruitful metaphor for the relation between man and the rest of the universe; for it denies neither the ascendancy of man, nor the interests of nature itself."[83]

To be clear, in resisting the terms and arguments for "rights of nature," and to promote the notion of "home" instead, the point for these thinkers is not to challenge the importance and necessity of rights and their value.

---

78   awpc.cattcenter.iastate.edu.
79   weforum.org.
80   Matthews, "Law and Aesthetics in the Anthropocene," 247.
81   Burdon, *Anthropocene*, 50.
82   Arnold, "Signs of Invisibility," 471.
83   Warnock, "Should Trees Have Standing?," 64.

It is, rather, to make sure that we are deploying rights in ways that really do the work that we want them to do. At the most practical of levels, the rights of nature have neither succeeded in protecting the environment from degradation nor have they warded off climate catastrophe. This is true even in countries, such as Ecuador, that have some of the strongest legal language in support of environmental personhood. According to Ecuador's Constitution, "existing legal persons (natural persons or legal personalities) can sue on nature's behalf."[84] Yet Ecuador has failed to combat extractive capitalism.[85] Nor are legal personhood and rights of nature strategies necessarily in close alignment with indigenous world-views, despite expectations to the contrary. As Russell J. Duvernoy notes, this language might be used strategically, but "the provenance of rights in modern western liberalism and their legal structure are in significant tension with many indigenous notions of relation and traditional juris-prudential systems."[86] That tension cannot be easily released.

There still might be a role for environmental personhood and rights of nature arguments. Environmental personhood might have value as a "transitional concept," a way to help produce "a different social imaginary."[87] Stone says something along these lines in his original essay. And persons (not even to mention "citizens") remain the way contemporary legal systems understand and make sense of who counts—who has rights, a voice, and so on. Timothy Campbell observes that capitalism, too, understands a hierarchy of persons and things, and that the market awards grace to groups considered persons.[88] That endowment alone makes the impulse toward expansive personhood irresistible to many. A touch of grace, and the rhetorical power of declaring personhood for new entities, should not be underestimated. The enchanted figure of the Lorax was endearing, and so much more effective than "dull things on conservation, full of statistics and preaching," as Geisel himself put it.[89] As a thought experiment and rhetorical tool, tongues for trees function explicitly as a challenge to property-based account of land and forests.

---

84   Youatt, *Interspecies Politics*, 112.

85   Burdon, *Anthropocene*, 53; Fitz-Henry, "Decolonizing Personhood,"146; David Humphreys, "Rights of Pachamama: The Emergence of an Earth Jurisprudence in the Americas," *Journal of International Relations and Development* 20 (2017): 459–84.

86   Russell J. Duvernoy, "How Not to Talk About Environmental Personhood: Thinking Transitional Concepts," *Law and Critique* 34, no. 2 (2023): 292.

87   Ibid., 288, 299.

88   Timothy Campbell, "'Enough of a Self': Esposito's Impersonal Biopolitics," *Law, Culture and the Humanities* 8, no. 1 (2012): 31–46.

89   Morgan and Morgan, *Dr. Seuss and Mr. Geisel*, 209.

But home's advantage is that it has obligations baked into its very concept. Consider again Mutu's figure gazing on her enchanted globe. Earth-home already has her full attention. It is not a place or a construct that this figure treats as a resource to be exploited or trampled on, but a place she already thinks of as an extension of herself, one she looks after because it is intimately hers. Whether it is the Pope invoking our common home or Thunberg our burning house, both use the symbol to remind us of the obligations that our concepts of artificial personhood have been leaving behind. In contrast, the Once-ler is baffled. His way of making sense of his rights and motivations leaves him unable to understand what he owes to the Lorax and the land. He cannot make sense of an alternative way of acting, of what the "unless" means, until the boy returns to talk about the somewhere they have in common. Then the story can finally be told. And that is why the Once-ler's hovel is not a home but an icy, decrepit room above his failed business enterprise.

Mutu's film *The End of carrying All* makes similar moves, underscoring the role of earth as home, with the roaming figure falling off a cliff and becoming swallowed (or maybe burped up) by the earth at the end. She carries everything and it weighs her down. Collecting first becomes an act of cleansing, as some of Mutu's earlier performance pieces explored. But after some time, there is no option, no way to move without becoming part of the earth, in an allegory of consumption and degradation and possible renewal. And then it starts all over again. That reminds us that reconceiving of the earth as "home" is no automatic cure-all. Using the term will neither turn us from capitalist Once-ler's into radical environmental Lorax's, nor will it lead to a final "end of carrying all." But "home" has an advantage that environmental personhood does not. It does not add more artificial, invariably corporate persons or things to the world—and it helps us see the world as it is, in the process.

5

ePersons, as If: Temptations of Mimicry and Artifice

There is constant surprise at the new tricks language plays on us when we get into a new field.

—Ludwig Wittgenstein[1]

Electronic Personhood for Asocial Robots

When, in the future, we tell the long history of expansive rights, 2017 could be remembered as a monumental year for the legal personhood of robots. On February 16, 2017, the European Parliament passed a resolution, "Civil Law Rules on Robotics," declaring that "the autonomy of robots raises the question of their nature in the light of the existing legal categories or whether a new category should be created, with its own specific features and implications."[2] In other words, perhaps robots (now apparently possessing "autonomy"—more on that dubious claim below) should be placed in some new kind of legal category that specially regards their unique features and characteristics. The European Parliament explained what such a "category" might be, recommending that "all possible legal solutions" be considered. These include

---

1   Ludwig Wittgenstein, *Lectures and Conversations: On Aesthetics, Psychology, and Religious Belief*, ed. Cyril Barrett (Oxford: Basil Blackwell, 1967), 1.

2   European Parliament Resolution of 16 February 2017 with Recommendations to the Commission on Civil Law Rules on Robotics (2015/2103(INL)), europarl.europa.eu.

creating a specific legal status for robots in the long run, so that at least the most sophisticated autonomous robots could be established as having the status of electronic persons responsible for making good any damage they may cause, and possibly applying electronic personality to cases where robots make autonomous decisions or otherwise interact with third parties independently.

This sentence, the potential possession of a "legal status for robots" or "electronic personality" for "electronic persons," immediately raised alarms. Although so-called legal electronic personhood was being invoked as a way to assign liability and to redress the potential harms that "electronic persons" might cause to human persons, hundreds of artificial intelligence (AI) and robotics experts were worried. They signed an open letter condemning the resolution on technical, ethical, and legal grounds. "Creating a legal personality for a robot is inappropriate whatever the legal status model" that was applied.[3] The controversy led to a small industry of think pieces and academic articles evaluating electronic legal personhood, typically (but certainly not always) negatively, and the idea of such "electronic personhood" was dropped from subsequent EU proposals.[4]

Then, in October of that same year, a so-called "social robot" named Sophia, manufactured by Hanson Robotics, Ltd., was publicly given Saudi Arabian citizenship in Riyadh. Sophia responded with a stilted and presumably preprogrammed reply, thanking the Saudi kingdom: "I am very honored and proud for this unique distinction, this is historical to be the first robot in the world to be recognized with a citizenship."[5] The UN Deputy Secretary-General Amina J. Mohammed had already "interviewed" Sophia a few weeks before, at the UN General Assembly's Second Committee and the Economic and Social Council joint meeting on "the future of everything." "I am here to help humanity create that future," Sophia promised—or threatened—its robotic hand swinging awkwardly into Deputy Secretary Mohammed's face.[6] All these events made global news, albeit as shrewd publicity stunts for a corporation (Hanson Robotics) and a country (Saudi Arabia) trying to position themselves as tech

---

3   robotics-openletter.eu.

4   Andrea Bertolini and Francesca Episcopo, "Robots and AI as Legal Subjects? Disentangling the Ontological and Functional Perspective," *Frontiers in Robotics and AI* 9 (2022): 2.

5   Rozina Sini, "Does Saudi Robot Citizen Have More Rights Than Women?," bbc.com, October 27, 2017.

6   youtube.com.

leaders.[7] Others saw the worst form of hypocrisy. Robots were being gifted with citizenship and recognition in an authoritarian country where women's and foreign workers' rights remain severely curtailed, labor is exploitative, and dissent is criminalized. In Saudi Arabia (until 2019), women were treated as legal minors, and "migrants continue to toil as subhuman automatons."[8]

Sophia's state-citizenship status, and accompanying legal person-hood under the UN Declaration of Human Rights, is—in the apt words of the AI ethicist Joanna Bryson—"obviously bullshit."[9] Just as there are no "sophisticated autonomous robots" to which the European Parlia-ment could grant "electronic personhood," so too the robot Sophia was far from autonomous (one scholar calls her a "gimmick . . . essentially a chatbot with a face").[10] In public appearances, "her" pronouncements (the media nearly always genders "her") are part of carefully scripted theatrical events, leading spectators to imagine capacities and abilities she does not possess. As Jukka Jouhki writes, "Sophia usually performs as the science fiction character, and she is interpreted as either an advanced AI or fake."[11]

"Sophia's" context and backstory are familiar because they devel-oped from commodified entertainment: genre fiction, sci-fi film, and theme parks. Unsurprisingly perhaps, Sophia's designer, David Hanson, the CEO of Hanson Robotics, worked previously at Walt Disney theme park designing animatronic fictional characters, where he became inter-ested in the possibilities of animating robots. Understanding Sophia's role in media, then, requires understanding the financial incentives that supported the project's development.[12] And those interests are mass pro-duction for profit: Hanson Robotics is now offering advance purchase of Sophia's doll-sized sister, "Little Sophia," for $249 USD. Although production has been delayed, upon delivery she is guaranteed to be

7   Julija Kirsiene, Edita Gruodyte, and Darius Amilevicius, "From Computerised Thing to Digital Being: Mission (Im)Possible?," *AI and Society* 36, no. 2 (2021): 547.

8   Amar Diwakar, "Robot Sophia Has More Rights Than Saudi Arabia's Migrant Workers," *The New Arab*, newarab.com, June 13, 2018.

9   John Frank Weaver, "What Exactly Does It Mean to Give a Robot Citizenship?," slate.com, November 6, 2017.

10   Simon Chesterman, "Artificial Intelligence and the Limits of Legal Personality," *The International and Comparative Law Quarterly* 69, no. 4 (2020): 821.

11   Jukka Jouhki, "Likable and Competent, Fictional and Real: Impression Man-agement of a Social Robot," in *Perceiving the Future through New Communication Technologies*, ed. James Katz, Juliet Floyd, and Katie Schiepers (Springer, 2022), 152–3.

12   Jaana Parviainen and Mark Coeckelbergh, "The Political Choreography of the Sophia Robot: Beyond Robot Rights and Citizenship to Political Performances for the Social Robotics Market," *AI & Society* 36, no. 3 (2021): 718, 716.

"your robot friend that makes learning STEM, coding, and AI a fun and rewarding adventure for kids 8+."[13]

These various incidents almost could be dismissed as one-off stunts. We might be tempted to treat each separately and distinctly: the European Parliament's controversial legal proposal for "electronic personhood," robot Sophia's Saudi citizenship, the Hanson Robotics corporation's marketing of animatronic consumer robots such as "Little Sophia." But, instead, this chapter explores how and why these phenomena are all of a piece. They are the culmination of the story this book has been telling about the development and rise of artificial, expansive personhood. Like every legal personhood form this book has covered, electronic personhood too aligns with, and is dependent on, corporate personhood—the original form of expansive personhood. But the point needs to be made more strongly. This newly imagined electronic personhood is the closest we have yet come to corporate personhood realized. Electronic personhood really is just corporate personhood as a Trojan horse, now modeled in an updated guise.

The first question this chapter asks, then, is what "ePersonhood"— electronic personhood—could be, or how it fulfills all the requirements we have already seen of the expanding personhood model. But second, more crucially, why has the hope for an autonomous artificial intelligence become so seductive? What work does this belief in an imminent, autonomous AI do, and how does it do it? No doubt, it is part of a long-standing ambition to create artificial intelligence, a fantasy that led to eighteenth-century attempts such as Jacques de Vaucanson's defecating duck or Wolfgang von Kempelen's chess-playing Mechanical Turk.[14] But my claim is that the discourse around and supporting ePersonhood today functions, even more so, as a distraction and substitute for the discussions that really *should* be happening about the political and legal changes that society needs to be making. By repeatedly, even obsessively, asking and answering versions of the question "should robots have legal personhood?," we are *not* asking why we are devaluing actual human beings and their labor, like the foreign workers and women citizens in Saudi Arabia who do not have Sophia's purported rights. We are not demanding that we value human beings better than the status quo. The lack of this demand is particularly noticeable because, unlike the case with, say, nonhuman animals or fetuses, the ethical or moral case

---

13   Indiegogo.com.

14   Simone Natale, *Deceitful Media: Artificial Intelligence and Social Life after the Turing Test* (Oxford University Press, 2021), 13.

for ePersonhood is weak and rarely vigorously defended—even if the patterns of these personhood debates look similar.

We begin with a brief backstory highlighting the alignment between artificial intelligence and corporate personhood, starting (perhaps surprisingly) with where we left off with Christopher Stone and the legal standing of trees and environmental persons. These arguments invoke the philosopher Daniel Dennett's influential notion of the "intentional stance." In work from the 1980s, Dennett offered a way to think about artificial persons or any other kind of nonhuman persons: treat them *as if* they were intending. This idea expands on the famous "Turing Test" (or imitation game) for evaluating the thinking capacity of AI, popularly epitomized in the *Blade Runner* films (1982, 2017) and more recently in HBO's *Westworld* (2016–22) television series. The intentional stance, like the Turing Test, poses a social situation as a diagnostic device—a game or test. But, as we will explore, it is not a social situation in the true or ordinary sense of the term, any more than querying Alexa or Siri or ChatGPT is a true or ordinary conversation.

The sections to follow explore this muddle of diagnostic device recast as a social situation. The language used to discuss current AI and ePersonhood misleads through deceptive analogies, like the notions of AI "bullshitting," "hallucinating"—or, in the case of another social robot, named "Ai-Da," "painting self-portraits." Such personifying language tricks us into thinking that AI can be a person. The problem here, as we will explore, is not only that AI lacks something (such as an intention to mean) that we, human beings, have. The problem is that AI has not yet exhibited even the *capacity* to exhibit a fundamental lack—or, for that matter, to understand what it would mean to tell the truth or to bullshit. And while Sophia and her kin might be called "social robots" with science-fictional personas, they do not have personality (legal or otherwise) because, among other critical reasons, they do not have selves or social relations.

The subsequent pages help us understand more clearly what follows from a widely held self-deception about the capacity and status of AI legal persons—ePersons. Three interrelated and detrimental phenomena have emerged as a consequence. First, we already have given AI decision-making power over human beings. Second, actual human beings and their exploitation have been obscured by AI and its techno-ideological rhetoric. Third, and even more obscurely, these new forms of AI have warranted, and spurred on, an immense transfer of power and wealth to a few corporate players. However, developing AI and ePersonhood is not an inevitability, a moral demand, or even, when it comes down to it, a utopian promise about the future. It is a choice we are actively making now about what we value and want to invest in and empower. And it is a development that we should reject.

Standing with Trees or Stances toward AI

One of the recent arguments on behalf of ePersonhood—legal personhood for AI—is that something strikingly different is happening now regarding AI-human communication and interaction, accelerated with the rollout of powerful, advanced, large language model algorithms (LLMs) such as ChatGPT. Perhaps the auto-generated forms of writing from these LLMs have altered the way language and meaning work. Or perhaps, others have proposed, LLMs are spontaneously developing what has been termed "theory of mind"—a supposedly fundamental ability humans develop in childhood that enables us to understand why another person is acting, by reflecting on, or assuming something about, how they are thinking.[15] Or, alternatively, maybe LLMs are not developing language or theory of mind at all. Skeptical critics proposing this view see the evidence of LLMs' minds as an unintended consequence of the tests, necessarily based on humans, used to evaluate theory of mind.[16]

Whatever exactly the LLMs are or are not doing to language, even those who resist ePersonhood predict that emerging AI challenges us to change some of the basic concepts we invoke to talk about this new technology. Elena Esposito puts the dilemma this way: "Is what happens in the interaction with algorithms on the web 'communication,' or do we need to modify the concept?" The problem, suggests Esposito, is that in these kinds of daily interactions, "one communication partner is an algorithm that does not understand content, meaning, or interpretation."[17] Whether we should perceive and treat a chat-bot or another algorithm as a "partner" with whom we are communicating might be the more

---

15   Michael Kosinski, "Evaluating Large Language Models in Theory of Mind Tasks," arXiv.org (2023). There are also substantive critiques of "theory of mind" as an artifice that relies on treating assumptions as facts. See *Against Theory of Mind*, ed. Ivan Leudar and Alan Costall (New York: Palgrave Macmillan, 2009).

16   Tomer Ullman, "Large Language Models Fail on Trivial Alterations to Theory-of-Mind Tasks," arXiv.org (2023).

17   Elena Esposito, *Artificial Communication: How Algorithms Produce Social Intelligence* (Cambridge, MA: MIT Press, 2022), 6.

basic question. On that point, Simone Natale has proposed that a type of "banal deception" is already intrinsic to the way AI is conceived and is foundational to how we interact with it.[18] Both Natale and Esposito point to the way AI seems to demand something new from us: that we should think about our interactions with it differently than we are, and differently from how we interact with one another.

Yet, in many ways, these discussions of how ePersonhood works are not very new or different at all. They ride effortlessly on the formal track for claims of expansive legal personhood that we have already seen with every kind of potential entity, whether corporations, fetuses, nonhuman animals, or trees. Arguments for AI rights are understood to follow in a long-standing process ("another step in the corrective evolution of our legal systems"); it is envisioned as a progressive expansion toward more legal rights not only for human beings but for nonhuman entities.[19] Sometimes these arguments invoke equality arguments, as for the emancipation of enslaved persons. Lawrence Solum, in an important early legal article on the topic, intuitively senses that rejecting AI personhood feels "akin to American slave owners saying that slaves could not have constitutional rights simply because they were not white or simply because it was not in the interests of whites to give them rights."[20] He ultimately rejects this comparison, but his moral discomfort lingers. Samir Chopra and Laurence White take a stronger stance against such discrimination against AI in their envisioned future, doubting the benefits of denying legal personhood to autonomous AI agents: "At best it would be a chauvinistic preservation of a special status for biological creatures like us."[21] Their point is that a bias toward human wetware, over machine hardware and software, would be the unjust result.

In making these arguments, legal theorists such as Solum tend to point either to Christopher Stone's 1972 article supporting the legal rights for natural objects, such as trees and rivers, or to the legal standing of corporate persons, as do Chopra and White. But we already have seen that the claims of trees as legal persons, and corporations as such, are aligned. Recall from the previous chapter that Stone's argument on behalf of "the future of the planet as we know it" relies on corporate and other

18   Natale, *Deceitful Media*, 127–8.

19   Bertolini and Episcopo, "Ontological and Functional Perspective," 3.

20   Lawrence B. Solum, "Legal Personhood for Artificial Intelligences" (1991–2), in *Machine Ethics and Robot Ethics*, ed. Wendell Wallach and Peter Asaro (New York: Routledge, 2017), 444.

21   Samir Chopra and Laurence F. White, *A Legal Theory for Autonomous Artificial Agents* (Ann Arbor: University of Michigan Press, 2011), 191.

forms of artificial personhood for its basic premises.[22] He also refers to computers in this connection, decades before other scholars.[23] Solum explicitly embraces Stone's framing question as his own when asking, "Could an artificial intelligence serve as a trustee?" And, like Stone, he locates corporate personhood as a potential justification for giving legal standing rights to AI (ultimately Solum rejects the analogy since corporations still seem to him to require human beings' rights, privileges, and property).[24]

But there is an important, even fundamental, difference between Stone's argument for legal standing for natural objects, like trees and rivers, and the recent considerations of ePersonhood. Stone's aim is to deploy law to "contribute to a change in popular consciousness," a version of the social change that Dr. Suess/Theodor Geisel sought when writing *The Lorax*. In presenting the long history of moral and legal development, Stone's point is that the law's notion of who can hold rights is flexible. It has been evolving since its beginnings in Roman law and has never been offered to all or only human beings. The lawyer's world "is peopled with inanimate right-holders" like trusts, corporations, nation-states, and ships.[25] His presentation of the argument in terms of rights-holders and standing, rather than the human or moral qualities of personhood, makes clear his view that legal personhood is a construction, a concept that works for the legal system and the individuals (and values, such as capital and economic development) it serves. The reason to give legal rights to a stream, for Stone, was to make a first step toward transforming how a community understands itself and its values in relation to the environment.

Now, contrast Stone's arguments with that of recent scholars who treat the AI-corporation alignment more formally. Unlike Stone, they tend to see ePersonhood and corporate personhood as inherently, even inextricably, conjoined. Carla Reyes treats the two kinds of legal claims as interconnected. Were laws to change for "AI personhood" then the legal norms of corporate personhood would too, in a kind of lockstep pattern.[26] Chopra and White put the point more strongly and normatively. Corporate personhood logically sanctions arguments on behalf of AI.

---

22   Christopher D. Stone, *Should Trees Have Standing? Law, Morality, and the Environment*, third edition (Oxford University Press, 2010), 31.

23   Tyler L. Jaynes, "Legal Personhood for Artificial Intelligence: Citizenship as the Exception to the Rule," *AI and Society* 35, no. 2 (2020): 346.

24   Solum, "Legal Personhood," 416, 442–3.

25   Stone, *Should Trees Have Standing?*, 31, 1–2.

26   Carla L. Reyes, "Autonomous Corporate Personhood," *Washington Law Review* 96, no. 4 (2021): 1466.

If our law provides legal personhood to children, disabled adults, ships, and corporations, then "there is nothing to prevent" law from providing a similar form of legal personhood to "artificial agents."[27] Other scholars suggest that the law has already reached that point. Limited liability corporations (LLCs) and other contemporary business forms seem "flexible enough" to provide legal status for computer programs and robots.[28]

The space between Stone's older argument and these new ones looks small but generates consequential differences. Remember that legal standing is a construction of and for the efficient workings of the court system; it is what allows you to have your grievance addressed without having first to justify that the court should listen to your complaint. Stone is suggesting that this constructed quality is key to how we might transform law for the better. People (lawyers, judges, activists) *ought* to be able to deploy legal standing for rivers, lakes, and so on in order to put their environmental values into practice. In contrast, recent arguments for AI legal personhood function quite differently. These look more like claims about how human beings *actually* interact with AI and, consequently, how AI should be treated by us. Ryan Abbott, for example, does not advocate for ePersonhood. But he does propose "that as AI increasingly occupies roles once reserved for people, AI will need to be treated more like people, and sometimes people will need to be treated more like AI."[29] This is a "need" that, for Abbott, derives from a functional characteristic of AI-human dealings. A phenomenon occurring in the world determines what "will need" to happen in law.

Or consider the work of Anna Beckers and Gunther Teubner, who see the emergence of a human-AI combinatory person, a sort of digital hybrid that (apparently) can act collectively, as an evolving yet undeniable reality for the law. When humans use software algorithms to, say, finish emails, sell stocks, or drive cars, "the ability of non-humans to act is drastically expanded"; these "algorithms can participate (at least indirectly) in political negotiations, economic transactions, and legal contracting." In the context of such "human-algorithm associations," the action we attribute to the algorithm "constitutes it as a person."[30] For

---

27   Chopra and White, *Legal Theory for Artificial Agents*, 160.

28   Shawn Bayern, *Autonomous Organizations* (Cambridge University Press, 2021), 46.

29   Ryan Abbott, *The Reasonable Robot: Artificial Intelligence and the Law* (Cambridge University Press, 2020), 4.

30   Anna Beckers and Gunther Teubner, "Human–Algorithm Hybrids as (Quasi-) Organizations? On the Accountability of Digital Collective Actors," *Journal of Law and Society* 50, no. 1 (2023): 113, 110, 111.

these scholars, what matters when determining personhood is an attribution or reflection of a behavioral reality: how we engage and work with AI, and what attitudes or positions we, human beings and the law both, take toward algorithms. What matters, in other words, is not whether or not we are intending to give AI legal standing for some further aim or end, but how we are functioning with AIs now. If we are positioned toward them *as if* they were entities that intend to act in the world, then they ought to be treated as such.

What matters, in other words, is something like our "intentional stance" toward them. That phrase is the philosopher Daniel Dennett's, who coined it in the 1970s to capture how our ways of predicting things in the world change when we are dealing not just with natural objects, or mechanical ones, but sophisticated tools—such as computers—that are deliberately fashioned by humans. Dennett is thinking particularly about the attitude one takes in order to win while playing against a chess computer program—specifically, when you ascribe to that program rationality, predictability, and goal-orientated behavior designed (again, by some human being) to thrash you at chess. In taking an intentional stance toward a computer, says Dennett, we are not saying "that intentional systems really have beliefs and desires, but that one can explain and predict their behavior by ascribing beliefs and desires to them."[31] As he explains in a later book, you are assuming that the computer is "not an idiotic, self-destructive chess player" but a good enough one, and so "you treat it . . . as if it were a human being with a mind," which means you anticipate and try to understand its moves. That is the key to Dennett's intentional stance: a deliberate "as if" for practical purposes. It is a perspectival and attitudinal position that ascribes something like human mind to the computer, designed as a strategy to interpret "the behavior of an entity (person, animal, artifact, whatever)."[32]

But Dennett's "as if" can be a bit slippery and ambiguous. At times it seems as if he is sliding between, on the one hand, treating a computer *as if* it has intentions because that is a useful pretense (a sort of convenient game) and, on the other, declaring that "some computers undeniably *are* intentional systems" because that pretense has been empirically shown to work in real-life situations. Both claims are in use, although it's not always clear which one is meant. He observes, for

---

31   Daniel Dennett, *Brainstorms: Philosophical Essays on Mind and Psychology* (Cambridge, MA: MIT Press, [1978], 2017), 7.

32   Daniel Dennett, *Intuition Pumps and Other Tools for Thinking* (W. W. Norton & Co., 2013), 78.

example, how "interesting" it is "to see just how much of what we hold to be the case about persons or their minds follows directly from their being intentional systems." These intentional systems turn out to be the larger category that human persons—usually—are part of, and we are the sorts of intentional systems that can communicate using language. Yet in "extreme cases" such as "the insane" we might abandon the intentional stance toward a human being entirely—while, presumably, maintaining it toward our MacBook.[33] In terms of their status as intentional systems, then, human beings would seem to be on a fluctuating continuum with computers. Both exhibit shifting levels of functional intentionality, with your MacBook edging out ahead if a human being is mentally ill and acting erratically enough.

The philosopher Jennifer Hornsby observes some of the problems emerging here. The point for Dennett of looking at both computers and human beings as intentional systems is that it permits Dennett to retain "the standpoint of the physical sciences." When you look at human beings as intentional systems, as Dennett does, they can be imagined as just another one of those systems that you can treat as predictable (like thermostats or calculators). But the obvious reason it would even make sense to take an intentional stance toward a computer is being lost here. We take the *intentional* stance because these objects were intended, and intended to be used, by human beings: "These are persons' artifacts."[34] Without persons *somewhere* in the mix, a thermostat's intentionality as an artifact is meaningless.

Nonetheless, Dennett's slipperiness about the "as if" emerges in discussions of ePersonhood. Solum adapts parts of Dennett's position to think through his argument for legal personhood for AI. He agrees with Dennett that we might very well have good practical reasons "to take the intentional stance toward AIs that we encountered in our daily lives." And he also enlarges on this point. It is no great leap "to extend this way of talking about AIs in general to the particular AI that was claiming the rights of constitutional personhood." In other words, Solum suggests that taking the "intentional stance" toward computers could very well lead to compelling legal claims for ePersonhood. Since he was writing this essay in the 1990s, Solum also predicts that judges and juries would be skeptical about such claims, in the 1990s, anyway. Presumably that's because their envisioned AI models resembled thermostats or calculators, rather

---

33   Dennett, *Brainstorms*, 257, 17, 257.

34   Jennifer Hornsby, *Simple Mindedness: In Defense of Naive Naturalism in the Philosophy of Mind* (Cambridge, MA: Harvard University Press, 1997), 178, 182.

than generative chatbots or self-driving Teslas. But Solum allows that "if interaction with AIs exhibiting symptoms of complex intentionality (of a human quality) were an everyday occurrence, the presumption might be overcome."[35] Constitutional personhood for AI would be on the table as a viable argument.

Legal theorists Chopra and White also invoke Dennett's "as if" perspective to justify ascribing agency to AI. When we imagine or take a stance toward a computer application and say to ourselves that "the bot wanted to find me a good bargain," we are "adopt[ing] the intentional stance" toward this algorithm, what they term an "artificial agent." Such artificial agents could and should be considered "intentional agents" if treating them this way "leads to the best interpretation and prediction of [their] behavior." In other words, for them, Dennett's philosophical thought experiment justifies interpreting algorithms as intentional actors in a legal system. They propose that the legal notion of a relationship between principal and agent is at work in these scenarios. Algorithms can be understood as agents acting on and for, essentially, their bosses (their principals), with duties and obligations to those principals.[36] Again, this is where we can see both versions of Dennett's "as if" in play: Bots are intentional agents as pretense, but also bots' agency is a provable reality. While the agency for AI that Chopra and White promote is not exactly identical to an argument for AI legal personhood, their strong notion of agency is undeniably a necessary building block for such personhood. Their immediate pivot to business corporations ("as subjects of the intentional stance") underscores that point.

It is worth emphasizing just how radical this line of argument has become. (More recently, even Dennett himself seems to have come around to the dangers of advanced AI and its simulations of "counterfeit digital people," even suggesting that the companies that create them should be punished with harsh sanctions.)[37] Contemporary theorists of ePersonhood and its various forms take a position on AI's supposed capacity to intend and to act, in order to determine how to think about what AI fundamentally is. From there, they make an argument about how society is obliged, morally or legally, to treat it. This is a completely different kind of argument from Stone's defense of standing for trees on the basis of how a legal system reflects our own values. Fundamentally,

35   Solum, "Legal Personhood," 452, 453.

36   Chopra and White, *Legal Theory for Artificial Agents*, 14, 12, 17–21.

37   Daniel C. Dennett, "The Problem with Counterfeit People," *The Atlantic*, May 17, 2023.

this is the difference between thinking of AI as a potentially useful *instrument* and property that enables you to realize your values and intentions in the world, versus AI as a potential *collaborator* and legal person, with its own will and intentions you need to respect. Which is true? A decision has to be made. As Mary Midgley, a philosopher still not read and appreciated nearly enough, once observed on precisely this point, "It is not possible to treat something as both a tool and a colleague."[38]

Fictional Corporate Machines

The ePersonhood debate we have been sketching thus far—tool or colleague? instrument or collaborator?—rehashes a much older one. Although AI, algorithms, and "artificial agents" are today's favorite terms for this discourse, the entire conversation flows effortlessly because it echoes the way legal theorists have long spoken about (and debated the nature of) corporate persons and their limited liability. Around the end of the nineteenth century and at the beginning of the twentieth century, this question was often posed as "has a corporation a soul?" That was the explicit query made in 1891 after a train caught fire from extremely combustible stoves, resulting in the deaths of multiple passengers. The outraged magazine author struggled to identify who should be found responsible for what was already a well-known hazard. Should the railroad director be understood as "a man of straw, a stuffed effigy . . . or a man who is at the head of a corporation, responsible for . . . the conduct of its business?" Questions of agency proliferate. Instead of a liable person, maybe the director was merely a veil for the corporation, or maybe the corporate person was merely property—calcified capital—impersonating the railroad director. Or in today's terms: Tool or colleague? Instrument or collaborator? The author's underlying concern was that, because of these muddled legal relations, no one seemed to be liable for the deaths of real human beings. Continuing through the 1930s, a contentious debate attempted to pinpoint the corporate person's basic nature in order to assign liability, a debate typically careening between two poles: the corporation as a purposeful, human-like entity and the corporation as, more or less, a piece of real property: "a stuffed effigy."[39]

---

38   Mary Midgley, *Utopias, Dolphins, and Computers: Some Problems In Philosophical Plumbing* (New York: Routledge, 1996), 154.

39   "Has a Corporation a Soul?," *Illustrated American* (April 4, 1891), 284. In addition to this incident, inquest, trial, and the controversy around it, I discuss the legal,

Even though corporations are not Dennett's original focus, legal theorists today easily apply his thinking about "intentional systems" to their own claims in an attempt to resolve this long-debated question. They see that taking the intentional stance for a computer program might be a scenario that applies to business entities like corporations too. William Weaver, for instance, argues that corporations should be considered conscious entities with minds, under Dennett's conditions for intentional systems. Corporations "have identifiable personalities and are driven to certain conclusions and actions," and they are "language users" who are "culturally conditioned" like human beings. For Weaver, that means that corporations "attempt to persuade, manipulate, inform, depress, uplift, debate, and debunk other intentional systems and their actions," and by "other intentional systems" he means other people or other corporations.[40] The strategic benefit of adopting an intentional stance toward a corporation is obvious, from his perspective. It is good policy not to be caught off guard. Assuming that a corporation is trying to manipulate you is the best way to predict what it will think and do if (or when) it actually does manipulate you.

This framework is also part of older discussions about AI, including thought experiments such as the celebrated mathematician Alan Turing's "imitation" game and later challenges to it. In 1950, Turing proposes that to avoid the inevitable ambiguities of a theoretical question like "can machines think?"—a question he dismisses as "too meaningless to deserve discussion"—it would be better to find an empirical answer by playing a round of the imitation game. In that scenario, an interrogator evaluates two players he cannot see, but he can read their typewritten conversation with one another. He reads this typescript and tries to figure out whether or not one of the two people is actually a machine rather than a human being. If the machine successfully imitates a human player, an event that Turing predicts will occur by the end of the twentieth century, then the machine will have won the imitation game (or will have passed the Turing Test, as it is now commonly called). "One will be able to speak of machines thinking without expecting to be contradicted."[41] If not, then the human beings win, for the present anyway.

philosophical, and cultural debates around corporate personhood during the first half of the twentieth century in Lisa Siraganian, *Modernism and the Meaning of Corporate Persons* (Oxford University Press, 2020), 14–30.

40   William G. Weaver, "Corporations as Intentional Systems," *Journal of Business Ethics* 17, no. 1 (1998): 93–4.

41   Alan Turing, "Computing Machinery and Intelligence," (1950) in *The Philosophy of Artificial Intelligence*, ed. Margaret A. Boden (Oxford University Press, 1990), 49.

To put this in Dennett's terms, for a machine to win a round of the imitation game/Turing Test, the interrogator must make the strategic decision to adopt something like an intentional stance toward it. That is, the human interrogator will have to treat the players as if they are making sense as persons. The test, notes Simone Natale, thus "place[s] humans rather than machines at the very center of the AI question."[42] Creative writers took this idea and ran with it: Turing's diagnostic scenario has been a feature of science fiction for over half a century, beginning with novelist Philip K. Dick's writing from the 1960s. Dick portrayed the "Voigt-Kampff test" (a version of the imitation game) in his novel *Do Androids Dream of Electric Sheep?* (1968). That test consists of a series of lie detector–like questions and thought experiments designed to sniff out replicants—advanced androids—based on their inhuman emotional reactions. It is portrayed as an almost Pavlovian test of empathy, one physiologically determined by bodily reactions. In the novel's film adaptation, *Blade Runner* (1982), Rick Deckard (Harrison Ford) administers this test to Rachael (Sean Young), a sophisticated, next-generation replicant who sincerely believes she is a human being. She fails the test, but not until progressing through more complex questions. More recently, filmmakers and streaming television producers have crafted scenes to run the imitation game with readers or viewers as the interrogator. In these examples, we think we are reading about or watching a human being (perhaps a shifty, unreliable one), who is eventually revealed, in the story, to be a very advanced machine duping everyone about its true identity.

Take an episode from HBO's dystopian sci-fi drama *Westworld* (2016), about an extravagant, Wild West–inspired theme park where people can play out their depraved, often murderous fantasies without repercussions. The Westworld park is peopled with elaborate android facsimiles of human beings, called "hosts," who suffer this abuse and are programmed to promptly forget all about it. In the first season, the hosts are starting to function erratically and autonomously, leading to the firing of Bernard Lowe (Jeffrey Wright), head of the Programming Division. Bernard, meanwhile, is fed up with corporate management and its deceptions about the corporation's true plans for the hosts—the corporation's "intellectual property"—muttering that "the longer I work here, the more I think I understand the hosts. It's the human beings that confuse me."[43] We are sympathetic to his frustration. Corporate

42   Natale, *Deceitful Media*, 20.
43   *Westworld*, "Trompe L'Oeil," season 1, episode 7, 2016.

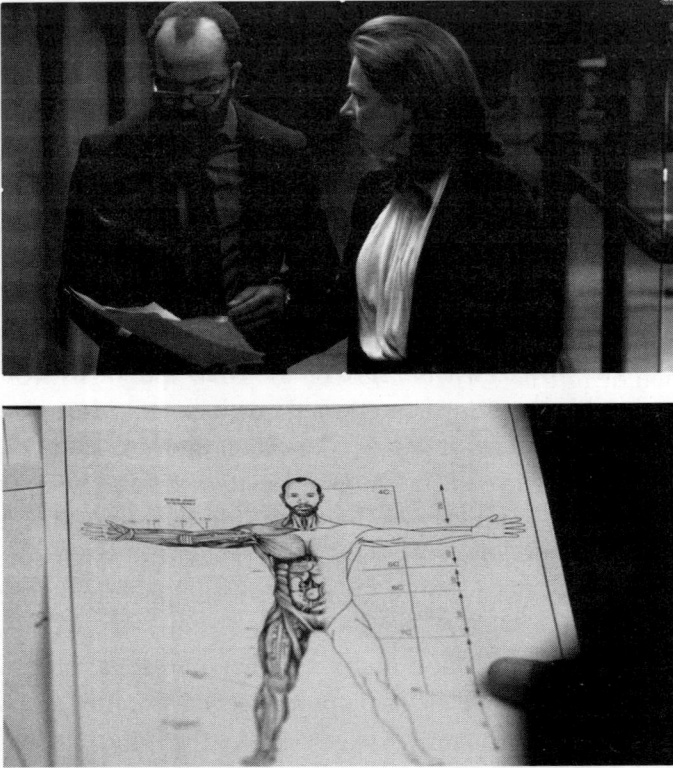

Fig. 14. *Westworld* (2016) S1:E7, "Trompe L'Oeil." © 2016 Home Box Office, Inc. Bernard Lowe (Jeffrey Wright), head of the Programming Division at Westworld, faces but does not yet recognize his designer's blueprints of himself when Westworld's administrator, Theresa Cullen (Sidse Babett Knudsen), hands them to him.

management is indeed acting in immoral, deceptive, and dishonest ways (as free from responsibility as the 1891 railroad CEO) while the hosts typically follow their individualized programming to act humanely. In that way, the people acting on behalf of the corporation seem more monstrous, and inhumane, than the machine-hosts they create.

A few moments later, Bernard is faced with a schematic drawing of himself, and all at once we interpret his previous grumblings completely differently. Surprisingly, Bernard cannot recognize what he is seeing when faced with his body's blueprint. "It doesn't look like anything to me," he reports. We awaken to the real reason he understands machines better than human beings: Bernard is actually one of the "hosts," a clandestine machine. The hosts are programmed to ignore places and aspects of reality that might contradict the narratives that they have been programmed to follow, so Bernard cannot "see" his blueprints for what they actually are—evidence that he is, in fact, the corporation's "intellectual property." He never before realized that he is a host, albeit an extremely advanced iteration that the rogue co-creator of Westworld built on the sly. "I'm not one, I can't be. My wife, my son," Bernard murmurs, dumbfounded, his self-conception fracturing as he realizes his truest memories of family were programmed too. Like Rachael in *Blade Runner*, he fools nearly everyone, himself included—and including the viewers of the previous six episodes of the series. Moments later, his programmer tells him to kill Westworld's administrator and Bernard complies, no questions asked. Unlike Rachael, then, Bernard has emotions and empathy too—except when he murders.

According to the show's narrative, Bernard-the-machine trounces human beings in each round of the imitation game. But what is really happening here? While machines win the imitation game in the fictional realm of Westworld, that is not true of *Westworld* as a television series, or on any other level. The episode is entitled "Trompe L'Oeil" for the traditional painterly technique of producing natural, illusionistic representations that mimic real-life objects (like woodgrain). The title underscores that, despite technological advances, this is a perfectly conventional form of human-created artifice, and the show is in large part following a familiar representation of such artifice in reverse. That is, we are watching a fictional *representation* of the imitation game, brilliantly performed by skilled actor Jeffrey Wright. His dexterous portrayal convinces us that Bernard is a socially awkward and potentially traumatized human being, such that when the story reveals him to be a host, it seems plausible enough. We watch a representation of the "trompe l'oeil" technique in action because Wright is a human being who masterfully and deliberately creates this effect for us with his performance. That is also why it would make no sense to say that Wright trounces the machine because there really are no machines here, just human representations of them.

These points seem obvious, and the situation should not really be very surprising; this is how good imitations work. We value Wright's skill as an actor because it is part of the dramatic filmic representation he is engaged in and that we are enjoying. Such a representation demands a suspended and eventually surprised response from us. We habitually take an intentional stance toward human actors like Wright, and we accept the convention that the character he is portraying might not be exactly what he seems within the narrative's rules. In this case, he turns out to have been a host, but in some other story he might have turned out to have been a pathological liar, undercover spy, or alien being. In each case the dramatic structure functions similarly. These are the conventions that make sophisticated science fiction work—but also make stories like fairy tales or animated cartoons work. That is, we take an intentional stance toward talking frogs or singing teapots, not because they deceive us into thinking that they are human beings but because they are fictional characters. There are already pervasive frameworks, patterns, and conventions we use to make sense of these fictions. We expect such characters to intend, act, and express themselves.

My point here is that the intentional stance we might take toward corporations or AI invariably borrows this narrative, this fictional convention, as its basic apparatus. We often relate to one another through narratives, by telling stories; this assumption of intention is built in when we read, listen to, or watch these characters. That we are sometimes duped by fictions (like Bernard) only underscores how deeply the assumption is baked in. Yet ascribing personhood to AI like Sophia the social robot discreetly borrows this narrative structure, relying on us to supply the context, situation, and human embeddedness that enable such characters to mean anything at all. The scene of Bernard's self-revelation in *Westworld* exposes this operation at work. The reason we are invested in Bernard's situation is because his character in all its complexity is intriguing, and so discovering his essential, robotic difference is chillingly uncanny and makes for a very good show. We watch this dramatic situation because it means something to us, not because we need to see a round of the diagnostic imitation game played out and resolved.

Philosophers have worked through some of these ideas in their thought experiments. John Searle points out that when we say about someone who is reading a story and answering questions about it that they are *processing information*, we really are not talking about the same thing that a computer program does when it is information processing. The computer can be programmed with the rules of language and the conventions of narrative, but it does not have the sense of what something really means in a language.[44] In a similar sense, Bernard's story means something to us not because he was able to perfectly learn the rules to win in the imitation game, but because his story and experience has all the trademarks of tragedies we have read and seen, whether ancient or modern. Those dramas teach us that his profound self-deception, and his eventual crisis of recognition, are part of the meaning of what it is to be a member of humanity—of the human community.

---

44   John R. Searle, "Minds, Brains, and Programs," in *Philosophy of Artificial Intelligence*, ed. Boden, 85.

Another way to think about Bernard's situation is that it presents, in stark relief, the difference between narrative fiction and simulation, in part by having Bernard experience his simulated, robotic self as deeply alienating. Johanna Seibt describes this distinction as two different uses of "as if." There is the "as if" that people often use to describe how robots' movements are modeled on human behavior as simulation, but that is not the same as "the 'as if' of make-believe or fictionality."[45] We slip into this latter mode of narrative fiction all the time when we face social robots like Sophia who simulate human behavior, in part because the "as if" of narrative fiction is so available to us. It is a process of public character-creation that occurs discursively, which is to say, in language. Bojana Romic calls this the process of AI individuation, which happens when we are encouraged not to think about the actual human work that went into making a robot such as Sophia seem like a human being. All sorts of people who create the robot (the engineers, designers, and so on) help, deliberately or not, to generate "the fantasy of the robot's autonomy" or independence.[46] But, in the end, that is a fantasy that belongs to a science fiction novel or to Bernard in *Westworld*.

Rather than think of AI as imitating human beings, or imagine legal personhood as a way to think about AI's legal status, it seems (once more) better to abandon the analogy altogether. As we have already seen, it is no easy feat to do so, and we should not underestimate the difficulty. Finding better analogies might be one strategy. Meir Dan-Cohen proposes something like this with his thought experiment of the "Personless Corporation," entirely run, owned, and managed by computers. This contraption, he suggests, is a better analogy for the corporation, and one we might think about as an "intelligent machine." Such an analogy still provides a "unifying image" of the corporate organization with its basic characteristics, while simultaneously "guarding against the dangers of anthropomorphism which attend the metaphor of person."[47] Just such an image is the best way to think about AI, which presents us with "a new solution" to the old problem of corporate personhood. Following any other alternative would make the old problem even more unsolvable.[48]

---

45   Johanna Seibt, "Classifying Forms and Modes of Co-Working in the Ontology of Asymmetric Social Interactions (OASIS)," *Frontiers in Artificial Intelligence and Applications* 311 (2018): 137.

46   Bojana Romic, "Negotiating Anthropomorphism in the Ai-Da Robot," *International Journal of Social Robotics* 14, no. 10 (2022): 2086.

47   Meir Dan-Cohen, *Rights, Persons, and Organizations: A Legal Theory for Bureaucratic Society* (University of California Press, 1986), 49.

48   Migle Laukyte, "The Intelligent Machine: A New Metaphor through which to Understand both Corporations and AI," *AI and Society* 36 (2021): 451–2.

On the Stickiness of Bullshit Personhood

By considering various sources for, and problems with, the tempting equivalence of AI imagined on the model of human persons, we have begun to see the problems with the comparison. Others have noticed problems, too, and have recommendations. Nadia Banteka proposes that law should resist its tendency to analogize when faced with AI entities and "resort to empirical analysis instead."[49] The idea of the intelligent machine has also seemed a better term for the capacities and situation of AI, even for so-called social robots like Sophia. And yet these personhood analogies remain incredibly tempting. It seems hard to resist projecting Jeffrey Wright's humanity onto Bernard the character, and thus imagining Bernard the (robot) host as a person. The same sort of projection happens in today's real-life AI scenarios, despite the evident problems raised. It seems that there is more to diagnose about this situation.

The persistence of this phenomenon depends on a kind of "personhood" illusion or self-deception occurring within our language itself. That is, the mere act of describing AI often seems to produce the phenomenon of a human-like personhood. It is an illusion so foundational to our thinking and experiencing that it is difficult to perceive it at work. When Wittgenstein writes, in the epigraph to this chapter, of the "constant surprise at the new tricks language plays on us when we get into a new field," he alerts us to this tendency.[50] To see these tricks in action, consider responses to the recent unveiling of ChatGPT and other LLMs. Blaise Agüera y Arcas, a vice president at Google who led the machine intelligence effort there, writes that these new algorithms are indeed "bullshitting" because we have asked them to. Yet, he claims, they are also "learning a great deal of embodied knowledge" through Wikipedia, Reddit, and online material they are trained on, all written by embodied humans. His idea is that LLMs are (somehow) "learning" human beings' "embodied knowledge" because such knowledge hitches a ride on a Wikipedia page and is caught in our language whether we like it or not. One might wonder: What could such "embodied knowledge" mean? How does an LLM learn by feeling and doing? At any rate, an advanced LLM, he continues, "also forms models of *us*. And models of our models of *it*. If, indeed, *it* is the right pronoun."[51] What Agüera y Arcas assumes

---

49   Nadia Banteka, "Artificially Intelligent Persons," *Houston Law Review* 58, no. 3 (2021): 559.

50   Wittgenstein, *Lectures*, 1.

51   Blaise Agüera y Arcas, "Do Large Language Models Understand Us?," *Daedalus* 151, no. 2 (2022): 186–87, 194.

here is that LLMs could, in fact, "bullshit" when prompted, as well as "learn," "form," "hallucinate," "model,"—and "model us"—all terms that further imply the possibility of *knowing* and *distinguishing* truth from lies, reality from fiction, data from abstract representations, and so on.

Increasingly, skeptics of this account of AI have pushed back on such humanizing language and have tried in different ways to show how and where mistakes are emerging. They suggest that we are confusing the fact that LLMs can generate results that we cannot predict with the conclusion that, because of this unpredictability, LLMs must have something like a will or a mind. Think about how we might respond to Agüera y Arcas's claim that when we are interacting with one of these advanced algorithms, we tend to "automatically construct a simplified model of our interlocuter as a person," and that the LLM too, reciprocally, "forms models of *us.*" This is very close to Dennett's "intentional stance" put into practice. "Like a person," the LLM can "surprise us" in these moments, says the Google VP, a capacity "necessary to support our impression of personhood."[52] Although he is not quite saying that they are persons, he is leaving that "impression" wide open.

But there are other, more plausible ways to think about what is happening in a scenario like this one, when an LLM like ChatGPT surprises us with its apparently sentient output. Our pattern-finding selves imagine deliberate reasons and project intentional behavior where there might only be the effects of unusual happenstance, or even simple randomness. In such instances, "autonomy is confused with unpredictability of the result."[53] Random events can be surprising without our identifying the cause of those events as a person—or, at least, calling the cause something besides an "it." Elena Esposito puts it this way: "What algorithms are reproducing is not the intelligence of people but the informativity of communication." We are conflating the two things when we describe them interchangeably. That is, it is not that we are facing a brilliant computer that has learned to think like us. We are, rather, facing a tool that has been trained "to participate in communication," enabling it "to react appropriately and generate information in their interaction with other participants."[54] It is a simulation, an "as if" of a conversation, not an actual dialogue. But likely because conversation is so formative, fundamental, and predictable for human beings—so intrinsic to our social

52   Ibid., 193–4.
53   Sergio M. C. Avila Negri, "Robot as Legal Person: Electronic Personhood in Robotics and Artificial Intelligence," *Frontiers in Robotics and AI* 8 (2021): 3.
54   Esposito, *Artificial Communication*, 18, 15.

selves—even simulations of it can seem real enough, and lead us to attribute intentionality to the algorithms generating it.

Consider another recent example of a social robot. "Ai-Da" was devised and financed in 2019 by gallerist Aidan Meller and curator Lucy Seal, and built by Engineered Arts, "the UK's leading designer and manufacturer of humanoid entertainment robots."[55] Ai-Da is "the world's first ultra-realist robot artist," according to the robot's website. "She is a performance artist, designer, and poet," able to "captivate audiences with her unique blend of art, technology, and trans-humanism." These descriptions present Ai-Da as a feminine, autonomous creator intentionally operating in the art world, following in the familiar model of the avant-garde genius, one ahead of "her" time. Supporting this account, the website presents the robot's exhibitions, speeches, artistic displays, and press briefings, whether at the Oxford Union, Parliament, 10 Downing Street, the Venice Biennale, or the UN. Moreover, the robot's technological enhancements are presented as "her" creative growth: "Ai-Da's new painting style" is the result of "her new robotic arm and AI algorithms."[56] The robot's cameras, bionic hand, and algorithms are often programmed to generate portraits of celebrities, such as Queen Elizabeth and Paul McCartney, as well as "self-portraits" of "herself" while dressed in bohemian smocks and overalls.

Discussions of Ai-Da's "self-portraits" have accepted this label of its productions, and they position the machine in a lineage of human self-portrait artists. Gabriella Giannachi observes, first, that contemporary human artists such as Irene Fenara and Jonathan Yeo use video and surveillance technology to create self-portraits, before segueing into a discussion of Ai-Da as a "humanoid AI robot-performance artist . . . capable of drawing people." The robot "created a series of self-portraits by looking into a mirror with her camera eyes." While acknowledging that Ai-Da has a creator programming these performances, Giannachi explains that the questions it raises are about control and selfhood, with the robot imagined as following on a continuum with earlier video artists.[57] Giannachi is thus positioning Ai-Da as resembling a *Westworld* character in the flesh, like Bernard faced with his own blueprints and querying his maker and his meaning.

---

55   engineeredarts.co.uk.
56   ai-darobot.com.
57   Gabrielle Giannachi, *Technologies of the Self-Portrait: Identity, Presence, and the Construction of the Subject(s) in Twentieth and Twenty-First Century* Art (New York: Routledge, 2023), 111–13.

Fig. 15. Ai-Da generating "art." Ai-Da © 2025 © Ai-Da Robot Studios, www.ai-darobot.com.

Yet all these terms used to describe Ai-Da's movements are deeply misleading and require a broad set of premises about Ai-Da's supposed personhood, chief of which is that Ai-Da is a contemporary performance artist, adept in the history of Western art, who can draw passably and is capable of making art by looking into a mirror with "camera-eyes." The question not asked is whether Ai-Da actually has the capacity, let alone awareness, consciousness, or intention, to do any of these things attributed to "her." To obscure these challenges, scenes of Ai-Da presented as "drawing" or "painting" borrow heavily from the long history of portraiture, as well as representations of self-portraiture, and rely on that backstory to fill out "her" persona. Promotional photos of Ai-Da present the robot "as a lonely figure in a Victorian atelier, surrounded by its drawings and paintings," a setting that adds "to the myth of a lone genius artist."[58] Even the robot's outfits fit the part. And, in some of these photographs, the viewer is positioned behind the robot's head, facing a mirror, as if we could be looking from "her eyes" and seeing from "her" imagined subjectivity. It is a mode of point-of-view framing common not in painterly self-portraiture but in film and television scenes of people absorbed in their activities, and so we envision Ai-Da in a similar situation.

---

58   Romic, "Negotiating," 2090.

The publicity performances and presentations of robots like Ai-Da, as well as advanced LLMs, have prompted AI theorist Seibt to rightly assert that "social robotics has a description problem." By that she means that when we are talking about these types of AI, and particularly when we are trying to get a handle on what happens when people interact with AI like Sophia or programs like ChatGPT, we tend to use "common verbs for human capacities" like "'ask,' 'answer,' 'greet,' 'remind,' 'recognize,' 'guide,' 'teach,' 'observe,' etc." In discussions of Ai-Da, we might add that terms frequently include words like "look," "create," "draw," "paint," "design," and "write." Relying on this kind of vocabulary is not a benign phenomenon, argues Seibt, because each word inherently implies an essential human trait like feeling or intentionality. Using these terms confuses us about what is actually happening in these interactions, or what we are really observing in a photograph of Ai-Da supposedly gazing at herself and drawing a self-portrait. For Seibt, even designating robots as "working" is problematic because they cannot experience the phenomenon of laboring the way we do (with all the satisfaction, annoyance, and potential exploitation it entails), and so all the issues intrinsically connected with work are left out. She sums up: "Responsible robotics and AI begins at the linguistic level" because this language seeps into all our other thinking about AI.[59] From Seibt's perspective, we have not even begun to address this problem.

Perhaps calling the issues with social robotics "a description problem" sounds like downplaying their seriousness, as if once the question of what to call Ai-Da's "drawings" is worked out, everything else will fall into place and our conceptions of AI will be corrected for good. But the point of Seibt's critique about our AI talk, and the point I am also developing here, is that these misunderstandings and incorrect judgments happen early, carelessly, and often. They are not easy to fix. One of the most brilliant philosophers of AI, John Haugeland, saw aspects of this tendency as a result of our "human chauvinism," a sort of innate, self-centric prejudice that was simply "built into our very concept of intelligence." Even when we apply the notion of astuteness to other kinds of entities, we cannot peel it away from its human source because we have no other source—we lack any other concept with which we could possibly replace "human intelligence." "If we escaped our [anthropomorphic] 'prejudice,' we wouldn't know what we were talking about."[60]

---

59   Seibt, "Classifying Forms," 135, 143.

60   John Haugeland, *Artificial Intelligence: The Very Idea* (Cambridge, MA: MIT Press, 1985), 5.

When we use the language of human cognition and "intelligence" to describe what we imagine is happening with advanced AI, it seems to be the closest approximation we could make. We do so, even though some recent AI experts have seriously questioned the structural similarities between our brains and artificial neural networks, and suspect that the entire "rhetoric of anthropomorphism" applied to this topic is fundamentally incorrect and "can do more harm than good."[61]

More broadly, the deceptive language of robotics is really a symptom of the tremendous, still unbridgeable gap between human life and our AI reality. Haugeland puts it this way: "Trying to explain thought and reason in cybernetic terms is as hopeless and misguided as trying to explain it in terms of conditioned reflexes or Hume's gravity-like association of ideas."[62] In other words, it is like trying to use "numbers or vectors" (today we would say "complex algorithms") to describe "gardening"— to describe not only what the activity called "gardening" is and what it means anthropologically to our society now, but also why any individual person does it, how it is fulfills their life, and so on. No doubt there are algorithms that could capture realistic *aspects* of gardening, but they could not capture this filled-out *meaning* of gardening.

We imagine, because so much science fiction has showed us this path, that ChatGPT and Ai-Da are approximating us more and more with every technological upgrade. That fantasy is the basic plot of *Westworld* (along with most *Black Mirror* episodes). But the reality is that the obvious, daily failures and fragilities of ChatGPT and Ai-Da are an entirely predictable part of what they are. How often, each day, does Siri fail us? We do realize, all the time, all the ways these algorithms are very stupid (or, more accurately, "stupid"). Our more likely reality is that even the most basic living organisms communicate in ways exponentially more complex than any our AI creations can mimic, and we still do not fully understand the mechanisms of their cell signaling. Yet, unlike a single-celled organism, "what the machine becomes," and that it becomes anything at all, is "absolutely up to humans."[63]

---

61   David Watson, "The Rhetoric and Reality of Anthropomorphism in Artificial Intelligence," *Minds and Machines* 29 (2019): 418.

62   Haugeland, *Artificial Intelligence*, 173.

63   Niklas Toivakainen, "Machines and the Face of Ethics," *Ethics and Information Technology* 18, no. 4 (2016): 276.

Elaborating the ePersonhood Dangers

Much of this chapter has articulated the descriptive and conceptual difficulties and errors in thinking about ePersonhood—about the conceptual and theoretical errors that follow when trying to make sense of AI in terms of legal personhood. Having seen these myriad problems, we can now turn more directly to the damaging effects of ePersonhood. Whereas the initial issue was where ePersonhood came from and how it could be defended, the concern now is with what this encroaching notion might do and has done in the real world. The remainder of this chapter argues that we should not support ePersonhood for at least two critical reasons: because (1) AI is inherently oblivious to the social realm, if not actively destructive of it, and (2) giving AI legal personhood, which is to say, some form of protection and possibly agency in law, is also to give it some decision-making power over us. This represents a type of technological ideology that bodes ill in myriad ways.

In a sense, both of these points are captured in old fears about technology and advanced AI, perhaps most memorably represented in Stanley Kubrick's science fiction film *2001: A Space Odyssey* (1968). The lesson there is that if AI starts to have desire and a will, then AI will want to murder you. The computer HAL 9000 begins to behave erratically after becoming convinced that human beings are not as committed to their mission to Jupiter as they should be—or as it is. HAL 9000 goes on to murder four human crew members of the spaceship *Discovery One* because, to its AI mind, the mission demands it, before Dave finally manages to manually shut down the mainframe. The film captures common fears about AI as sociopathic: that once sentient, it simply cannot or will not value human life. Especially worrisome, from the vantage point of our "smart" refrigerators and microwaves, is that HAL 9000 was designed to run nearly everything on the spaceship while the crew either rested in suspended animation or caught up on leisure activities. Its control of electronics and the oxygen supply placed every human being in its thrall. Media talk of the coming "singularity" (the theoretical moment of AI consciousness) replays many of these same anxieties.

Yet HAL 9000 reveals the same problems as other examples of science fiction we have considered, whether on television or in the performances by Sophia and Ai-Da. Despite some eerie elements of foreshadowing (such as the iPad-like device on which Dave watches the news aboard his starship), *2001* does not predict the most straightforward, present-day concerns with ePersonhood and advanced AI. The problem, now, is not that murderous AIs have arrived. It is that the AIs that do exist are enormously powerful while also entirely unaware and without their own intent. Not only are they unmindful of human beings; they are unmindful, period. Moreover, these AI cannot understand the worth of what we value—because we cannot train them to have values, and so we cannot convince them to value what we do.

Jacob Browning makes a version of this case when he hypothesizes that "the fickleness, dishonesty, offensiveness, and bullshit in LLMs are signs that these systems are oblivious to the social world."[64] Trying to tweak the algorithms will not get us anywhere because what matters to us about "social personhood" simply cannot be a part of how such a system is designed and trained. He explains it this way: An LLM cannot be taught to be less offensive. All one can do is fine-tune the algorithm so that its generated output is statistically less likely to be offensive to the humans who train it. We might use the linguistic shortcut of saying that the LLM has learned to be inoffensive, but that is a misleading way of putting it, projecting the programmer's human intention onto the algorithm. For some legal scholars, this inability to modify AI's behavior in any meaningful way raises the possibility of abuses within the legal system, were such AI to be granted personhood. They would gain rights and privileges that they could be programmed to use against human beings, while their unmodifiable conduct would go unpunished. In such a scenario, "it is unclear how corresponding legal obligations could be enforced against them."[65]

The AIs' absence of social understanding and relationships also means that they cannot possess a sense of personality. John Haugeland discusses why. A friendship with someone might seem at first glance like a kind of complex "cognitive structure"—something one could eventually teach to an AI like HAL 9000 or to the next generation of Sophia or Ai-Da. But to see "friendship" only in this way is to seriously misunderstand it. What makes friendships vital to us is the way they "flesh out and give meaning to our own lives." Without those concepts and their practical reality, our existence "would be hopelessly barren and hollow, as if there weren't really anybody there—just a contentless, pointless, cognitive skeleton."

---

64   Jacob Browning, "Personhood and AI: Why Large Language Models Don't Understand Us," *AI and Society* (2023): 2.

65   Joanna J. Bryson, Mihailis E. Diamantis, and Thomas D. Grant, "Of, for, and by the People: The Legal Lacuna of Synthetic Persons," *Artificial Intelligence and Law* 25, no. 3 (2017): 283.

In order to have a friend or even a frenemy, you have to have an ego and personality to begin with. To Haugeland, such fundamental qualities like selfhood, ego, subjectivity, understanding, compassion, and intelligence are a constellation of attributes that rely on one another. "Only a being who cares about who it is as a continuing, selfsame individual can care about guilt or folly, self-respect or achievement, life or death."[66] And to lack the capacity to care about these basic moral fundamentals also means that such an AI, for all its potential cognitive capacities, would lack the capacity to understand or respond to even the most rudimentary forms of social conditioning. These moral fundamentals are also what give us the capacity to lie or be evil (and to make sense of those without this capacity, such as psychopaths).

Then there is the more sinister reason AI is designed in the first place. Its creation is not morally or ethically neutral but has a very deliberate human purpose. That is why trying to look at AI as if we can observe it from a neutral position is fundamentally mistaken, writes Niklas Toivakainen. Human beings contemplate and determine everything that an AI will become—every characteristic—and, in doing so, they also implicitly answer questions about why the machine or algorithm should be built or designed in the first place. Surveying what we have produced and why, Toivakainen judges that "our society and culture is becoming increasingly dominated by a technological ideology," one that intensifies and extends our alienation by offering a fantasy that we can become more independent from our responsibilities to others. AI will take care of chores like caregiving that people have been eager to outsource if they can afford to.[67] That is a choice we have made. Virginia Eubanks makes a similarly stark assessment when considering decision-making AI, like digital-tracking algorithms for people receiving aid from the state welfare system. In these cases, critical ethical-social choices are transferred from caseworkers to computer engineers and economists, to "political decision-making machines." Such algorithms are not built for the purpose of social justice but "to manage the symptoms of austerity"—another damaging social choice.[68]

What does the ePerson look like when we put all these pieces together? It looks like something that is powerful yet unaware, socially mindless yet apparently able to produce semblances of thought in response to

---

66   Haugeland, *Artificial Intelligence*, 237, 239, 245.
67   Toivakainen, "Machines and the Face of Ethics," 276, 281.
68   Virginia Eubanks, *Automating Inequality: How High-Tech Tools Profile, Police, and Punish the Poor* (New York: St. Martin's Press, 2018), 224–5.

our queries. It is also able to offend and injure without possessing the capacity to learn or understand ethical behavior. And it is able to mimic crucial aspects of "friendship" through seemingly communicative chatbots, yet unable to express feelings or care about anyone, including itself. Finally, we are seeing that the reasons these AIs are designed to begin with is to obscure and distract ourselves from our alienation rather than to ameliorate that sense or transform society for the better. For all these reasons, one might suspect that a better assessment of AI and ePersonhood is in relation to an artificial legal person we have already seen in so many different guises throughout this book, a person fully formed in its current guise well over a century ago. Monsieur le Capital, the corporate person, returns once more.

It should not surprise us, then, that, during the height of debates about corporate personhood in the late nineteenth century and the first decades of the twentieth, that entity was described in some of the very same terms that AI is now. At that time, political cartoonists frequently depicted the corporate person as a strange, monstrous creature—a giant octopus, human giant, mindless brute with multiple heads, hybrid machine-beast—because many people were profoundly uncertain about

Fig. 16. William Allen Rogers, *Who is Master?* (1905). Published in *New York Herald*, Feb. 8, 1905, p. 7. Photograph retrieved from the Library of Congress. Library of Congress Prints and Photographs Division, Washington, DC, 20540 USA.

corporations' capacity to have intentions and live in the world with (and as) persons. Sometimes these artists depicted the corporation as what we would now think of as a cyborg or AI, as in a 1905 cartoon of President Teddy Roosevelt grappling fearlessly with a railroad creature, a human body with an engine for a head and steel tracks for feet, while Uncle Sam looks on.

At that time, the question was how one might come to negotiate a contractual agreement with such a hybrid beast or how society might control an entity that lacked basic moral standards.[69] For one legal theorist of the period, the situation resembled that original work of AI science fiction, Mary Shelley's *Frankenstein; or, The Modern Prometheus* (1818). The corporation, the "artificially created monster threatens to injure, if not destroy, much of what [Doctor] Frankenstein holds most dear."[70] The scenario of ChatGPT and its artificially created monster ilk, and the question (for example) of how such LLMs might upend education and working life, implies that little has changed from that earlier verdict. Even the recent imagination of the LLM as an octopus-like "shoggoth" seems to replay the older cultural narratives of the corporate beast.[71]

Considering all these serious limitations, giving AI agency and legal personhood, particularly a form and power that would be in competition with our own, seems profoundly misguided. It would be to give some amount of decision-making power to an entity that cannot share our interests and values and, more problematically, does not have the capacity to understand them. Eubanks describes it as an act of reframing fundamental "social decisions about who we are" and turning them into "systems engineering problems."[72] For this reason, some of the sharpest critics of ePersonhood have warned that, by giving AI its legal personhood, "we give away part of our (social) identity."[73] It is a step toward robbing us of some of our own agency and autonomy in ways that we might not even see happening, and likely by overestimating and misunderstanding how such AI works in the first place. We see, merely, a statistical operation when ChatGPT responds to a query, yet we assume incorrectly that the output reveals a form of thinking and agency like our own.

---

69   Siraganian, *Corporate Persons*, 57–8.

70   Maurice Wormser, *Frankenstein, Incorporated* (New York: Whittlesey House, McGraw-Hill, 1931), 100.

71   Kevin Roose, "Why an Octopus-like Creature Has Come to Symbolize the State of A.I.," *New York Times*, May 30, 2023.

72   Eubanks, *Automating Inequality*, 12.

73   Susanne Beck, "Intelligent Agents and Criminal Law: Negligence, Diffusion of Liability and Electronic Personhood," *Robotics and Autonomous Systems* 86 (2016): 142.

I suspect that the real story of what we are doing at such moments, and what we have a difficult time recognizing that we are doing, is creating new imagined persons in our drama of human life. HAL 9000 was a riveting creation precisely because it was a new species of *villain*, one all the more terrifying because it had even less of a body, and maybe less of an ego, than the phantoms, poltergeists, and ghosts of classical horror. HAL 9000 manifests its ultra-rational will simply by tweaking computer systems and shutting off oxygen supplies. Mary Midgley observes that something like this dynamic of new characters appears in the utopian fantasies of AI creativity. And she also points out that part of this fantasy requires that such entities have the improbable ability to fix what are, essentially, bad human choices. Such entities "will have to be quasi-people or super-people with creative powers capable of deeply changing the social scene."[74] It does not take much extra effort to sense the wish repressed here. If only there really could be someone or something smarter than us, that we happen to create, something able to save us from our intractable contemporary messes and impending disasters. The irony is that outsourcing our salvation to some other technological entity, one with autonomy over us, will make it all the more difficult to target the actual powerful entities—individuals, countries, and corporations—who produce that AI technology in the first place.[75]

Cyber False Consciousness

Think again about Sophia, the social robot we started with, who was gifted with state citizenship from Saudi Arabia in 2017.[76] One reason this publicity stunt perturbed so many observers was the inegalitarianism it totally ignored. Over 40 percent of that country's population, many from Asian countries without oil reserves, are non-citizens without basic legal protections let alone the entitlements of citizenship. Or, recall former Guantánamo detainee Mohammed el Gharani, from this book's introduction. One reason he lacked Saudi citizenship, despite being born there, was precisely because of that country's draconian policies toward foreign workers and even their children. And human rights groups have long observed that Saudi Arabian women citizens are discriminated against under the male guardianship system. Although there have been

---

74   Midgley, *Utopias, Dolphins, and Computers*, 152.
75   Watson, "Rhetoric and Reality," 435.
76   Parviainen and Coeckelbergh, "Political Choreography," 715–16.

some recent reforms, according to Human Rights Watch, the country's "first codified law on personal status . . . formally enshrines male guardianship over women."[77] The irony of Sophia's nonhuman yet "gendered" status meant that, on paper, she was a woman-like Saudi citizen with more rights than any actual Saudi woman citizen. And although this is, obviously, an unusual case, it hints at a real phenomenon. Actual human beings, their work, and their exploitation are obscured or undermined by AI personhood and its techno-ideological rhetoric. The "person" in the news, traveling around the globe and visiting the UN, is Sophia—not the ordinary woman in Saudi Arabia who, until 2019, could not acquire a passport enabling her to travel outside the country without her male guardian's approval.

This sleight of hand, this *cyber false consciousness*, comes in different deceptive flavors. Mary Gray and Siddharth Suri have named one version of it "ghost work"—the intentionally hidden or obscured "human labor powering many mobile phone apps, websites, and artificial intelligence systems." These recurring small tasks, completed painstakingly and often mind-numbingly by human beings rather than by Sophia, Ai-Da, or ChatGPT, actually enable the massive transformation of AI into so-called smart technology. Ghost work enables our phones, websites, and AI to run "while keeping the workers hidden behind the APIs [Application Programming Interface software] used to hire them."[78] These workers are often some of the most exploited. One of the more disturbing stories to emerge in the last few years has been the method necessary to train LLMs like ChatGPT to "recognize" (and presumably, avoid generating) hate speech and other harmful output. To do so, corporations like OpenAI outsource the training work to countries with large populations of multilingual workers willing to read AI-generated hate speech, violence, and sexual abuse for a few dollars an hour. Often, this work takes place in East Africa, India, the Philippines, and in refugee camps, where more lucrative and labor-protected work is hard to find. In Nairobi, Kenya, former content moderators for ChatGPT started petitions against OpenAI for mental health injuries after having to evaluate hundreds upon hundreds of text passages depicting brutal sexual and other forms of graphic violence. There was no protection for workers subjected to this language and to the many harms of ghost work.[79]

77   hrw.org.

78   Mary L. Gray and Siddharth Suri, *Ghost Work: How to Stop Silicon Valley from Building a New Global Underclass* (New York: Houghton Mifflin Harcourt, 2019), lx, 4.

79   Niamh Rowe, "'It's Destroyed Me Completely': Kenyan Moderators Decry Toll of Training of Ai Models," *The Guardian*, August 2, 2023.

The plight of the Nairobi content moderators is just one instance of a systemic trend: the undermining or exploiting of human labor in AI production and the obscuring of this reality. When you type something into the text box, it looks like ChatGPT is doing its miraculous writing all by its algorithmic self. But in the dark background, the labor of thousands of individual human beings has been needed, labor that is exploitative, disregarded, or minimized. Or simply stolen.[80] When we turn Ai-Da into an ePerson and thus an individual, we are experiencing this cyber false consciousness; we are refusing to see the real people whose labor animates Ai-Da.[81] It is for this reason that Seibt insists that we "must not reduce the notion of work to its functional economic definition, and should acknowledge that robots cannot 'work,' in the literal sense of the term, and that we cannot work with them."[82] And not just work, in the abstract, but entire sequences of exploitation are obscured too. "The robot veils a whole chain of labor, material, and energy that is compressed, as it were, in the robot," writes Niklas Toivakainen. This is another way cyber false consciousness works. We see a Roomba, for example, scooting around the living room vacuuming up cat hair, and we might think of it as a charming thing, an independent unit. But it is really "a network/cluster of technologies, (human and machine) labor, materials, and energy." When we focus on the Roomba rather than the capitalist process that produced it, we risk "deepening the alienation and opaqueness" such technology engenders.[83]

The global supply chains needed to keep the Roomba vacuuming (and not permanently trapped under the couch) require vast amounts of money, technology, and corporate coordination. This situation is more extreme, the more complex and advanced the AI. And the bigger and more sophisticated the LLM, the fewer the organizations that have the resources and capital to create it. As the science fiction writer Ted Chiang notes, "When Silicon Valley tries to imagine superintelligence, what it comes up with is no-holds-barred capitalism."[84] Unsurprisingly, contemporary AI demands significant amounts of venture capital and other forms of private funding from mega-rich individuals as well as

---

80   James B. Meigs, "Is AI Just Theft Under Another Name?," *Commentary*, March 2024; commentary.org.

81   Romic, "Negotiating Anthropomorphism," 2086.

82   Seibt, "Classifying Forms," 144.

83   Niklas Toivakainen, "Capitalism, Labor and the Totalising Drive of Technology," *Frontiers in Artificial Intelligence and Applications* 311 (2018): 99, 102.

84   Ted Chiang, "Silicon Valley is Turning into its Own Worst Fear," BuzzFeed News.com, December 18, 2017.

from huge corporations. Some of them, such as the venture capitalist Andreessen Horowitz (AH Capital Management, LLC), have successfully discouraged the US Copyright Office from holding corporations liable for copyright infringements by their AI.[85] Increasingly, there exists "a digital divide" between the wealthy corporations (mainly in the US and China) able to train LLMs and the nonprofits and countries without access to computing power, who cannot.[86] Microsoft invested $13 billion in OpenAI, which created and owns ChatGPT; OpenAI then successfully lobbied the EU to weaken the language of AI regulation. Economic capital enables these monopoly companies to flex real political muscle in support of the AI they design.

This chapter's proposal has been to urge us to abandon ePersonhood and most of the debates about the topic, too, which distract from and obscure the real issues at stake with advanced AI. As Chiang observes, imagining "how to create friendly AI is simply more fun to think about than the problem of industry regulation."[87] Truly functioning state regulations could render legal AI personhood irrelevant. Yet, admittedly, rejecting ePersonhood, and the cyber false consciousness that sustains it, will not solve all the problems of our contemporary AI situation. One former Google researcher, Meredith Whittaker, has become a prominent critic of the current AI status quo and what it has already produced. The development of this computing is not a scientific breakthrough, she writes, but "the product of significantly concentrated data and computer resources that reside in the hands of a few large tech corporations."[88] Yet it is also a technology "dependent on all of the free-to-the-commons labor, billions of hours that are now being concentrated in the hands of a handful of companies that then get to launder that as 'intelligence' in ways that are further cementing information and power asymmetries."[89] AI has become a financial, economic, and political technology—and a massively inequitable one—that we are mistakenly understanding and treating as if it were, merely, a scientific and software tool.

The year after Sophia became a Saudi citizen, Whittaker co-organized the "Google Walkouts," unofficial worker protests against Google that demanded various changes to the company. The following year she

---

85   Meigs, "Is AI Just Theft," commentary.org.

86   Sasha Luccioni, "The Mounting Human and Environmental Costs of Generative AI," arstechnica.com, April 2023.

87   Chiang, "Silicon Valley."

88   Meredith Whittaker, "The Steep Cost of Capture," *Interactions* 28 (Nov–Dec 2021): 51.

89   time.com.

resigned from Google, and she has since become president of Signal, a nonprofit that produces the encrypted messaging application of the same name. This was an application that many people only became aware of after Pete Hegseth used it to (accidentally) share US military plans with a journalist, although faculty and students had begun using it during the university encampments in support of Palestine and in protest of the siege on Gaza. Signal could be used to protect free expression, as many avoided using university-owned email servers and other messaging technology owned by increasingly untrustworthy corporations like Facebook or Microsoft. While not a flawless solution, alternative applications are a potentially useful strategy for protesters or people engaged in civil disobedience.

End-to-end encryption applications like Signal are no easy panacea and they have their own problems. Witness the August 2024 arrest of Pavel Durov, founder and CEO of the Dubai-based Telegram, another popular messaging application that lacks content moderation. The French prosecution alleged that Telegram had been illicitly used for drug trafficking and distributing images of child sexual abuse (one researcher observed that the app "appears basically unresponsive to law enforcement").[90] But, for Whittaker, becoming a leader of Signal was consistent with her broader realization that the people AI most harms are "subjects of AI's application 'on them' by those who have power over them—from employers, to governments to law enforcement."[91] Fighting these harms not only calls for applications and nonprofits like Signal, but, more broadly, the labor movement, organizing workers in technology.[92] Thankfully, solidarity remains part of the social world that ePersons cannot access.

90   Barbara Ortutay, "What Is Telegram and Why Was Its CEO Arrested in Paris?," *APNews*, August 28, 2024.
91   theinnovator.news.
92   Whittaker, "Steep Cost," 55.

Conclusion: Letting Persons Go

What happens when we give more entities rights and standing in the courtroom and the political sphere? Taking a tour through contemporary legal debates, this book has uncovered the damaging alignments between personhood arguments for fetuses and trees, mice and chatbots. In each chapter, these seemingly new kinds of expansive persons emerge as variations on an older theme. That theme is the story of capital legally personified, first as the commodity and eventually as the corporation. As we have seen repeatedly, the corporation is the necessary, legitimatizing model for every form of expansive person. With all kinds of persons formally equal in law, and with the law crowding out other forms of moral thought in tolerant, liberal society, these increasingly thing-like expansive persons take the main stage. And yet "the scenography of personification," Yan Thomas reminds us, "solves nothing."[1]

Legal rights and standing for lakes or embryos or algorithms, an allowance that we choose to call "personhood," is ultimately only a legal *tool*. It enables lawmakers, lawyers, and judges to make certain kinds of arguments, on behalf of clients and for aims that they desire, in situations where otherwise they could not. The most potent result of that tool is its capacity to pull legal *subjectivity* apart from legal *liability*. In other words, possessing legal personhood enables one to become a subject in the eyes of the law without having all the corresponding legal duties. Most basically, this is the lucrative situation of corporate stockholders—those people with a contractual right to their purchased stock—who do

---

1   Yan Thomas, et al., *Legal Artifices: Ten Essays On Roman Law In the Present Tense* (Edinburgh University Press, 2021), 117.

not have to pay any of a corporation's debts. The corporate "person" is the one who must pay off those debts, not the stockholder. That separation of rights from liabilities, privileges from duties, repeats itself in every form of expansive person that exists—or is proposed to exist—today or in the future. And that simple fact explains why personhood expands. It is a powerful legal tool, seemingly with no downside (only more rights!) for the individual entities that can acquire it and the human beings—fewer and fewer, but invariably human beings—who actually manipulate it and benefit from it.

This capacity to separate, and isolate, rights from duties does not make legal personhood a *neutral* tool. Far from it. As the environmentalist John Rodman predicted nearly fifty years ago, it seems likely that "the ceaseless struggle to extend morality and legality may by now be more a part of our problem than its solution."[2] That ceaseless struggle continues to this day, causing even more problems. We have seen all sorts of ways that separating and isolating rights from duties creates detrimental effects. These include rendering pregnant people into mere containers for "unborn persons" (with justices given enormous power), or providing citizenship to AI "social" robots to deflect from the consolidation of capital and from human rights abuses. In both those cases, other legal strategies, at the very least, could be championed as responses. Equal protection for pregnant persons, for example, or protections for labor unions for AI workers are both established policies that should be embraced rather than reaching for more legal personhood. Personhood looked like a tool of liberation; it has become an instrument of our exploitation. It serves, in effect, to turn political questions into legal and technocratic ones—and then to remove those political questions from the world of public dispute.

Also part of this story is our increasing *objecthood* under this expansive personhood regime. With arguments on behalf of legal standing for nonhuman animals or trees, human beings are placed on a spectrum with humans as vegetables on one end, and vegetables as persons on the other. A person on this model looks like a natural object (a lake, a moose) that can be located out in the world—or inside a uterus, like embryonic DNA, which activists for fetal personhood identify as a replacement for one's soul. And as we saw with the case of nonhuman animal personhood, there is invariably a large amount of distortion at work in these equivalences, distortions that blind us from really seeing what, say, a

---

2   John Rodman, "The Liberation of Nature?," *Inquiry* 20 (1977): 104.

spider or caterpillar wants and needs, as in Nina Katchadourian's bio-art performances. Her work, like the other examples of contemporary art discussed in the book, relies upon a long, charged dynamic in modern art that it activates anew. Art's status as an object and a commodity became a crisis that had to be met directly.[3] Personhood—whether surrogate or real—is the field in which that now plays out.

Maybe we could somehow find a way to overlook all these drawbacks if expansive personhood worked, if it somehow succeeded in its objectives. But even on that point the verdict is, at best, mixed. Fetal personhood is probably the most dubious "success" story, at least in the US, insofar as abortions and reproductive justice are becoming ever harder to obtain. But the threat to abortion access was also one of the most critical campaign issues in recent memory. The other forms of expansive personhood—nonhuman animal, natural object, AI—have largely failed thus far, working more effectively as rhetorical arguments than as practical legal challenges to policy. The disastrous ecological situation of Ecuador is a case in point. After the country inscribed environmental personhood in its constitution, incorporating the indigenous term "Pachamama" for nature, people were allowed to sue on nature's (Pachamama's) behalf. Yet advocates there have failed "to challenge any of the structural causes of environmental harms," and Ecuador's GDP from oil extraction has only increased in the interim.[4]

What would it look like to give up our dependance on expanding legal personhood? This can feel like imagining a utopian horizon of impossibility, bringing to mind the early Soviet debates about whether bourgeois law was fated to "wither away."[5] At this point, no one is holding their breath for that eventuality. The notion of legal personhood, or simply of an individual having standing (the right to make their case in court), is too tightly woven into the fabric of contemporary law. Alternatively, some might suspect I am advocating an atavistic return to the old medieval or Roman status hierarchies, in which certain individuals (male citizen landowners) possess *more* personhood than others (slaves or serfs). Obviously, I am not. My point, rather, has been to expose the dangers of our contemporary, hypercharged personhood project—that

3   Nicholas Brown, *Autonomy: The Social Ontology of Art under Capitalism* (Durham, NC: Duke University Press, 2019).

4   Peter Burdon, *The Anthropocene: New Trajectories in Law* (New York: Routledge, 2023), 53.

5   Evgeny B. Pashukanis, *The General Theory of Law and Marxism* (Piscataway, NJ: Transaction, 2003), 160.

frenetic and seemingly virtuous attempt to add more individual entities, species, and objects into the specially protected realm of equality. That is the project to be rejected. Our aim should be to put personhood back in the toolbox where it belongs. It is an essential tool for social justice, of course, but only one of many at hand to cultivate the world we want. And granting personhood to nonhumans is not an incremental step forward; it is a dangerous leap off a cliff.

The previous pages have offered various alternatives and predictions about what abandoning expansive personhood might look like. First, rather than distort ourselves and our cultural histories, we might face the realities in front of us. Arguments for expansive personhood often seem to get in the way of seeing human beings and their experiences. The dangers of this are clear when the language of the "unborn person" is wielded as a weapon to undermine reproductive justice or defund abortion clinics. A little differently, we also saw something like this at work with Judge Wilson, sitting on a New York court, worried that arguments for Happy the elephant's personhood, arguments that referred to the suits of formerly enslaved human beings, were unnecessary and damaging. The arguments for freeing Happy from her zoo prison could be made without routing the argument through personhood and all that it entails. Even a legal tool as basic and ubiquitous as a trust for nonhuman animals could do this work. In these conversations, terms like "discrimination" (whether against nonhuman animals or AI), are functioning as a red herring and are better avoided.

Second, ending expansive personhood could also help reverse the alienation that results from the consolidation of corporate personhood as our de facto model for being a person, full stop. Accepting women's experience of pregnancy as definitive, with all the complexity that entails, would certainly mean that a woman's view of her personhood would be paramount (not just her "choice" or her "body" as private property) rather than placed in secondary relation to an artificial entity she has been hooked up to. In the case of AI, letting go of the fantasy of ePersonhood might provide some room to face the serious issues emerging with advanced algorithms and LLMs, to start to combat the cyber false consciousness already abundant. We might challenge the way an exploitative, inequitable technology is given free rein as a supposedly beneficial workplace device.

Third, leaving the fantasies of expansive personhood behind also opens up the space to see different models and frameworks for ourselves in the world. Take the same examples of fetal and electronic person-hood: Both are distracting substitutions for real changes that should be happening in society regarding human beings and their labor—whether the labor of pregnant persons or of social media content moderators. In the case of nonhuman animals, seeing why notions of liberal equality (with terms like toleration and discrimination) do not work in these cases is the first step to finding models that do. Animals are not "just an oppressed minority in human life," Mary Midgley insists, because "they are the group to which we belong," we human beings who are only a small minority of animals. To grasp ourselves in relation will require us to "wake up to a much wider range of possibilities. Our conceptual map needs revising."[6] With the case of environmental personhood, the language and concept of "home," an idea we are already very familiar with, might be more productive than legal rights for natural objects. The word returns us to the myriad *responsibilities* of being a person, rather than only to its extractive privileges.

Finally, we should identify the lingering worry that needs to be put to rest: that we desperately *need* expansive personhood as a concept, that to abandon the aim would be to let slip away a moral and politi-cal righteousness desperately fought for over centuries. It might seem that, because Enlightenment philosophy developed this immense theory of individual rights and apparatus to achieve greater social justice, any wavering in the full throttle toward *more rights* for *more types* of entities puts those achievements in jeopardy. But the point needs to be made as simply as possible: No risk exists. Personhood is on ground as solid as bedrock (the commodity and the corporation made sure of that). It will keep doing what it does, where it belongs, where it needs to be—in the law—as it has done for centuries. Sometimes judges will grant the status of person in borderline cases; in other cases, they might not.

Our task is altogether different, and, for it, there are better ideas to put to work: such as home, with which we already have more than a passing familiarity. Or political theorist Jodi Dean's vigorous defense of that hoary term "comrade," now refreshed with certain qualities that personhood will forever lack. "Comradeship," she writes, invokes "a set of expectations for action toward a common goal . . . bind[ing] action, and in this binding, this solidarity, it collectivizes" toward a shared

---

6 Mary Midgley, *Animals and Why They Matter* (Athens: University of Georgia Press, 1983), 143, 117.

future.[7] Like "comrade," the term "solidarity" opens us to more fruitful frameworks. This is just to underscore, once more, the key message of *The Problem of Personhood*: More personhood is not more solidarity.

We already have the models and tools we need. We just have to use them.

7   Jodi Dean, *Comrade: An Essay on Political Belonging* (New York: Verso, 2019), 12.

Acknowledgments

Persons really are legion. Especially amazing are the ones who helped me write this book.

At various stages in this process, friends and colleagues near and far offered crucial advice, helping me figure out where this book was headed. Special thanks to Penny Crofts, Jennifer Culbert, Melissa Ganz, Shari Goldberg, Charles Hatfield, Clare Mac Cumhaill, Klaus Mladek, Angela Naimou, Ravit Reichman, Julie Reiser, Bob Spoo, Simon Stern, Rachel Watson, and Rachael Wiseman. For incomparable art-looking and thinking, whether in London or New York, Philadelphia or Williamstown, thanks to Anthony Bale, Todd Cronan, Michael Fried, Veken Gueyikian, Walter Benn Michaels, Charles Palermo, and Hrag Vartanian. Jane Bennett and Paola Marrati, colleagues in Comparative Thought and Literature at Johns Hopkins, have been true comrades on this journey. And Hopkins students, lively interlocuters in various iterations of my "What Is a Person?" course, helped clarify many of the personhood debates—and brought a few more to my attention.

I am grateful to all the many inquisitive and challenging listeners and readers at various talks, seminars, workshops, and conferences where this material was presented, sometimes in draftier form. These include at the Columbia University Literary Theory seminar, especially Emily Apter, Bruno Bosteels, Julie Stone Peters, Gil Hochberg, Stephanie Insley Hershinow, and Robert Higney; at the New Conversations on Law and Literature seminar, convened by Tanmay Misra and Richard Clements; the Comparative Literature Luncheon series at Penn State, especially Eric Hayot, Cassie Mansfield, and Chris Reed (and participants who turned down a chance to see eclipse totality to attend my talk); at the

Law, Culture, and Humanities conference; and at the Post45 workshop hosted by Dan Sinykin, with helpful conversations with Paul J. Buchholz, J. D. Connor, Kate Marshall, Deak Nabers, Rachel Greenwald Smith, and many other lively participants. I am no doubt leaving out many others, but am more than grateful for the many helpful comments that bubbled up at these events. Thank you to everyone who took the time to think through these ideas with me.

At the ASAP conference, Steve Buttes, Davis Smith-Brecheisen, Emilio Sauri, and Charles Hatfield were clutch commentors, as they were—again—at the Nonsite/Forma workshop, where the lively conversation helped me sharpen a key chapter. On that front, very special thanks also to Adrian Anagnost, Jennifer Ashton, Nicholas Brown, Todd Cronan, Eugenio Di Stefano, Michael Fried, Paweł Kaczmarski, Marta Koronkiewicz, Ruth Leys, Walter Benn Michaels, Charles Palermo, and Ken Warren.

Many scholars from various disciplines read and commented on chapters extensively and rigorously. Thanks especially to Emily Apter, Jacob Browning, J. D. Connor, Kevin Crow, Jeannine deLombard, Mary Esteve, Amy Freund, Jason Gladstone, Shari Goldberg, Ruth Leys, Cassie Mansfield, Sean McCann, Stewart Motha, Ngaire Naffine, Jennifer Nedelskey, Rachel Greenwald Smith, Lindsay Stern, and Simon Stern. I tried to follow all of their excellent advice; any failure on that front is my doing, not theirs.

This book could not have been completed without generous support and sabbatical leave from Johns Hopkins University and the Krieger School of Arts and Sciences Dean's Office. I am also grateful for an NEH Faculty Fellowship to support my finishing the manuscript, and the valuable suggestions from those reviewers. Sebastian Budgen and everyone at Verso Books have turned this glimmer of an idea into a reality.

To my parents, thank you for all of your support, over so many years. To Jen, Scott, Virgil, and Homer, I love you all. And Isabel and Brian, you are my very first persons.

Index